ADVOCACY PRACTICE FOR SOCIAL JUSTICE

Advisory Editor
Thomas M. Meenaghan, *New York University*

Related books of interest

Social Policy in an Information Age
John McNutt and Richard Hoefer

Policy, Politics, and Ethics: A Critical Approach, Third Edition
Thomas M. Meenaghan, Keith M. Kilty, Dennis D. Long,
and John G. McNutt

New Perspectives on Poverty: Policies, Programs, and Practice
Elissa D. Giffords and Karen R. Garber

**Essential Skills of Social Work Practice:
Assessment, Intervention, Evaluation, Second Edition**
Thomas O'Hare

Straight Talk about Professional Ethics, Second Edition
Kim Strom-Gottfried

Navigating Human Service Organizations, Third Edition
Rich Furman and Margaret Gibelman

**Writing Clearly for Clients and Colleagues:
The Human Service Practitioner's Guide**
Natalie Ames and Katy FitzGerald

**Social Service Workplace Bullying:
A Betrayal of Good Intentions**
Kathryn Brohl

ADVOCACY PRACTICE FOR SOCIAL JUSTICE

Third Edition

Richard Hoefer
University of Texas
at Arlington

LYCEUM
BOOKS, INC.

Chicago, Illinois

Published by

Lyceum Books, Inc.
5758 S. Blackstone Ave.
Chicago, Illinois 60637
773+643-1903 (Fax)
773+643-1902 (Phone)
lyceum@lyceumbooks.com
http://www.lyceumbooks.com

6 5 4 3 2 1   15 16 17 18 19

ISBN 978-1-935871-82-8

Printed in the United States of America.

Library of Congress Cataloging-in-Publication Data

Hoefer, Richard.
    Advocacy practice for social justice / Richard Hoefer, University of
Texas at Arlington— Third edition.
        p. cm.
    Includes bibliographical references and index.
    ISBN 978-1-935871-82-8 (pbk. : alk. paper)
  1. Social advocacy. I. Title.
    HV40.H628   2016
    361.3—dc23
                                                                2015009108

To my family, for shaping the past,
making the present, and creating the future

CONTENTS

Preface   xi

Chapter 1: The Unified Model of Advocacy Practice   1
Defining Advocacy and Advocacy Practice   2
The Broader Context for Advocacy Practice   17
Conclusion   21

Chapter 2: Social Justice and Advocacy Practice   23
Advocacy in the National Association of
    Social Workers' Code of Ethics   25
Social Justice in the National Association of
    Social Workers' Code of Ethics   27
Distributive Justice   28
What Are Social Workers Trying to Accomplish with Advocacy?   35
Examples of Ethical Issues in Advocacy Practice   36
Conclusion   40

Chapter 3: Getting Involved   43
Why Are Some People Active in Politics?   43
Are Social Workers Politically Active?   46
Influencing the Factors That Lead to Getting Involved   49
Conclusion   60

Chapter 4: Understanding the Issue   62
Step 1: Define the Issue   63
Step 2: Decide Who Is Affected and How They Are Affected
    by the Issue   71
Step 3: Decide What the Main Causes of the Issue Are   74
Step 4: Generate Possible Solutions to the Issue   75
Step 5: Review Proposed Solutions to Determine Their
    Impact on Social Justice   79
Conclusion   83

Chapter 5: Planning in Advocacy Practice   86
Definition of Planning   87
What Do You Want? Using Advocacy Mapping to
    Describe Your Agenda   87
Who Can Get What You Want? Identifying Your Target   100
When Can or Should You Act to Get What You Want?   101
Conclusion   102

Chapter 6: Advocating through Education, Persuasion,
         and Negotiation   104
Education   104
Persuasion   108
Negotiation   126
Conclusion   131

Chapter 7: Presenting Your Information Effectively   133
Information   133
Presenting the Information   135
Working with the Media   150
Conclusion   158

Chapter 8: Electronic Advocacy   160
What Is Electronic Advocacy?   160
Organizational Attributes of the Use of Electronic Advocacy   162
The Growing Influence of the Information Age   163
Using the Web and Social Media in an Advocacy Campaign   167
Conclusion   178

Chapter 9: Evaluating Advocacy   180
Observation Phase   182
Judgment Phase   194
Difficulties in Evaluation   198
Conclusion   200

Chapter 10: Ongoing Monitoring   202
Differences in Advocacy between Legislative and
    Executive Branches   206
Influencing the Regulation-Writing Process   208
Influencing the Budgetary Process   212
Influencing the Implementation Process   214
Conclusion   217

Chapter 11: Integrating Advocacy Practice into
               Your Social Work Practice   220
The Progressive Era   220
The Great Depression and the New Deal   222
The 1960s: War on Poverty and the Great Society   223
Between the 1960s and the End of the
    Twentieth Century: Keeping Hope Alive   225
Advocacy Practice in the Twenty-First Century   226
Integrating Advocacy Practice into Your Social Work Practice   227

References   235

Index   245

PREFACE

My introduction to advocacy came early in life, and the examples came from my father. He did not always have a good idea of the best way to go about his advocacy, but I learned from him that it is important to tell those with decision-making authority what is wrong with the world so that something can be done to fix it. One of my early attempts at advocacy was a spontaneous protest at a high school pep club rally that resulted in me being suspended for several days. It also led, however, to a high level of name recognition and to a successful campaign to become sophomore class president. From that position I was able to make at least one or two important changes for the better, probably because I had the reputation of being willing to work at making change happen.

I carried these early experiences with me as I planned and wrote this book, but I also had a great deal of additional knowledge that I had acquired over the years. Some of this knowledge was "book learning," gained during my education in social work, political science, and sociology. Some of the knowledge was from serving as a board member and president of T-PACE, the National Association of Social Workers' political action committee in Texas—an honor I have had twice. Some of the knowledge came from leading a neighborhood organization and other activities. I've also learned a great deal from the students with whom I've worked on advocacy projects for the past two and a half decades. In writing this book, I want to share the fruits of my study and experience.

Still, there are already good books on advocacy available, and I had to figure out what I could add that would make the effort worthwhile when I wrote the first edition and updated the material in the second edition. Since this text first came out in 2006 and this writing in 2015, several additional books on the topic have been written.

Back in 2005 I found at least two areas where I thought I could bring something fresh, interesting, and useful to the field: First, books published before that year tended to describe advocacy as apart from and distinct from the rest of social work. Sure, every social worker should *do* advocacy, it was argued, but these other books, nonetheless, described advocacy as a special endeavor that should be examined as something in its own category. I, too, believe that advocacy practice is unique, but only in the same way that all practice modalities are unique—different skills may be needed and different techniques may be used. But what strikes me about advocacy is how much it is similar to all other social work practice approaches.

Advocacy is conceived of in this book as a process designed for problem solving, and, thus, it easily fits into a generalist model of social work. No other book on advocacy when I wrote the first edition listed "generalist social work practice" in its index, so bringing a problem-solving perspective to the presentation of advocacy practice was an addition to the field. Interestingly, books on generalist practice, even those on generalist practice in macro settings, do not apply the larger generalist approach to advocacy. Again, those books see advocacy as part of social work practice, but not in the form of a problem-solving technique. Conversely, this book is laid out in a way that follows a typical problem-solving pattern that should be familiar to almost every social worker in the United States. By showing how similar advocacy is to other types of social work practice, I hope to remove the seemingly foreign nature of advocacy and help make social workers more comfortable in taking on this vital work. I believe that this approach also clearly shows the interconnections between the different theaters of advocacy, such as within the legislative, executive, and judicial branches of government.

The second contribution I made with my first edition of this book was to show the large amount of empirical research that applies to advocacy. I had to learn a great deal about topics that are not necessarily first thought of as being related to social work advocacy in order to write this book. The political science literature was an especially useful source, but so too were other fields, such as psychology, sociology, and business. Compared to the authors of other books that were written in prior years, I have the advantage of several years of additional research to comb through for insights and evidence. Thus, I establish an evidence-based advocacy practice that builds on the practice wisdom that has been the norm for the area. Certainly, other authors have used the research available to them, but this book has the most recent information available from a variety of academic disciplines. With this third edition the evidence base has again been expanded. As readers will note, this book updates many details.

The most obvious difference between the second and third editions however comes in the form of a new chapter discussing the infusion of the Internet into all aspects of advocacy. The material on electronic advocacy is in its own chapter in order to highlight the importance of the topic. As far as I can tell, the extensive treatment of the subject is a unique feature compared to other texts on advocacy in the social work field.

Another feature of the third edition that is unique is the cross-walking of the book's content with the Council on Social Work Education (CSWE) Standards for Accreditation. While this material may not be of much interest to the typical student, it will be helpful to instructors and programs seeking new accreditation or reaffirmation of accreditation.

Finally, in all editions I wanted to put all of this information in a compact and highly readable book that would support the strengths of other texts or be read on its own by someone interested in advocacy who did not have the time to read a very long book.

WHO IS THIS BOOK FOR?

Advocacy Practice for Social Justice is designed primarily for students at both bachelor of social work (BSW) and master of social work (MSW) levels and for practicing social workers who need a focused yet comprehensive reference on advocacy. This book is primarily intended for two types of courses: First, it is intended for *introductory or specialized social welfare policy courses* in which only part of the course is devoted to understanding and conducting advocacy; the rest of the course is an overview of social welfare policy or a deeper look within a particular policy arena, such as mental health or child welfare. Second, it is intended for *macropractice courses* that teach more information on advocacy than is found in the generalist texts currently available.

As the research tells us, administrators and executives of human service agencies tend to be tasked the most often with conducting advocacy. While I believe this is not the best way to promote advocacy for social justice—all social workers should be trained and encouraged to advocate—it does indicate an additional audience. Administrators and students in administration courses who desire to learn the steps of advocacy can read this book and achieve excellent results.

Other potential audiences include students in elective courses focusing on advocacy (particularly those on a quarter or shortened term calendar), or courses with a service-learning component, in which an assigned project requires the student to attempt to influence policy.

THE PLAN OF THE BOOK

As noted above, *Advocacy Practice for Social Justice* is based on the generalist approach to social work practice. As such, I present a step-by-step idealized approach to advocacy, even while admitting that advocacy in real life frequently returns to earlier steps and sometimes skims over other steps rather quickly. Still, I designed the bulk of the book to be used in a front-to-back way.

Chapter 1, "The Unified Model of Advocacy Practice," introduces advocacy practice as a specialized practice modality within the larger generalist framework. That chapter also introduces three major contextual trends affecting social work practice and shows how the material in the book helps advocates handle those trends. Students who are thoroughly familiar with the generalist approach to social work practice may find some of this material familiar, but the chapter provides an overview of most of the book so is important.

Chapter 2, "Social Justice and Advocacy Practice," discusses the reason social workers conduct advocacy: to promote social justice. The ethical imperatives for advocacy, as set forth in the National Association of Social Workers' Code of Ethics, are explored, as are the terms "social justice" and "distributive justice." With the foundation of the reasons to engage in advocacy laid, the next several chapters explain the steps of the advocacy process. I provide several examples of situations where ethical conflicts may be present as a critical thinking activity and application of chapter material.

Chapter 3, "Getting Involved," discusses the first step. Going beyond mere exhortation to be involved, this chapter provides a clear, research-based understanding of why people are involved. It describes a model of involvement and the variables that front line practitioners and administrators can influence to increase the level of involvement in advocacy. In that sense, then, it is a blueprint for advocacy capacity building. Readers can examine their lives to determine which factors are promoting their interest and abilities in advocacy and how they might affect these variables in their own situation.

Chapter 4, "Understanding the Issue," begins with a vignette about one of my real-life situations. I present a five-step process for gaining understanding of an issue. Of special note in this chapter are several techniques that I present to aid decision making, particularly when developing solutions to addressing the issue and in understanding the impact of various solutions on social justice. These techniques are very appropriate for immediate use in a group role-play situation or for individual reflection.

Chapter 5, "Planning in Advocacy Practice," provides information on what planning is, how to conduct it, and how to know when it is time to move from planning to action. A tool called an advocacy map is introduced as an aid to the planning process. An offshoot of the logic model concept often used in program planning, the advocacy map assists advocates in keeping the big picture goals in mind even while planning the details of who will do what and why, when taking action. I provide two examples of advocacy maps, and readers can use the blank template in thinking about their own advocacy projects.

Chapter 6, "Advocating through Education, Persuasion, and Negotiation," presents information on education, persuasion, and negotiation. Using the latest research on these topics, I present readers with a comprehensive way to plan their pitch, from how to frame an issue to understanding the mind-set of the target of advocacy and what works to change it. Readers can quickly use this material in everyday situations at home and at work, as well as within an advocacy context.

In chapter 7, "Presenting Your Information Effectively," I rely on recent scholarship to assist readers in showcasing what they have to say in the most effective way. The information in this chapter links with the previous chapter to allow readers to see the full range of options available to get the word out to indirect targets as well as to the direct targets of an advocacy effort.

Chapter 8, "Electronic Advocacy," is a new chapter in this third edition. The influence of the Internet is the most profound change in advocacy tactics that most of us will ever encounter. Still, as noted in the chapter, new tools for advocacy do not necessarily change underlying strategies, nor do they eliminate the need to understand education, persuasion, and negotiation. Social justice advocates need to understand how to use all the tools at their disposal, however, and this chapter presents both theory regarding implementing innovations and suggestions for using mainstream social media applications such as Facebook, Twitter, and YouTube.

Chapter 9, "Evaluating Advocacy," returns to the advocacy maps introduced in chapter 5 to show how this planning tool can be extremely useful in evaluation. In addition to the usual aspects of evaluation, such as process and outcome evaluation, I also introduce the idea of context monitoring, which is used to keep abreast of how an organization is perceived by others in the policy arena. Context monitoring is an essential, though frequently overlooked, element of an advocacy group's effectiveness.

After an advocacy project is completed and evaluated, the tendency is to pack up one's bags and move on to the next campaign or issue. The purpose of chapter 10, "Ongoing Monitoring," is to squash this tendency. Monitoring the regulation-writing process and implementing a policy are important to creating and maintaining social justice. I include specific recommendations for how to be an effective advocate in each part of this phase of the advocacy process.

Chapter 11, "Integrating Advocacy Practice into Your Social Work Practice," presents a brief history of advocacy in social work and the lessons learned throughout the book. I could have presented this material earlier in the book to provide the historical context of advocacy in social work for readers, and, in fact, some may want to read this chapter before the chapters on the advocacy process. I have put it at the end, however, because many students have told me that they have a much greater positive regard for the history of social work advocacy *after* they have tried to do it. Too often historical overviews are seen as nonessential fluff by readers who want to get to the meat of the topic. It is often only when students have tried to emulate the pioneers of advocacy, and seen the difficulties and barriers that can block the way, that they can truly appreciate what others have done. By leaving this material until the end, I hope the inspiration of others' actions is blended with the lessons learned in today's environment.

CONNECTIONS TO THE COUNCIL ON SOCIAL WORK EDUCATION'S EDUCATIONAL POLICY AND ACCREDITATION STANDARDS

The CSWE, the accrediting body for social work education programs at the bachelor's and master's levels, uses its Educational Policy and Accreditation Standards (EPAS) to help educational programs understand the outcomes it expects for students (CSWE, 2012). The latest EPAS (from 2008) were updated in 2012; we refer to that version of these standards here. CSWE uses a model of education that is competency based rather than input based, looking at what graduates can do rather than what was in their educational program. CSWE (2012) defines competencies as "measurable practice behaviors that are comprised of knowledge, values, and skills" (p. 3).

CSWE (2012) has created ten core educational policies that reflect the desired competencies. This book can be used to address all of these core competencies. Each educational policy is listed below, and the sections or elements of this book that apply are described afterward.

Educational Policy 2.1.1—Identify as a professional social worker and conduct oneself accordingly. Social workers serve as representatives of the profession, its mission, and its core values. They know the profession's history. Social workers commit themselves to the profession's enhancement and to their own professional conduct and growth. Social workers

- advocate for client access to the services of social work;
- practice personal reflection and self-correction to assure continual professional development;
- attend to professional roles and boundaries;

- demonstrate professional demeanor in behavior, appearance, and communication;
- engage in career-long learning; and
- use supervision and consultation. (CSWE, 2012)

The entire book presents information for students to serve as representatives of the profession, using advocacy to work for social justice, empowerment, and other embodiments of social work's core values. The final chapter describes social work's vaunted history of advocacy and social activism. Chapters 3 through 10 provide what students need so they can advocate for client access to services of social work or anything else. Exercises throughout the text assist students in reflecting on their growing professional development and provide ethical dilemmas that allow students to grapple with professional roles and boundaries. Material is presented regarding professional behavior, appearance, and communication in the process of negotiation and persuasion. The model of advocacy delivers a strong message of the need to continually learn about social work values, social justice, and advocacy skills. The unified model of advocacy also provides information on how to work with others in one's practice.

Educational Policy 2.1.2—Apply social work ethical principles to guide professional practice. Social workers have an obligation to conduct themselves ethically and to engage in ethical decision-making. Social workers are knowledgeable about the value base of the profession, its ethical standards, and relevant law. Social workers:

- recognize and manage personal values in a way that allows professional values to guide practice;
- make ethical decisions by applying standards of the National Association of Social Workers (NASW) Code of Ethics and, as applicable, of the International Federation of Social Workers/International Association of Schools of Social Work Ethics in Social Work, Statement of Principles;
- tolerate ambiguity in resolving ethical conflicts; and
- apply strategies of ethical reasoning to arrive at principled decisions. (CSWE, 2012)

Chapter 2 presents a detailed explanation of the ethical basis for advocacy in the social work profession, drawing heavily on the NASW Code of Ethics, theories of distributive justice, and the antioppression framework. In doing so, it shows readers how, despite what may seem to be clear guidelines, ambiguity is rampant. The book provides methods for arriving at principled decisions to help resolve ethical dilemmas.

Educational Policy 2.1.3—Apply critical thinking to inform and communicate professional judgments. Social workers are knowledgeable about the principles of logic, scientific inquiry, and reasoned discernment. They use critical thinking augmented by creativity and curiosity. Critical thinking also requires the synthesis and communication of relevant information. Social workers:

- distinguish, appraise, and integrate multiple sources of knowledge, including research-based knowledge, and
- practice wisdom;
- analyze models of assessment, prevention, intervention, and evaluation; and
- demonstrate effective oral and written communication in working with individuals, families, groups, organizations, communities, and colleagues. (CSWE, 2012)

Chapter 4, which shows the steps to understanding an issue, and chapter 5, which provides a model of planning using an advocacy map, present vital material relating to critical thinking skills to inform and communicate professional judgments. Building on a problem-solving generalist model, *Advocacy Practice for Social Justice* demonstrates the importance of analysis and use of knowledge for professional practice. Chapter 4, "Understanding the Issue," relates to assessment. Chapter 5, "Planning in Advocacy Practice," assesses models of developing solutions, including prevention of future problems. Chapter 6, "Advocating through Education, Persuasion, and Negotiation," is the intervention component of the book, which, along with chapter 7, "Presenting Your Information Effectively," provides detailed, evidence-based instruction in oral and written communication for maximum effectiveness. Chapter 8, "Electronic Advocacy," brings forward tactical knowledge regarding electronic advocacy, a must for social justice advocates, as the use of social media has become standard operating procedure. Chapter 9, "Evaluating Advocacy," indicates the importance of evaluation and how to conduct one. All of this information is written with the ultimate goal of promoting social justice.

> **Educational Policy 2.1.4—Engage diversity and difference in practice.** Social workers understand how diversity characterizes and shapes the human experience and is critical to the formation of identity. The dimensions of diversity are understood as the intersectionality of multiple factors including age, class, color, culture, disability, ethnicity, gender, gender identity and expression, immigration status, political ideology, race, religion, sex, and sexual orientation. Social workers appreciate that, as a consequence of difference, a person's life experiences may include oppression, poverty, marginalization, and alienation as well as privilege, power, and acclaim. Social workers:
>
> - recognize the extent to which a culture's structures and values may oppress, marginalize, alienate, or create or enhance privilege and power;
> - gain sufficient self-awareness to eliminate the influence of personal biases and values in working with diverse groups;
> - recognize and communicate their understanding of the importance of difference in shaping life experiences; and
> - view themselves as learners and engage those with whom they work as informants. (CSWE, 2012)

The philosophical underpinnings of the book are rooted in an understanding of the value of diversity and difference. Social work advocates are shown, repeatedly, how to work with others by teaching them the skills of advocacy so that they can, whatever their age, class, color, culture, disability status, ethnicity, gender, gender identity and expression, immigration status, political ideology, race, religion, sex, or sexual orientation, work on their own behalf, for their own causes, in their own ways. The planning and advocacy processes employed throughout the book provide ways to ensure that oppressed, marginalized, alienated, and relatively powerless people can increase the odds that their needs will be met and their lives will be made easier.

Educational Policy 2.1.5—Advance human rights and social and economic justice. Each person, regardless of position in society, has basic human rights, such as freedom, safety, privacy, an adequate standard of living, health care, and education. Social workers recognize the global interconnections of oppression and are knowledgeable about theories of justice and strategies to promote human and civil rights. Social work incorporates social justice practices in organizations, institutions, and society to ensure that these basic human rights are distributed equitably and without prejudice. Social workers:

- understand the forms and mechanisms of oppression and discrimination;
- advocate for human rights and social and economic justice; and
- engage in practices that advance social and economic justice. (CSWE, 2012)

The advancement of human rights and social and economic justice are cornerstones of this book, starting with the title itself. At every turn, and with every page, the material stresses the importance of basic human rights, the need to battle oppression, and the vision to see how oppression can be fought using a strong ideology of Rawlsian distributive justice. Working at individual, organizational, institutional, and societal levels, *Advocacy Practice for Social Justice* discusses tools to understand issues such as oppression and discrimination, provides proven methods to advocate for human rights and social and economic justice, and leads the way in assisting social workers to engage in activities to promote social and economic justice.

Educational Policy 2.1.6—Engage in research-informed practice and practice-informed research. Social workers use practice experience to inform research, employ evidence-based interventions, evaluate their own practice, and use research findings to improve practice, policy, and social service delivery. Social workers comprehend quantitative and qualitative research and understand scientific and ethical approaches to building knowledge. Social workers:

- use practice experience to inform scientific inquiry; and
- use research evidence to inform practice. (CSWE, 2012)

Chapter 4 addresses this educational standard in particular. Titled "Understanding the Issue," the material underscores how vital it is for social workers to conduct policy-related research in a credible, scientific manner. The chapter highlights, as does chapter 9, "Evaluating Advocacy," that the best social workers mix quantitative and qualitative approaches as they use practice experience to inform their research activities and also apply the lessons from research to their practice activities.

Educational Policy 2.1.7—Apply knowledge of human behavior and the social environment. Social workers are knowledgeable about human behavior across the life course; the range of social systems in which people live; and the ways social systems promote or deter people in maintaining or achieving health and well-being. Social workers apply theories and knowledge from the liberal arts to understand biological, social, cultural, psychological, and spiritual development. Social workers:

- utilize conceptual frameworks to guide the processes of assessment, intervention, and evaluation; and
- critique and apply knowledge to understand person and environment. (CSWE, 2012)

Decision making is the result of many human behaviors. Ultimately, advocacy is a process designed to change the thinking and behavior of humans. Social workers should understand theories and conceptual frameworks as they look at improving the world at all levels of intervention. Assessment for, intervention by, and evaluation of advocacy requires the ability to understand, critique, and apply knowledge of decision making and policy development. In addition, knowledge about human behavior is crucial for social workers to be able to develop effective solutions for which they advocate. This book provides readers with a great deal of evidence-based information relating to the topic of advocacy.

Educational Policy 2.1.8—Engage in policy practice to advance social and economic well-being and to deliver effective social work services. Social work practitioners understand that policy affects service delivery, and they actively engage in policy practice. Social workers know the history and current structures of social policies and services; the role of policy in service delivery; and the role of practice in policy development. Social workers:

- analyze, formulate, and advocate for policies that advance social well-being; and
- collaborate with colleagues and clients for effective policy action. (CSWE, 2012)

It is as if this particular educational policy standard had been written with this book in mind. *Advocacy Practice for Social Justice* is especially valuable for any program that needs to strengthen its curriculum to meet this standard.

Educational Policy 2.1.9—Respond to contexts that shape practice. Social workers are informed, resourceful, and proactive in responding to evolving organizational, community, and societal contexts at all levels of practice. Social workers recognize that the context of practice is dynamic, and use knowledge and skill to respond proactively. Social workers:

- continuously discover, appraise, and attend to changing locales, populations, scientific and technological developments, and emerging societal trends to provide relevant services; and
- provide leadership in promoting sustainable changes in service delivery and practice to improve the quality of social services. (CSWE, 2012)

In addition to the material previously cited, chapter 10, "Ongoing Monitoring," indicates that social workers can provide the leadership to monitor dynamic postadvocacy conditions and to ensure that policies are implemented correctly, that all appropriate locales and populations continuously receive services that are mandated or desirable, that emerging social trends do not negatively affect oppressed or minority populations, and that changes in society are most targeted to benefit the worst-off among us.

Educational Policy 2.1.10(a)–(d)—Engage, assess, intervene, and evaluate with individuals, families, groups, organizations, and communities. Professional practice involves the dynamic and interactive processes of engagement, assessment, intervention, and evaluation at multiple levels. Social workers have the knowledge and skills to practice with individuals, families, groups, organizations, and communities. Practice knowledge includes identifying, analyzing, and implementing evidence-based interventions designed to achieve client goals; using research and technological advances; evaluating program outcomes and practice effectiveness; developing, analyzing, advocating, and providing leadership for policies and services; and promoting social and economic justice. (CSWE, 2012)

Educational Policy 2.1.10(a)—Engagement

Social workers:

- substantively and affectively prepare for action with individuals, families, groups, organizations, and communities;
- use empathy and other interpersonal skills; and
- develop a mutually agreed-on focus of work and desired outcomes. (CSWE, 2012)

Educational Policy 2.1.10(b)—Assessment

Social workers:

- collect, organize, and interpret client data;
- assess client strengths and limitations;
- develop mutually agreed-on intervention goals and objectives; and
- select appropriate intervention strategies. (CSWE, 2012)

Educational Policy 2.1.10(c)—Intervention

Social workers:

- initiate actions to achieve organizational goals;
- implement prevention interventions that enhance client capacities;

- help clients resolve problems;
- negotiate, mediate, and advocate for clients; and
- facilitate transitions and endings. (CSWE, 2012)

Educational Policy 2.1.10(d)—Evaluation

Social workers critically analyze, monitor, and evaluate interventions. (CSWE, 2012)

The model of advocacy practice described in this book follows this educational standard exactly, providing students and other readers the material to engage, assess, intervene, and evaluate in the context of advocacy practice. The student who completes this book will have an excellent grounding in the ten competencies required by the CSWE. An instructor who adopts this book will have a clearly enunciated connection with all ten core competencies of generalist social work practice. The program or school of social work that endorses this book will most likely find the reaffirmation process a bit easier.

ACKNOWLEDGMENTS

The writing of a book requires a substantial investment of time and energy, thought and learning, writing and revision. Without an array of understanding people around me, particularly Paula Homer, this manuscript would never have been completed. My family is my greatest support system and they deserve every kudo possible. I want to thank David Follmer, who has supported this project from the beginning, and those who critiqued the completed draft. I have tested these ideas on hundreds of students at the University of Texas at Arlington, and those students deserve extra credit for helping me understand better ways to present specific material. Their questions have helped me form the answers I present in this book.

—Richard Hoefer

Chapter 1

THE UNIFIED MODEL OF ADVOCACY PRACTICE

Ms. Jones enters your office, head hanging down, two young children at her side. After she sits down, you ask how you can be of help to her today. "Nobody can do anything for me today!" she exclaims. "The air conditioning is out in my apartment building, and the weather forecast is for highs over 100 degrees for the rest of the week. This is the third time this summer that the air has broken down, and the landlord sure is no good. He just wants the rent paid on time. It's bad for my kids' health—Michael here's got asthma. My neighbors and I are sure fed up with this nonsense! But there's nothing we can do."

Social workers are called on to assist people in need. Needs can be physical, mental, social, or societal, and social workers must be able to provide help for all types of needs. People come with problems, hoping that social workers will be able to assist them in resolving their issues. Social work education prepares students with a set of knowledge and skills to enable them to help clients. Situations that social workers face in their professional lives certainly include problems that bedevil individuals and families. But one of the defining elements of social work practice is that social workers are trained to see the connections between problems happening to individuals and problems occurring to larger numbers of people. These problems can be due to organizational or governmental policies that impose costs on or deny services to people in need.

Examples of these costs include spending time waiting for assistance in a first-come first-served line to apply for financial assistance, paying higher prices at local markets in low-income areas because public transportation is not available to other shops, paying high fees to cash checks because banks are not located nearby, and having

1

higher levels of cancer and other diseases because low-income housing is located near industrial dumping zones or other sources of significant pollution.

Changes in legislation and shifts in administrative rules affect what benefits are available and for whom. Organizations and governments sometimes deny services to people in need because they have changed the definition of eligibility for a service. Benefits are also denied when levels of income are lowered, leading to fewer people being eligible for services because they earn too much. Another way to deny services is to restrict the benefits available.

Advocacy is a core concern of social workers. Social workers are not content with only understanding current policy, the forces that shaped it, and what its effects are. Such analysis and understanding is but a first step in assisting clients with their situation. In fact, because policy shapes what social workers can do to assist their clients and how they can practice social work, the importance of understanding and being able to conduct effective advocacy is vital to all social workers. Advocacy is not the only method social workers use, but it is one of the techniques that make social work unique among professions. Thus, all social workers should know and be able to use the principles and processes of advocacy.

The purpose of this book is to provide readers a concise but thorough understanding of advocacy practice: what it is, why to use it, and how to apply it in real life. I present advocacy in the context of generalist social work practice, thus developing a unified model of advocacy practice. The main purpose of advocacy practice is the pursuit of social justice. This chapter begins by defining advocacy and advocacy practice, and compares the stages of generalist social work practice and advocacy practice. It concludes with information regarding current trends in the field of social work.

DEFINING ADVOCACY AND ADVOCACY PRACTICE

Advocacy is a term with many definitions. Barker (1995), in *The Social Work Dictionary,* defines advocacy as "the act of directly representing or defending others" (p. 11). Mickelson (1995), in *The Encyclopedia of Social Work,* states that advocacy is "the act of directly representing, defending, intervening, supporting or recommending a course of action on behalf of one or more individuals, groups, or communities, with the goal of securing or retaining social justice" (p. 95). Richan (1996) equates advocacy with lobbying. Jansson (2003) links the term "advocacy" to efforts to change policies to help relatively powerless groups. According to Gibelman and Kraft (1996), "The many definitions of advocacy share in common an action orientation that is systematic and purposeful and which is undertaken to change some condition" (p. 46).

Social workers are not the only ones talking about advocating. Daly (2012) argues that good ideas need skillful advocacy if they are to be adopted in the face of resistance. He sees advocacy as bringing persuasive arguments to bear effectively. In his view, marketing an idea is advocating for it, and vice versa. He does not have a values orientation regarding the purpose of advocacy—the term "advocacy" simply refers to a set of actions an effective proponent uses to persuade. Lawyers also are trained in advocacy, seeing it as a set of techniques they use to build the best possible case for their client (Messing, 2013). This view is similar to that of rhetoricians who study persuasion as a goal in itself, regardless of the goals of the advocate (Rybacki & Rybacki, 2011). People who study rhetoric differ from social workers not in what they do, but rather in that they discuss advocacy outside of any values orientation. To them, advocacy (i.e., marketing and persuasion) is a tool to serve whatever purpose the advocate desires. There is an important difference between rhetoricians and social workers, who are trained to use advocacy to promote social justice.

Advocacy practice is, then, that part of social work practice where the social worker takes action in a systematic and purposeful way to defend, represent, or otherwise advance the cause of one or more clients at the individual, group, organizational, or community level in order to promote social justice. The usual targets of advocacy practice are decision makers in elected or appointed positions who create and legitimize laws, regulations, rules, and other types of policies, or decision makers who apply the policies others have created. These targets can be in government or in other organizations, such as nonprofits or businesses that make decisions that affect people's lives.

This book proposes a unified model of advocacy that aligns with the generalist, problem-solving approach to social work. The importance of seeing advocacy as a unified field of practice can be seen when one looks at the nonunified approaches to advocacy that are sometimes found in the literature and in the field.

The first nonunified description of advocacy describes two types of advocacy: case and cause. The difference between them is the level of intervention: Case advocacy is related to individuals or families, such as in assisting them to receive benefits or services for which they are entitled. Cause advocacy is related to larger groups or social movements, such as an effort to expand the range of benefits and services available to a segment of the population. While dividing advocacy into these two categories is useful for some purposes, it also runs the risk of ignoring the commonalities of advocacy, no matter what level of client system is addressed, and of making important information less accessible to advocates who need it. Lens (2005), for example, writes an excellent article describing details of argumentation and rhetoric for persuasive communication but, for some reason, limits the application of these tools to cause advocacy: "Social workers engaged in cause advocacy need rhetorical skills" (p. 231). The information in the article is as useful for convincing a target of advocacy at the micro level as it is at the macro level. Unfortunately, someone who searches using the key words "cause advocacy" will find the article; someone who uses the key words "case advocacy" may not. A unified approach to advocacy avoids such problems entirely and clearly demonstrates how persuasion, negotiation, and other aspects of advocacy practice can be used at all levels of advocacy.

Another problem related to subdividing the topic of advocacy emerges routinely. Authors focus on the venue of advocacy, such as the legislative, executive, and judicial branches of government, as another way to discern differences in advocacy practice. Again, while there are certainly differences in the activities associated with advocating in these different arenas, the focus on the differences tends to mask the underlying similarities. This chapter presents a unified model of advocacy based on the generalist approach to social work.

The Generalist Model of Social Work and the Unified Model of Advocacy Practice

You may recall from introductory classes in social work something called the generalist model of social work. This model links all of social work practice, from the micro scale of individuals, couples, and families to the macro scale of organizations, communities, and larger entities. Although there are many different approaches to generalist social work practice, all agree that generalist social work practice is a problem-solving method (Perlman, 1957). This method consists of a number of generally agreed-on stages. According to its proponents, this method can be used to address virtually any problem.

Table 1.1 shows the stages in the generalist model of social work as presented by Kirst-Ashman and Hull (2011) as well as the corresponding stages in the unified model of advocacy. Although these models are shown as linear processes, experience teaches that life does not always move smoothly or easily from one stage to another. Thus, a social worker must remain flexible enough to recognize the process, intercede at whichever stage is occurring, and approach the situation at the correct level of intervention.

Engagement is the first stage in the generalist social work process. It consists of getting to know the client and deciding to work with him or her. The relationship built at this time is the foundation for the rest of the social work intervention. The client must also choose to work with the social worker, or else the process becomes something that is done *to,* rather than *with,* the client. In advocacy practice, the first stage is getting involved. When social workers get involved, it means

TABLE 1.1   Comparing Generalist Social Work and the Unified Model of Advocacy

Generalist Social Work (Kirst-Ashman & Hull, 2011)	Unified Model of Advocacy (Advocacy Practice)
Engagement	Getting Involved
Assessment	Understanding the Issue
Planning	Planning
Implementation	Advocating
Evaluation	Evaluating
Termination	
Follow-up	Ongoing Monitoring

that they are willing to expend time, energy, and other resources on behalf of a client, with the ultimate goal of promoting social justice.

Assessment is Kirst-Ashman and Hull's (2011) second stage of generalist practice. This is when social workers determine the extent of their clients' problems, and what their strengths and goals are. During this stage, client and social worker agree about which issues they will work on. Proper data collection and assessment are vital at this stage to lay the groundwork for future stages in the helping process. Similarly, in advocacy practice the second stage is understanding the issue. Social workers at this stage are working to know what the issue is and to be able to define it in a way that is mutually agreeable for key stakeholders, including the client system. Social workers work to understand who benefits from the current situation and who suffers. Social workers also strive to define causes in this step and to generate possible solutions. Finally, in the unified model of advocacy, a social worker assesses the possible solutions according to how well each promotes social justice.

Planning, the third stage in both generalist and advocacy practice, is when the agreed-on goals of intervention are connected with the techniques of the intervention. This stage is sometimes the most difficult to conduct because there is a desire by both the social worker and the client to "make things happen now!" But without careful planning, the result too often is minimal accomplishment and maximal disillusionment. The planning process in advocacy practice has five steps: (1) identifying what is wanted, (2) determining the targets of advocacy, (3) assessing when to act, (4) understanding what to do, and (5) gathering the appropriate information and incentives to cause the target to adopt the advocate's position.

Implementation is the fourth stage of the generalist model. The most wonderful plans are worthless if they are not put into effect. Because even the best-laid plans often do not work out exactly as designed, core skills at this stage are the ability to be flexible, to roll with the punches, and to quickly develop alternative plans to achieve desired outcomes. The same is true in advocacy practice—the advocacy that was planned is put into effect. Continued measurement and assessment during the implementation stage allows everyone involved to see where progress is and is not occurring.

Evaluation is the next stage, in both generalist practice and advocacy practice. In the generalist model, evaluation usually consists of measuring clients' gains toward solving their problems, whether at the individual, family, group, or larger level. In the unified model of advocacy practice, evaluating is the process of comparing expected changes in clients' conditions with what actually occurred. Social workers also judge the extent to which they were able to implement their plans. If barriers arose to putting their plans into effect, it is reasonable to expect that fewer of the desired outcomes will be achieved.

Kirst-Ashman and Hull's (2011) model of generalist social work includes a stage labeled "termination." This stage exists to provide a formal exit for the social worker and to provide a way for clients to resume their lives on their own. In this regard, social workers hope to work themselves out of their job (at least with the currently engaged clients). The unified advocacy model does not have an analogous step. While social work advocates may indeed move away from certain clients who have attained their immediate needs and understand how to advocate on their own behalf, the struggle for social justice never ends. There is always something else to do, another case to take on, and, hopefully, many more victories to celebrate. Termination of caring for the overall cause of social justice is not part of social workers' approach to advocacy.

The final stage in the Kirst-Ashman and Hull (2011) generalist approach to social work is follow-up. (Not all models of generalist social work include this concept.) Social workers periodically check back with former (now terminated from regular contact) clients to ensure that they continue to function better than before. Advocacy practice has a final step called ongoing monitoring. In this step, social work advocates continue to watch for social injustice to reappear or look for ways to further improve conditions or policy. Monitoring provides additional information on which new planning, advocacy, and evaluation of efforts may occur.

This brief overview of advocacy practice shows that it is similar to other types of practice that you may be familiar with and that it uses the same generalist problem-solving approach pioneered in social work many years ago. While the techniques are different from the techniques in direct or other types of macro practice, many of the skills you learn elsewhere will be important in advocacy. Social work advocates must be good listeners, be able to reflect back to others what is said, build on others' strengths, gather information from many sources, move discussions to solutions, and act in ethical ways to achieve client goals.

Comparing Generalist and Advocacy Practice: The Case of Ms. Jones

Ms. Jones is the client who appears in the short vignette at the start of this chapter. This section compares what a generalist practice social worker (we will call her Ms. Generalist) who does not employ an advocacy practice approach might do with that situation with what a social worker (we will name her Ms. Advocate) using the advocacy practice approach might do. (Please review the vignette before continuing this section.)

Stage 1: Engagement/Getting Involved

- Both Ms. Generalist and Ms. Advocate listen carefully to the concerns of Ms. Jones and work diligently to address the immediate needs of the family members for a safe and cool place to live in the short term. Ms. Generalist takes Ms. Jones at her word when she says, "Nothing can be done." Ms. Generalist has many more clients to listen to today and does not think she has time to delve into greater detail about conditions and actions relating to the apartment building and the property owner.

- Ms. Advocate, also knowing that she has many more clients to talk to, asks Ms. Jones what she and her neighbors have done in order to bring about a permanent solution to the ongoing problems with the air-conditioning of the apartments. She is willing to get involved with the larger issue of property owner irresponsibility, knowing that solving this one problem may prevent many smaller problems for this family and others.

Stage 2: Assessment/Understanding the Issues

- Ms. Generalist has assessed the situation as one that needs immediate attention to keep Ms. Jones and her family members safe from heat stroke or other reactions to the extreme heat in their apartment. While it is problematic that the property owner is not following the law to keep the units habitable, Ms. Generalist does not know of any way to force the property owner to comply with city codes.

- Ms. Advocate asks questions to understand the issues that Ms. Jones is facing. The information that Ms. Jones shares leads Ms. Advocate to understand the situation as one requiring both immediate attention to solve the family's housing crisis and a longer-term solution to the property owner's multiple violations of the housing code.

Stage 3: Planning

- Ms. Generalist, working with Ms. Jones, sketches out a plan to solve the immediate problem of safe housing. She checks out various possibilities, always checking with Ms. Jones to ensure that she is acknowledging and following the client's wishes as much as possible.
- Ms. Advocate also works with Ms. Jones to understand what she might like to choose from the range of possibilities available. Ms. Advocate also gives Ms. Jones information relating to property owner responsibilities to provide habitable housing. She brainstorms with Ms. Jones about what can be done to make sure the problems do not happen again to herself or her neighbors.

Stage 4: Implementation/Advocating

- Ms. Generalist does what she has agreed to do for Ms. Jones and her children. She first secures a spot for them all in a Red Cross–sponsored emergency shelter set up in the nearby elementary school that the children attend. She promises to check on the availability of a donated window air-conditioning unit and an emergency discount in rates for electricity so that the family can afford to use any air-conditioning unit that they hope to receive.
- Ms. Advocate uses her resources to secure the family a cool place for the next few nights at the nearby elementary school that has been set up as an emergency shelter. Ms. Advocate also adds Ms. Jones's name to a list for donated air-conditioning

units. A third task is to download and print instructions from the city's Web site on how to file a housing code violation complaint. She realizes that Ms. Jones and her neighbors may want this information and suggests that, while the neighbors are at the elementary school together, they talk about ways to use the city's power to force the property owner to act responsibly. Ms. Advocate also looks up and gives Ms. Jones information relating to making an appointment with a legal aid clinic lawyer.

Stage 5: Evaluation/Evaluating

- As far as Ms. Generalist is concerned, the key aspect of this case is that the family has a safe and cool place to live until the heat spell breaks. It is also important to her that the family receive an air-conditioning unit at least until the one at the apartment building can be fixed. She is concerned about Ms. Jones's son who has asthma, and realizes that this malady may cause future problems unless it can be controlled. That problem, however, must wait for a while, until all of these other, more-urgent, cases can be dealt with. Just knowing that the family will be taken care of by the Red Cross shelter means that the problem is being handled appropriately and satisfactorily.
- Ms. Advocate is pleased that a cool spot is available for Ms. Jones and her family, keeping them all together and out of danger. She is glad that the Red Cross is working to solve the immediate health issues that Ms. Jones faces. Ms. Advocate checks over the planning documents she developed and sees that, while the immediate problem is covered, additional work will be required to determine what, if anything, the neighbors in the apartment building will want to do to make a longer-term solution possible. She notes that just giving information about filing a code violation complaint and giving a referral to a legal aid clinic does not make the property owner behave responsibly. She knows there is more to do.

Stage 6: Termination

- Ms. Generalist feels good about the way she handled Ms. Jones's case. She listened well, was empathic, took into account Ms.

Jones's preferences in developing a plan and then was able to get the entire family into the same nearby shelter. She knows the Red Cross does an excellent job, given their resources. Ms. Generalist was unable to secure an air conditioner due to the agency allocation policy; she felt bad about that, but the few available units had been promised to elderly clients who were less mobile than the members of this family. While Ms. Generalist believes that she will need to help this family again in the future, she puts the file back in the file cabinet.

- Ms. Advocate looks in her planner and notes that she needs to follow up with Ms. Jones because of the larger issues at stake.

Stage 7: Follow-up/Ongoing Monitoring

- Ms. Generalist looks up to see Ms. Jones and her family coming in the door. "How can I help you today?" she asks. Ms. Jones begins, "Well, it's the same old thing. The landlord isn't keeping up the building right."

- Ms. Advocate contacted Ms. Jones while the heat wave was still in full force. Ms. Advocate contacts two other residents of the building. She speaks with them and Ms. Jones and listens while they express their ideas and fears relating to filing a complaint against the property owner. She acknowledges what they are saying and provides support for the idea of using the legal process. Ms. Advocate agrees to facilitate a meeting of the neighbors with a legal aid clinic lawyer to identify their options.

This illustration shows that an advocacy practice viewpoint leads to additional work for the practitioner in the short run, but may lead to higher levels of client empowerment and less overall work in the long run.

The remainder of this chapter provides additional details on the advocacy practice process. We take each stage in turn, even while realizing that advocacy may take steps out of order, return to stages we thought were completed, and not always end up where we thought we were going when we first began. In these ways, and many others, advocacy practice is like all social work practice: helping human beings change themselves and the world around them is not an exact science, so we must always be ready to develop and implement Plan B, Plan C, and even Plan D in order to achieve something close to what we really are striving for.

Stage 1: Getting Involved

The task of promoting social justice can sometimes seem daunting because there are so many unjust situations in the world. It can seem for people who are interested in advocacy, both in and out of their job settings, that any effort they might make is merely a token one. As Margaret Mead once said, however, "Never doubt that a small group of thoughtful, committed individuals can change the world. Indeed, it is the only thing that ever has."

The getting involved stage is analogous to the engagement stage of the generalist model of social work. The notion of getting involved implies a psychological readiness to expend energy, time, and possibly other resources in the pursuit of social justice, if only in the sense of helping one person to be treated more fairly. Getting involved often stems from a sense of outrage about how someone or some group is being treated. Parents might become outraged by seeing their child being unfairly affected by school policy (as when a head cheerleader was prevented from participating in her extracurricular activity all semester for drinking off campus, but a football player was removed for only two games for the same offense) (KWCH12 News, 2014). Social workers might become outraged that gays and lesbians are declared ineligible in some states for providing foster care or adopting because of their sexual orientation.

Other motivations are possible, too. Just as one of the most powerful predictors of volunteering is previous volunteer experience, present or future advocacy is often related to prior advocacy. Thus, even if the motivation for a person's first efforts at advocacy is to make a good grade in a class, to impress a potential partner, or to feel that he or she is a part of the action, there is likely no wrong motivation for advocacy in the name of social justice. In the end, continued advocacy is most likely linked to a person's ethical standards and sense of efficacy when employing advocacy practice skills. Therefore, it is important to understand the ethics of social justice (covered in chapter 2), as well as to learn the most effective ways of acting as an advocate (examined in chapters 3 through 9).

Stage 2: Understanding the Issue

Issues are situations and conditions that affect people. Some issues affect people positively and some affect people negatively. Usually, though, situations and conditions affect some people positively and other people negatively. Although there are several steps to understanding an issue, the first is to figure out what the issue is. This is often both overlooked and more difficult to do than expected. It is an overlooked step because the answer seems obvious—everybody knows that poverty, domestic violence, unemployment, and so on are issues with societal causes, except, of course, that some people believe that these same problems are, at least in part, caused by the affected individuals. Thus, particularly when people come at social justice issues from different value positions, the first step is to agree on a mutually acceptable definition of the problem to be addressed.

This step is harder to do than expected because of the difficulty in overcoming other people's—and our own—belief systems. Again, we may believe that the answer is obvious and be very surprised that there is another stance. Bridging the various viewpoints can be a challenge for advocates, but a challenge that we must meet before moving to the next step in understanding the issue.

The second step is to determine who is being positively affected and who is being negatively affected by the identified issue. Poverty, for example, is an issue that has both positive and negative effects. It is, of course, a negative condition if you are a member of a family of four with a combined income below $16,000 a year. You are probably not eating nutritiously, and you probably either do not have a home or have a poor-quality home that needs repairs. You may live in a part of town that has inferior schools, poor access to public transit, and few job opportunities.

For those of us who are not poor, however, the condition has some positive elements. The existence of poverty means that wages in the United States can be held down to the minimum wage or lower. This helps us stretch our earnings further by making everyday items and the cost of eating out lower. Worldwide disparity in income is particularly helpful to us because so many things we like to own are made outside our borders, where wages and working conditions are much worse than in the United States. Poverty, it may be argued, continues to exist in our country and around the world largely because it is such a positive condition for so many people.

Once it is clear who benefits and who loses from a particular condition or situation, the third step is to understand the causes of the issue. The issue of the existence of poverty, for example, has had many explanations. Some of the explanations have more evidence to support them than others.

The fourth step is to view the various solutions that are proposed and determine how likely they are to lead to social justice. The basic approach to creating and looking at possible solutions is to ask the following questions repeatedly: What would be the results of adopting this solution? Who would be assisted? Who would be harmed? How would this solution act on people currently affected negatively by this issue? How would this solution act on people currently affected positively by this issue?

You should rank proposed solutions that lead to greater social justice higher in preference than solutions that do not improve social justice as much. (Chapter 2 addresses what social justice is in greater detail.) This stage, understanding the issue, in advocacy practice parallels the generalist model's assessment stage. In both cases, it is the prerequisite for the planning stage.

Stage 3: Planning

Planning is vital for effective advocacy practice. Based on their understanding of the issue, social workers and clients will have developed possible solutions and chosen one to be the primary approach. This solution, if successfully adopted and implemented, will lead to greater social justice. Planning, then, is detailing the actions needed to make the preferred solution the solution that is eventually chosen by targets of advocacy.

Step 1 of the planning stage is to identify what is wanted. This may seem easy, as the primary solution has been determined in stage 2, understanding the issue, but that is only the first part of the planning process. The overall solution, which might also be known as the advocacy goal or outcome, needs to be broken into smaller and more manageable outcomes, which in turn are connected to advocacy activities and participants. A tool called an advocacy map (see chapter 5) can be used to assist moving from the here of a problematic situation to the there of a better future.

Step 2 in the planning process is to determine who the targets of advocacy are. Trying to influence people who have little or no say on the issue you wish to affect is a waste of time for everyone concerned. A state senator, for example, is not likely to assist in an effort to reallocate community development block grant funds. City council members in most cities, however, will be very active in making these decisions. Thus, it is vital to identify the decision maker(s) who can help you reach your goal.

Once you identify the targets, step 3 is to assess when you can or should act. Immediate action is not always possible, so it is important to lay the groundwork for later success, including finishing planning, making contacts, and gathering information.

Step 4 is to understand the way(s) that you can act so that you get what you want. This requires an understanding of the principles of education, persuasion, and negotiation. As decision makers tend to have strong individual preferences on how they receive information, it may seem impossible to have general rules of how to educate, negotiate, and be convincing, but practice wisdom and research have made strides in these areas.

Step 5 is to gather the appropriate information and incentives for bringing the target over to your side of the issue. The most important task of someone who wants to use advocacy to make a difference is to have information that is accurate and convincing. Most decision makers like to have not only tables of numbers and other facts, but also case stories of how the issue is harming someone or examples of the kinds of people who would benefit from a change in policy. Proponents of abolishing the estate tax, for example, argued that heirs of family farmers and small businesspeople were being harmed by having to sell their parents' farm or business in order to pay taxes on their inheritance. Opponents of removing the tax countered that people like Bill Gates (founder of Microsoft and one of the world's wealthiest people) do not need to receive any tax relief. Both sides on this argument had figures about the number of people affected by the decision and how their lives would be affected.

Once you have what you want, have determined who the targets are, decided when to act, understood what the best ways to persuade are, and possess the information to be optimally convincing, the next stage is to put plans into action and actually advocate.

Stage 4: Advocating

This stage is where the planning pays off. The stage of advocating is where social workers may speak to a supervisor or board of directors, talk to legislators, call allies for action, write memos detailing grievances, or walk a picket line. You now put into effect the tactic(s) you chose during the planning stage. Change may occur quickly in some cases, although bigger changes and decisions often take years, if not decades, to make visible progress toward greater social justice.

Most social policy advocates understand the slow nature of true change. They keep one eye on the future and outcomes to be achieved, and another eye on the present to ensure that plans are followed and conditions are assessed. Only by doing both can advocates truly make progress.

Stage 5: Evaluating

Advocacy practice performed without evaluation efforts is inadequate. People involved in change efforts must keep track of their level of success, whether the effort is aimed at changing the life of one person or a million people. Without the stimulus of an evaluation, even a fairly informal evaluation, advocates will be less likely to examine why their efforts achieved what they did. Lessons for more skillful advocacy in the future can be derived from both success and failure. Learning, not assessing blame, is the goal of a healthy evaluation process. In general, evaluations use the planning documents created early in the advocacy effort to compare what was sought with what was achieved.

Stage 6: Ongoing Monitoring

Once evaluation determines that sufficient progress is being made, most social work texts indicate that termination of the helping relationship should occur. You should follow up later to ensure that client progress is maintained. However, high caseloads often prevent follow-up. In the advocacy practice model, termination rarely happens. In some ways, social workers who are advocates for social justice have taken on their issue(s) "until death do us part" because social justice is such a worthy, yet far-off, goal. Ongoing monitoring of specific conditions is required to provide information for new planning, new advocacy, and new evaluating.

Naturally, specific interventions with particular clients do terminate, even in advocacy practice. Advocates who do the job of training and empowering their clients can often step away, knowing that the former clients are now capable of advocating for themselves. Even so, social workers may wish to continue their quest for social justice with regard to one particular issue with other clients, in other communities, or at different levels of intervention. Ongoing monitoring is thus necessary to ensure effective advocacy.

The use of advocacy, whether or not it is conceived of as part of the generalist practice perspective, is also part of a broader context. The next section discusses three trends that affect the profession of social work and its use of advocacy.

THE BROADER CONTEXT FOR ADVOCACY PRACTICE

This section describes three trends affecting advocacy practice in the social work profession. (Another trend, the growing importance of the Internet, is so important that it needs its own chapter.) These trends are the increase in support for evidence-based advocacy practice and evaluation, the rise in ideologically consistent political beliefs, and the increasing role of wealth in American politics.

Increase in Support for Evidence-Based Advocacy Practice and Evaluation

One of the key movements throughout the field of social work is the evaluation of practice, whether at the individual case level or at the program level. The term "evidence-based practice" is increasingly used to describe social work practice that has been evaluated as being effective. The knowledge base being developed in order to show the efficacy of social work interventions is based on increasingly rigorous research (Briggs & Rzepnicki, 2004; Roberts & Yeager, 2004). Advocacy, however, is in a primitive place in terms of the development of an ethos of evidence-based practice—indeed, evaluation of advocacy efforts is a topic almost unmentioned in most social work practice texts, even those primarily directed at helping students and practitioners to improve their advocacy skills.

Fortunately, efforts at fresh thinking about the evaluation of advocacy have gathered steam in the past decade. This book, for example, provides research-based information and a clear, tested, and practical approach to guide advocates promoting social justice. Panelists at the American Evaluation Association's national conference present trainings and research findings regarding advocacy evaluation. Enough evaluators are interested in the topic that a special group has been formed to promote additional advances in practice. As these ideas are tested and refined, social workers must keep up with what works in the advocacy evaluation arena.

The Rise in Ideologically Consistent Political Beliefs

While it is incorrect to paint all the members of a political party with the same brush, in American politics members of the Republican Party are generally more conservative than members of the Democratic Party. One of the key differences between the parties is the amount of action they believe the government should take in defense of economic equality. Republicans favor less government in the economic sphere than do Democrats. This means the Republican Party is on record against environmental regulations, intervention in the market (such as minimum wage increases), and mandating equal pay for women and men doing the same job. In general, Republicans think government is part of America's problems, and not an engine for good. Republicans are seen as protecting the right for individuals to own firearms with minimal regulation or governmental control. Many Republicans also desire to reduce or eliminate the ability of women to obtain abortion services and to legislate that marriage can only be between one man and one woman.

Democrats, on the other hand, generally promote government efforts to reduce inequality and extend equal protection to all. They are often supporters of the rights of racial, ethnic, and gender minorities. Democrats tend to favor less military spending and more welfare benefits. They are also less opposed to higher taxes.

According to a recent Pew Research survey (Pew Research Center, 2014), the American electorate has become more polarized in the past decade. This means that Republicans are becoming more conservative and Democrats are becoming more liberal. As a result, there is less common ground to agree on in terms of policy, and compromising to enact policy is less likely. Among those highly engaged in politics, the polarization is stronger than among the general members of the party, whether Republican or Democrat. Naturally, elected officials follow the trends within their parties, so the gridlock in politics that has existed in recent years is only to be expected. In addition, intense negative feelings about the "other" party (whether one is Republican or Democrat) have increased dramatically (Pew Research Center, 2014). Working across party lines is difficult when voters and officials believe that the other party's policies are dangerous for the country.

This situation means that advocates working in the political arena to support social work's generally liberal views will be less likely to find anyone to compromise with. It will be more difficult to find officials of either party willing to work with members of the other party or to find policies that are middle-of-the-road. This suggests that advocates for social work positions may want to focus more on getting Democrats elected, as it will be difficult to find relatively moderate Republicans. It may also suggest that advocacy efforts in the administrative or judicial arenas could be more successful than legislative advocacy.

The Increasing Role of Wealth in American Politics

While wealth has always been an important correlate of political power in the United States, it seems to have become even more influential in recent years. The conservative Koch brothers have poured millions of dollars from their private fortune to support conservative causes and to create a network of office holders who believe in far-right-wing ideas. Democrats also have some large funders who donate to support their causes. Because campaigning for office is so expensive, people running for office ask for donations early and often. There is a strong belief that large donors receive extra attention in recognition of their role in a campaign.

Recent decisions by the U.S. Supreme Court have increased the role of money in elections. In *Citizens United v. Federal Elections Commission* the court held that the First Amendment right to free speech for individuals extended to nonprofits, corporations, and labor unions. This means that independent commentary or efforts to sway voters' minds (such as through the purchase of television broadcast time) cannot be regulated by government. In response, super political action committees (known as Super PACs) have been created to accept donations to spend on influencing elections, with no requirement to disclose who the donors are.

Another noteworthy recent change (in April 2014) in election financing was caused by the ruling in *McCutcheon v. Federal Elections Commission*. This case eliminated aggregate contribution and spending limits in federal elections. This means that a person may contribute to as many campaigns at the national level as he or she desires.

This trend toward even more importance for large campaign donors, facilitated by Supreme Court rulings, can lead social work advocates to despair. Combined with the other trends mentioned, workers can become fatalistic and wonder if there is any reason to bother with advocacy. My answer, and that of countless other social workers, is a resounding call to action.

Social justice is under attack. It is under attack in families, groups, organizations, cities, counties, states, the nation, and throughout the world. It is under attack every day. While social workers do not have a monopoly on good ideas or the correct set of values, the profession of social work has firm ideas about the values that should dominate the decision-making process and the outcomes that should be achieved through individual and social action. Victories occur and we should celebrate them. Clients do receive more equal treatment, agency budget cuts are reduced or reversed, and social policy is made on the basis that people do matter, particularly those on the bottom of the economic and social ladder. Yet, too often, the advocates for increased concentration of power, wealth, and prestige win. One reason for this is that social workers do not know how to advocate well for their clients and for themselves and their agencies. The core premise of this book is that knowledge is power—that knowledge of how to engage

20

in a structured approach to advocacy will lead to more-successful advocacy. This, in turn, will lead to greater social justice across the country and perhaps even the world. We must all do our part, and the first step is to know what to do. After completing this book, any reader can be a better advocate for social justice.

CONCLUSION

This chapter has examined briefly one model of generalist social work practice. It introduces the unified model of advocacy practice, which is conceptualized as a specialized form of social work practice with stages that parallel the generalist problem-solving approach. It also provides an overview of the six stages of advocacy practice—getting involved, understanding the issues, planning, advocating, evaluating, and ongoing monitoring. Finally, three broad societal trends affecting social work are described and their implications for advocacy are explored. Laying the groundwork for the rest of the book, this chapter allows readers to understand the place of advocacy practice in the big picture of social work practice and society. In the next chapter, social justice, the goal of advocacy practice is examined in detail.

Suggested Further Reading

Jansson, B. (2013). *Becoming an effective policy advocate* (7th ed.). Pacific Grove, CA: Brooks/Cole.

This textbook first identified advocacy and working within the policy-making arena as an area of social work practice equal with other types of social work practice. The text organizes a massive amount of information pertaining to politics, policy making, and social work advocacy.

Perlman, H. (1957). *Casework: A problem-solving process.* Chicago: University of Chicago Press.

More than 200,000 copies of this classic book have been sold, and it has been translated into at least ten languages. Adhering to neither the Freudian nor the Rankian approach to clinical practice prevalent at the time, Perlman relied on her social work experience and keen mind to reject long-term psychotherapy as a model for social work practice. Instead, she developed social casework, a short-term approach based on the idea that people come to social workers with problems that often need to be broken into solvable pieces. Solving one piece of the client's problems often leads to gains in other areas as well. Perlman's approach is still the backbone of social work practice.

Discussion Questions

1. Why is advocacy an important function of social work?
2. How does advocacy practice fit in with what you already know about social work?
3. Choose one of the three trends discussed at the end of the chapter. Apply the implications to your field placement, volunteer work, or other social work setting. Describe the impact the trend is having there.
4. Look back at the differences in approach between Ms. Generalist and Ms. Advocate. On your own or in a group take a look at several case examples you have been involved with. For each, lay out the steps a Ms. Generalist and a Ms. Advocate might take.

Chapter 2

SOCIAL JUSTICE AND
ADVOCACY PRACTICE

*Social workers have a professional responsibility to make ... choices
and to participate in the broader societal debate to resolve issues of
social change.* D. Iatridis, *Social Policy*

Mara Liasson, reporter for National Public Radio, started a presentation
to a NASW Political Action Institute by defining her subject. The word
"politics," she said, "comes from *polis*, a Greek word meaning community, and *tics*, meaning small, bloodsucking insects. Politics is thus a
domain of life controlled by a group of people leeching off the rest of
us" (Liasson, 1996). Unfortunately for the field of social work and the
United States at large, this facetious definition is widely accepted.

The belief that politics and thus advocacy is a dirty arena, popu-
lated by the worst kinds of people, and something that no decent person would want to be associated with, is all too common in social
work. There is, however, another view of politics. A political scientist,
Harold Lasswell (1936), wrote that politics is the process by which it
is decided "who gets what, when and how" (p. 5). Politics, in this view,
is simply a tool that can be used for good or bad purposes.

Reisch and Jani (2012) provide a set of ideas that inform their
more-academic approach to understanding the term "politics": they
focus on how power differences are created and perpetuated by institutions, language, and other socially constructed actions. They also
include in their perspective how power affects the allocation of all
aspects of the social welfare enterprise, from worker-client relations to
the selection of policies.

A similar, though simplified, version of this definition is that politics (or policy making) is "deciding how stuff gets spread around," and

the underlying processes that support that decision process. The only question, then, is whether social workers (or any other group of individuals with common interests) want to help make these decisions. If you are not the decision maker yourself, then advocacy is the process by which you help make the decisions on these matters. Former Texas state senator and mayor of Fort Worth, Texas, Mike Moncrief is fond of saying that social workers and politicians have a common goal: to help people. Barbara Mikulski, U.S. senator from Maryland, says, "Politics is simply social work with power" (Reisch, 1995, p. 1). If social workers want to assist clients, it is imperative that enough of them are active and capable advocates in the policy-making arena to ensure that things happen.

Social workers must be involved in advocacy practice if clients' situations are to improve. If social workers do not act as advocates, their policy ideas and, even more importantly, their values will not be represented in policy-making circles. When social workers engage in advocacy practice, they bring with them specialized knowledge about the human condition and a belief that service provision to clients must consider individuals within their environment. Social workers also want to focus on client strengths, rather than on pathology. When social workers share their knowledge and beliefs, decision makers are exposed to a fresh and important point of view.

Decision makers are encountered in many different places, and not just in the legislative branch of the government or in the top strata of other organizations. Decision makers can be found everywhere in organizations because even low-level workers have to interpret ambiguous regulations, rules, and customs in their place of employment (Lipsky, 1980). Organizational culture may make some choices "obvious," even if they run counter to client interests. These decisions are just as appropriate for advocacy practice as is passing a law.

Because values are such an important component of social workers' advocacy practice, it is important to identify the source of these values. The next section looks at NASW's professional Code of Ethics to explore the connection between professional responsibility (as defined in the NASW Code) and advocacy practice. (Web sites for other codes of ethics are provided in this chapter's Discussion Questions and Exercises.)

ADVOCACY IN THE NATIONAL ASSOCIATION OF SOCIAL WORKERS' CODE OF ETHICS

According to social worker and member of the Detroit city council Maryanne Mahaffey, "What the social worker brings [to the advocacy process] is a value system that, if implemented, along with the [proper] skills, makes the difference" (Haynes & Mickelson, 2009, p. 40). One of the best places to look at the values used to justify advocacy practice is in the Code of Ethics of the primary professional organization of social workers in the United States, NASW.

There are several parts of the Code of Ethics (last revised in 2008) that indicate that being involved in advocacy is one part of a professional social worker's job description. Section 6.01 states this idea most clearly: "Social workers should promote the general welfare of society, from local to global levels, and the development of people, their communities, and their environments. Social workers should advocate for living conditions conducive to the fulfillment of basic human needs and should promote social, economic, political, and cultural values and institutions that are compatible with the realization of social justice" (NASW, 2008, Sec. 6.01).

The code further explains this responsibility in Section 6.04:

(a) Social workers should engage in social and political action that seeks to ensure that all people have equal access to the resources, employment, services, and opportunities they require to meet their basic human needs and to develop fully. Social workers should be aware of the impact of the political arena on practice and should advocate for changes in policy and legislation to improve social conditions in order to meet basic human needs and promote social justice.

(b) Social workers should act to expand choice and opportunity for all persons, with special regard for vulnerable, disadvantaged, oppressed, and exploited people and groups. (NASW, 2008, Sec. 6.04)

The code addresses involving the public in politics in Section 6.02: "Social workers should facilitate informed participation by the public in shaping social policies and institutions" (NASW, 2008,

Sec. 6.02). Thus, social workers not only have an obligation to participate actively in advocacy themselves, but also to empower others to do so. Social work administrators have a specific duty along these lines, too, according to the Code of Ethics: "Social work administrators should advocate within and outside their agencies for adequate resources to meet clients' needs" (NASW, Sec. 3.07[a]).

Despite the specificity and clarity of the Code of Ethics, a historical concern in the literature is that social workers do not have the skills necessary to be policy advocates and to encourage others to shape social policy (Wolk, 1981). Many blame this situation on social work education programs' lack of student training in these skills (Ezell, 1993; Haynes & Mickelson, 2009; Mary, Ellano, & Newell, 1993).

Reisch and Jani (2012) add a contemporary analysis of the issues involved in lack of student preparation. They argue that social work educators need to stress the development of critical consciousness regarding power differentials on policies, promote theoretical perspectives that emphasize change and conflict, and question the underpinnings of intervention research. Reisch and Jani acknowledge that students would be resistant to these measures because they often have limited knowledge about politics, and are perplexed by the strain between an emphasis on social justice and the desire to practice objectively validated social work. Students also lack the skills of conflict management, and so do not want to be active in inherently conflictual arenas.

It is not only students who stay away from politics and training in advocacy, but also others: practitioners, even administrators of human services nonprofits, are not flocking to the banner of advocacy. According to Almog-Bar and Schmid (2014), "Most studies reveal low levels of advocacy, indicating that political advocacy is marginal and limited in scope. Resources are not allocated and very few staff positions are assigned for this purpose" (p. 7).

Despite the lack of formal advocacy skills training for social work students and the current low level of advocacy effort that nonprofit human service organizations put forth, it is vital to learn how to approach issues relating to the denial of social justice, and it is important to continue to seek knowledge about advocacy and learn its place in the social work profession. The next section examines what social workers are trying to accomplish with their efforts. Identifying with the goal of social justice can help us all overcome the inertia that seems to keep society and our peers stuck in place.

SOCIAL JUSTICE IN THE NATIONAL ASSOCIATION OF SOCIAL WORKERS' CODE OF ETHICS

The 2008 NASW Code of Ethics sets forth six core values of the profession: service, social justice, dignity and worth of the person, importance of human relationships, integrity, and competence. A complete description of these values is beyond the scope of this book, but it is important to take a closer look at the value of social justice because it is the value that most directly encourages advocacy practice.

The Code of Ethics states, "Social workers challenge social injustice" (NASW, 2008, Ethical Principles). The code elaborates on what this principle means by declaring, "Social workers pursue social change, particularly with and on behalf of vulnerable and oppressed individuals and groups of people. Social workers' social change efforts are focused primarily on issues of poverty, unemployment, discrimination, and other forms of social injustice. These activities seek to promote sensitivity to and knowledge about oppression and cultural and ethnic diversity. Social workers strive to ensure access to needed information, services, and resources; equality of opportunity, and meaningful participation in decision making for all people" (NASW, 2008, Ethical Principles).

The NASW Code explicitly mentions some of the main, concrete issues for social workers who want to work for greater social justice. The concept of "social justice" is difficult to define definitively, however, as it means different things to different people. Making matters difficult for social workers who want to follow the Code of Ethics' call to work for social justice is that the code does not define the term. Other references are available, however, and step in to help us understand the term more fully.

The Social Work Dictionary, for example, defines social justice as "an ideal condition in which all members of a society have the same basic rights, protections, opportunities, obligations, and social benefits" (Barker, 2003, pp. 404–405). Finn and Jacobson (2008), in *The*

27

Encyclopedia of Social Work, give a wide range of perspectives on social justice. They provide a capsule review of utilitarian, libertarian, egalitarian, racial contract, human rights, processual, and capabilities perspectives. Van Soest (1995) discusses three views of social justice: Legal justice, the first view, is concerned with what a person owes society. Commutative justice, the second view, is concerned with what people owe each other. Distributive justice, the third view, is concerned with what society owes its members. The third view is the type of social justice most often discussed in a social work context. The relative importance of these three types of justice fuels many policy debates.

DISTRIBUTIVE JUSTICE

One of the most important elements of the struggle over social welfare policy is the difference in interpretation of the term "distributive justice." Distributive justice "concerns the justified distribution of benefits and burdens in society. . . . The distribution of benefits and burdens is a cooperative social process structured by various moral, legal, ideological, and cultural principles" (Iatridis, 1993, p. 62). Thus, politics, "the process of distributing stuff," is the way that distributive justice either is or is not made a reality; therefore, the debates of political philosophers deserve considerable attention from social workers (Reamer, 1993).

Allingham (2014) discusses four main theories of distributive justice. The first, justice as fairness (associated with John Rawls), considers any distribution of goods as if the persons with the least get more of the current distribution in order to bring them up to the level of others. The second, equality of resources (associated with Dworkin), indicates that a distribution is fair if everyone has the same amount of resources from which to live.

The third viewpoint (linked to libertarian theorists), that of common ownership, states that a distribution is just if everyone starts off at the same level but allows for individuals to make voluntary transactions that may alter this initial beginning. Finally, the entitlements theory of Robert Nozick defines a just distribution as one that comes about from voluntary transfers of resources. In this situation, all inequality is acceptable.

Although the literature on this topic is extensive, we focus in this section on two of the four approaches described by Allingham: that of John Rawls and that of Robert Nozick, because these are the most "fundamentally opposing. . . . In essence, Rawls emphasizes equality while Nozick emphasizes liberty" (Allingham, 2014, p. 4). John Rawls and Robert Nozick each penned very influential works on the subject of distributive justice in the early 1970s. Their different interpretations of the concept have provided a great deal of material for debate since that time.

John Rawls's Views on Distributive Justice

Rawls (1971) asks his readers to imagine that they are going to develop the rules for a society knowing that people will be randomly "assigned" different places in society once the "game of life" begins. Participants in this thought experiment must agree ahead of time to live within the rules they develop, but they do not know what position in society they are going to be given. This is what Rawls calls the veil of ignorance. A person may be assigned a position among the wealthy elite, with many resources and privileges, or a position among those with very few material resources. However, for this type of inequality to exist, the rules agreed to have to allow for the inequality. Given the veil of ignorance about one's future assigned position in society, Rawls argues that people will want to create the fairest set of rules possible, if only to protect themselves from being placed into a very difficult situation. According to Rawls, this set of "the fairest possible rules" would be based on two main principles. The first principle is that "each person is to have an equal right to the most extensive total system of equal basic liberties compatible with a similar system of liberty for all" (Rawls, p. 302). This ensures that all are treated equally within the context of the rules, which are addressed in the second principle. This principle states that "social and economic inequalities are to be arranged so that they are both (a) to the greatest benefit of the least advantaged and (b) attached to offices and positions open to all under considerations of fair equality of opportunity" (Rawls, p. 302).

The second principle is an especially important point. Inequality is not seen as an evil in and of itself, but rather as a condition that can be harnessed for the good of all. An example may help illustrate this idea: The rules set forth under the veil of ignorance might allow some positions in society to be more appealing than others; examples for the former might be those with higher pay, better working conditions, and so on. In the case of physicians, for example, we want very capable practitioners because they make life-and-death decisions that require considerable levels of skill and many years of difficult training. Because there are a limited number of people with the required aptitude and because the training process is arduous, members of society may wish to encourage those few people with the requisite aptitude to become doctors. Furthermore, people who become physicians could earn more than others without breaking the second principle if they are required to use some of their time to assist the least advantaged in society. Point b above ensures, moreover, that the position of physician is open to everyone with the appropriate aptitude and is not limited by reasons of race, gender, social class, or other non-merit-based considerations.

Rawls's approach to distributive justice has considerable appeal to many social workers. Those who have tried to apply his principles quickly run into practical difficulties, however. No matter which set of rules is agreed to under the veil of ignorance, even when using Rawls's two principles, it is difficult to determine whether that structure is "to the *greatest* benefit of the *least* advantaged" and, therefore, just. It is also seemingly impossible, without drastic interventions, to keep the children of the advantaged from maintaining their early lead in health, schooling, and connections.

Robert Nozick's Views on Distributive Justice

A very different interpretation of distributive justice is set forth by Robert Nozick (1974) in *Anarchy, State and Utopia*. Nozick argues that Rawls and others who focus on end-states or patterns of a distributive process are wrong. In order to maintain a fair distribution of resources, there would have to be a central distribution mechanism, and there is not. In other words, the end-state, or the point at which people have been assigned their positions and given the rules, is theoretically a rather equal distribution of economic goods. However, the distribution is constantly made less equal because people put forth unequal effort and have unequal skills, and under Rawls's system they are paid according to effort and skill. The only way to prevent inequality is to have government constantly redistribute wealth.

In a free society, diverse persons control different resources, and new holdings arise out of the voluntary exchanges and actions of persons. There is no more a distributing or distribution of shares than there is a distributing of mates in a society in which persons choose whom they shall marry. The result is the product of many individual decisions that the different individuals involved are entitled to make (Nozick, 1974, pp. 149–150).

The proposed solution is a procedural approach to distributive justice in which "a distribution is just if everyone is entitled to the holdings he possesses under the distribution" (Nozick, 1974, p. 151). To simplify this theory, "From each as they choose, to each as they are chosen" (Nozick, p. 160).

An example illustrates his approach clearly. An end-state theorist might object to a distribution of income that left many people with little and a few (such as sports stars) with much. But suppose that the many choose to buy tickets to football games where the stars play. The football team makes a large profit and pays the players quite well. Nozick argues that this voluntary transfer of holdings (income) from the many to the few is completely just and that any move to redistribute it through governmental action (coercion) is unjust. He makes this last point very strongly when he states, "Taxation of earnings from labor is on a par with forced labor" (Nozick, 1974, p. 169).

Under Nozick's approach, the main principle to ensure social justice, then, is to set up a way for fair, voluntary exchanges to take place. This market should be as unfettered as possible. Once the rules are set and followed, any result, no matter how unequal, is socially just. Government's major duty is to ensure that everyone follows fair rules, because enforcement leads to a just outcome. The idea is similar to political freedom. As long as the rules of one-person, one-vote are followed in an election and everyone has a chance to vote, the result of such a free election is just and fair. It is not just, however, to decide who should win an election ahead of time in order to distribute elected positions fairly—that is, to give those positions to different types of people. Similarly, it is not just to determine if the outcome of an economic distribution is fair by looking at the amount of inequality that ensues. As long as fair rules are followed in the marketplace, the distribution of money that results is just.

Comparing Rawls's and Nozick's Views

The practical implications of these two interpretations of the term "distributive justice" are staggering. Nozick's formulation would eliminate many, if not all, government efforts at redistribution and would return the country to a system where charity giving was the only support for people who could not earn their own living. This harsh state of affairs would mean that social work values would be under great duress. Inequality would certainly increase. It is a very individualistic approach to how society should operate, although it is consistent with many of the basic tenets of American values.

Rawls's viewpoint requires many calculations to be made that may be beyond most persons' abilities, but the general thrust of his approach is congruent with social work values. The approach focuses on the least advantaged members of society and seeks to improve their condition. Despite the practical difficulties of determining the exact level of justness that is involved in any one situation, it is clear that the NASW Code of Ethics is written with an eye on the needs of the least advantaged members of society. This viewpoint, too, has a place among American values but is clearly not the dominant value. Nonetheless, the Rawlsian view is the dominant value amongst social workers: "[The view] supports the normative aspects of social policy practice and the ethical commitments of social work. It emphasizes humanness and the enhancement of being human. It also promotes welfare-state programs that redistribute goods and services in favor of the poor, the disadvantaged, and populations at risk" (Iatridis, 1993, p. 69).

Antioppression Framework

A more recent and alternative approach to understanding social justice emerges from the antioppression framework. Young and Allen (1990) argue that distributive theorists such as Nozick and Rawls who argue for fairness in distributive justice terms depoliticize policy making and accept, in most ways, the existing methods of decision making. Furthermore, distributive justice theorists downplay or deny difference, place insufficient emphasis on the role of group identity, and believe in the ability of decision makers to act impartially. Young and Allen state that the idea of equal treatment began as a positive approach to ensure fair, equal treatment, but that it in fact suppresses difference. Sometimes, they argue, in order to reduce oppression, equal treatment must give way to "the politics of difference" (Young and Allen, p. 11).

The elements of the antioppressive framework and the meaning of antioppressive practice are loosely defined. Even though ideas around antioppressive practice are decades old, they have not yet become standardized. Baines (2007) indicates, "Rather, than a single approach, AOP [antioppressive practice] is an umbrella term for a number of social justice oriented approaches to social work, including feminist, Marxist, post-modernist, Indigenous, post-structuralist, critical constructionist, anti-colonial and anti-racist" (p. 4). Thus, in this discussion of oppression and antioppression, a considerable amount of subtlety will be missing, just as it was in the earlier sections regarding Rawls's and Nozick's ideas of distributive justice. Suggested additional readings on the topic are provided at the end of this chapter to extend your thinking concerning this important topic of advocacy for social justice.

Before delving into what antioppression is, we need to understand the concept "oppression." Young and Allen (1990) state, "Oppression happens to social groups," and the existence of social groups is "fluid and often shifting, but nonetheless real" (p. 9). One aspect of Young and Allen's identification of oppression is that it occurs through systemic and structural phenomena—aspects of society that are not necessarily intentional. This perspective immediately challenges the social justice advocate to look beyond individuals who are "the oppressors" and those who are "the oppressed" to look at systemic barriers preventing social justice from being realized. Young and Allen provide extended discussions of what they call the five faces of oppression, which provide concrete ways to look for oppression: exploitation, marginalization, powerlessness, cultural imperialism, and violence. Each face of oppression can overlap others, in some ways, but each is distinctive enough to be named and described separately.

Exploitation. Exploitation refers to using people to make profits. Even if the workers are paid, the amount of payment is low in relationship to the income for the exploiters. Capitalism is the mechanism by which exploitation occurs.

Marginalization. Marginalization occurs when groups are excluded—that is, kept out of meaningful social participation and relegated to lower social standing. While racial groups are often targeted for marginalization, other groups, such as the elderly, those with mental illness, women, gays, lesbians, bisexuals and transgendered people, as well as many other groups, are often oppressed using marginalization.

Powerlessness. Powerlessness refers to the inability to give orders or make choices, even while being ordered and having choices made for them by others. Extreme powerlessness results in a culture of silence, meaning that those who are oppressed do not speak of their oppression or, at the most insidious levels of powerlessness, do not even know they are oppressed. Indoctrination is used as a method of keeping the oppressed silent: they come to believe that they are inferior, and that they deserve their place at the bottom of society.

Cultural Imperialism. Cultural imperialism is the process of taking the culture that the powerful have and making it the norm. In this way, members of the dominant culture ignore or look down on nonconformists. People who follow the dominant cultural expectations make those who do not feel different from and worse than themselves.

Violence. Violence is an obvious form of oppression. It results in oppressed groups being subject to physical harm at any time and for no reason. News shows tell the tale of sexual violence against women, police violence against blacks and other minority groups, and hate-motivated assaults on individuals from numerous groups.

Thus, one approach to antioppressive social work practice analyzes the situation to be addressed using one or more of the types of oppression, and works to overcome it or them. Barnoff (2001) describes the difficulties of implementing this framework in feminist social service settings, but also provides examples of enabling processes. It is important to note that the antioppression framework is not universally accepted at a conceptual or practical level for social workers. Tester (2003), for example, strongly challenges the use of an antioppression framework for social work practice and is an interesting example of the conceptual and practical debates around the topic. This debate is still in full swing and can be an important alternative way of viewing the role of social work in advocating for social justice.

WHAT ARE SOCIAL WORKERS TRYING TO ACCOMPLISH WITH ADVOCACY?

It is all well and good to be an advocate: indeed, some might argue that a democratic society needs people to be active simply because engagement in the process is good. Social work, however, takes a normative view of the desired outcomes of the advocacy process. Many purposes for social work advocacy are listed in the NASW Code of Ethics. Meeting client needs, both material and emotional, should be uppermost in the minds of social worker advocates. The workers' primary goal should be to "confront discrimination, oppression and institutional inequalities" (Barker, 2003, p. 405). This is a lofty goal, and we may wonder if social workers actually believe in these values.

Research by Abbott (1988) indicates that social workers consistently rank higher than other professional groups in their belief in four important social work values: respect for basic rights, sense of social responsibility, commitment to individual freedom, and support for self-determination. This is true even for beginning MSW graduate students, as compared to students in other professional programs (Abbott, p. 44). Social work students, at both the BSW and MSW levels, "report high levels of social work idealism" in response to the following statements: "Access to opportunities and resources should be open to all" and "Social workers have an obligation to advocate for change in their communities" (Csikai & Rozensky, 1997, p. 537). The mean scores on these statements indicate that social work students "agree" to "strongly agree" with these ideas.

Interestingly, however, Csikai and Rozensky (1997) also found that the social work students surveyed had comparatively little agreement with statements such as "Advocacy is the main thrust of social work" and "Social workers' responsibilities should include active involvement in lobbying for political change" (p. 533). Both of these statements had a mean score placing them between "uncertain" and "agree" on the scale used. Perhaps most disturbing for those who see a strong need for advocacy practice because of the impact of policy decisions on social work practice, students in this study indicate considerable agreement with the statement, "Political issues have no bearing on direct social work practice with individuals" (Csikai & Rozensky, p. 533).

There was a shift in social workers' attitudes toward poverty and social action between 1968 and 1984 (Reeser & Epstein, 1987). Surprisingly, respondents in 1984 were more likely both to believe that poverty was due to structural factors and to be less committed to activist goals than were social workers in 1968. This shift in attitude may have two causes: first, casework and psychotherapy had become the primary social work methods, and, second, in 1984 there was a sense of futility about social change due to the insensitivity of President Reagan's administration toward social work concerns.

There has been a long gap in this type of research, however, so it is unclear if these findings still hold. Recent work by Felderhoff, Hoefer, and Watson (2014) suggest that the pendulum has swung back to strong support for political action. Results indicate that social workers in Texas strongly support political activity by the state chapter of the NASW. An overwhelming majority (82%) report that they are "more likely" or "much more likely" to join or rejoin NASW as a result of NASW's political advocacy. Only 3 percent were "less likely" or "much less likely" to join or rejoin as a result of the advocacy efforts by their professional organization.

In summary, it appears that social workers believe in social work values. This finding underscores the importance of social workers engaging in advocacy practice because their beliefs and values are unique. It is thus important for social workers to receive education and training in the how-tos of advocacy practice.

EXAMPLES OF ETHICAL ISSUES IN ADVOCACY PRACTICE

Up to now, this chapter has focused on the ethical responsibility social workers have to address societal and client problems through advocacy and the need to focus on social justice in their practice. Still, the questions remain, How do these principles operate in the real world? Is everything fair in love, war, and advocacy practice, or should social workers be held to some other standard of behavior?

Saul Alinsky (1972), in his classic essay "Of Means and Ends," argues forcefully that people who extensively debate the morality of means and ends "wind up on their ends without any means" (p. 25). Organizers must use what is available to enable them to accomplish their goals:"He who sacrifices the mass good for personal salvation has a peculiar conception of 'personal salvation'; he doesn't care enough for people to be 'corrupted' for them" (Alinsky, p. 25). It is appropriate to be concerned with ethics only when there is a choice of means. Thus, if the ends are just and the means are limited to one tactic, that tactic, no matter what it is, is fair. It is only the powerful who call the effective tactics of the dispossessed "unfair" (Alinsky).

The NASW Code of Ethics may be used to support Alinsky's (1972) view in part, but the overall message is clear that social workers should be held to a higher standard. Maryanne Mahaffey maintains this point vigorously:"There are people who tell me that the ends justify the means. This is antithetical to social work values. . . . For social workers the ends and the means must be consistent. Another way to put it: If the method you use to arrive at your ends are [sic] dirty, then the end result will be dirty" (Haynes & Mickelson, 2009, p. 52).

Although social workers are called on to engage in advocacy practice, the code is often silent on the subject of how to do so ethically. In addition, there might be some contradictions inherent in the code. The very first sentence of the detailed ethical standards states plainly, "Social workers' primary responsibility is to promote the welfare of clients. In general, clients' interests are primary" (NASW, 2008, Sec. 1.01). This is immediately followed, however, by the statement, "However, social workers' responsibility to the larger society or specific legal obligations may on limited occasions supersede the loyalty owed clients" (NASW, Sec. 1.01). Reporting child abuse is given as a specific example of when loyalty to the client is overcome by legal obligations.

The fifth ethical principle described in the code is integrity. Social workers must be "continually aware of the profession's mission, values, ethical principles, and ethical standards" and to "practice in a manner consistent with them." More specifically, "Social workers act honestly and responsibly and promote ethical practices on the part of the organizations with which they are affiliated" (NASW, 2008, Ethical Principles). Honesty is certainly an important element in being effective in advocacy efforts, but is honesty always the best policy? Is it permissible to lie if it better accomplishes social work's primary mission to "enhance human well-being and help meet the basic human needs of all people, with particular attention to the needs and empowerment of people who are vulnerable, oppressed, and living in poverty" (NASW, Preamble)?

There are no firm answers to these questions. At best we can do what Jansson (1994) suggests be done when ethical principles conflict: "When issues reflect important values and consequences, they should not be resolved impulsively. We should feel tugged in different directions, as if each alternative is serious and cannot be lightly dismissed. Were we to hurriedly resolve such issues, we might later decide that we had compromised important values and overlooked important consequences" (p. 59). In the end, "reasonable differences of opinion exist among social workers" (NASW, 2008, Sec. 3.10[b]). Not every social worker will solve a problem the same way. Nevertheless, "Social workers should carefully examine relevant issues and their possible impact on clients before deciding on a course of action" (NASW, Sec. 3.10[b]).

The following are some examples of situations for which there are no clear answers, and reasonable social workers may indeed disagree on how to proceed.

You are chair of a statewide social work political action committee. A major newspaper writes a disturbing story on Maria Rodriguez, a candidate your committee has already endorsed for state senator in the primary race, which she won. The report says that she has falsified her academic credentials. Ms. Rodriguez first denies then admits the deception. The committee did not endorse this candidate based on her academic record, but rather on the twenty years of good work she has completed on behalf of low-income Mexican Americans in south Texas. Some of the members of your political action committee want to continue as if nothing has happened: "Her strong voice is needed in the state senate to protect against conservatives of both parties!" Others want to renounce the earlier endorsement and ask her to remove herself from the race altogether: "She lied to us!" A third group thinks it best to express disappointment in her, but support her privately: "She let us down, but she is still the better of the two candidates."

You are asked by your state NASW chapter to help organize a get-out-the-vote drive in your city because you have done similar work with the League of Women Voters, a nonpartisan group. You are willing to do this because you believe that "social workers should facilitate informed participation by the public" (NASW, 2008, Sec. 6.02). The main organizers are clear, however, that the vote they want to get out consists only of registered Democrats, as Democratic voters are much more likely to vote for Democratic candidates than are members of other parties or nonaffiliated voters. When you object, the organizer explains that Laura Smith, the Democratic candidate, is a strong supporter of equal rights for sexual minorities while the Republican candidate in the race is antigay. Ms. Smith has also been endorsed by NASW. "The far right religious groups and the Tea Party–types are mobilizing their forces to get out only Republican voters," says the organizer. "Why shouldn't we do the same for our side?" Although you understand this logic, you are still not convinced that this is entirely ethical for NASW, which is officially a nonpartisan group.

You are a longtime member of NASW and consider yourself to be a political conservative. You believe that NASW is too liberal and especially disagree with its prowelfare position. You are convinced that, despite changes to end traditional welfare, the welfare system created a generation of people who believe that they are entitled to public support. Even with the threat of being cut off from government assistance, some able-bodied recipients and their children have little hope of becoming self-sufficient because the aid they receive from charities and government eliminates incentives for them to seek gainful employment. Although you do not mind having a different opinion about policy compared to most social workers, you have noticed (starting in graduate school) a tendency for conservative social workers to be frozen out of social circles. This is a problem for you because you want to keep on other social workers' good side to maintain their referrals, which your practice relies on. Should you remain in the organization and try to change its policies to be more in line with your values, should you remain a member of NASW to keep the good insurance benefits available to members but otherwise quietly work against its proposals, or should you give up your membership because of your philosophical differences with the organization?

A client of yours in a nonprofit agency could make good use of a special fund set aside for buying back-to-school clothes. When you mention this to your supervisor, she agrees but cautions you to provide only half the allowed amount of funds in order to keep money available for other clients. You believe that special circumstances make it vital to assist your client with more than half the amount possible, yet you know that there are limited funds for this purpose. You are also aware that you are only four months into your six-month probationary period. Social work jobs as good as this one are hard to come by in your small community. What should you do?

In order to address situations such as the one above in a systematic way, first choose which ethical principles are in conflict. Refer specifically to the NASW Code of Ethics and other ethical codes that may apply, such as those that cover licensed social workers in your state. Ask which principle, in this situation, is more important. Gather opinions from other social workers you trust. In the end, you may need to prioritize one principle over another in order to resolve the conflict.

CONCLUSION

Although this lengthy discussion of distributive justice may seem beyond the scope of a class on advocacy, the reason to include it is simple: if social workers are going to use advocacy to promote social justice, they need to understand what social justice really means. Because there are different ideas relating to distributive justice, and because these different definitions have significant impacts on policy, we must explore where we stand in this philosophical debate. The NASW Code of Ethics makes clear that every social worker has the responsibility to advocate for social justice. Every social worker must then understand what is meant by the different views of social justice and be able and willing to support the definition most in line with social work values.

Social workers have important information about client needs and a distinctive view of social justice. Social workers tend to believe that people at the bottom of economic and social ladders should be helped to climb more quickly than people who are already higher on the ladder.

The rest of this book covers the most effective ways to advocate for these values to be adopted by decision makers and thus translated into laws and regulations. Each chapter covers one of the steps in advocacy practice. The final chapter summarizes and brings together the lessons from the book.

Suggested Further Reading

Allingham, M. (2014). *Distributive justice.* New York: Routledge.

This short book might best be recommended for people highly interested in philosophy, but it is also very useful for understanding the different conceptions of distributive justice. Each of the four theories mentioned in this chapter has its own chapter in Allingham's book, which then compares the theories in a clear way. It will not tell you which approach is "correct" but you will be well prepared to discuss the issues around "fairness" at any family gathering with a wealth of knowledge and arguments.

Lasswell, H. (1936). *Politics: Who gets what, when, and how.* New York: Free Press.

Although this is an older book, it continues to enlighten discussion of politics. Lasswell, a psychologist who studied political communication and propaganda techniques, begins the book stating, "The study of politics is the study of influence and the influential" (p. 3). The remainder of the book justifies this position. The second chapter, about the use of political symbols, is still astonishingly illuminating and easy to apply to current political concerns.

Young, I., & Allen, D. (1990). *Justice and the politics of difference.* Princeton, NJ: Princeton University Press.

This book lays out the authors' approach to antioppression. While it is not an easy read, it is far ranging and influential. With its emphasis on difference and the role of the social group as the key determinant of oppression, it challenges much conventional wisdom in social work education and practice.

Discussion Questions and Exercises

1. Do you generally agree more with Rawls or Nozick? How do you incorporate the views of antioppression framework authors such as Young and Allen? Are there specific issues on which you agree more with one viewpoint than the other?

2. Look up codes of ethics from other social work groups, such as the Clinical Social Work Association (http://www.clinicalso cialworkassociation.org/about-us/ethics-code), the National Association of Black Social Workers (http://nabsw.org/ ?page=CodeofEthics), or the International Federation of Social Workers/International Association of Schools of Social Work (http://ifsw.org/policies/statement-of-ethical-principles/). How do they compare with NASW's code regarding advocacy? Do you prefer some aspect of one of the other codes to the NASW code?

3. Can you think of codes of ethics from other professions that you might wish to follow, such as the American Psychological Association, the American Society for Public Administration, or the American Bar Association?

4. Discuss a current controversial issue regarding social justice from the perspective of Rawls, Nozick, Young and Allen, or others. For example, what is the "correct" response to police use of deadly force in a racially disproportionate way? How do the debates regarding distributive justice apply here? Or in what ways do energy-related policies allowing oil pipelines across farm land, or using fracking techniques that may pollute groundwater and lead to earthquakes but provide natural gas and jobs, have distributive justice implications? What position do you agree with?

Chapter 3

GETTING INVOLVED

For politics ought to be the part-time profession of every citizen who would protect the rights and privileges of free people and who would preserve what is good and fruitful in our national heritage. D. D. Eisenhower, *Address Recorded for the Republican Lincoln Day Dinners*

According to the generalist social work practice model described in chapter 1, the first step of the helping process is engagement. In advocacy practice, the first step is getting involved. This chapter examines the research on why people get involved in political action and then extends the conclusions to why people become involved in advocacy, whether they are advocating for one individual or thousands.

Getting involved requires making a decision—choosing between doing nothing and doing something. Although motivation varies from one person to the next, research indicates that several prerequisites are usually in place before the choice is made to do something. Although the research cited here refers mainly to being active in politics on a macroscale, the same thinking process and prerequisites need to occur no matter what level of advocacy is being undertaken. The next section looks explicitly at political activism, but later in the chapter I extend the discussion to advocacy in general.

WHY ARE SOME PEOPLE ACTIVE IN POLITICS?

All is not well in the American political system. Political cynicism is rampant, and trust in government is at an all-time low. One of the more popular beliefs about politics is that people in other industrialized and democratic countries are more active than those in the United States. This is not entirely true historically or currently. There is considerable political activity in the United States, especially in an international context.Voter turnout, as a percentage of the eligible population, is relatively low in the United States, but Americans are more active in other ways: they are active members of local groups that are working on community problems, working for a political party, or contacting officials about problems. Still, people often ask why Americans are not more active in politics.This section addresses a different question:Why is *anybody* active in politics?

In his classic study, *Who Governs?,* Robert Dahl (1961) wrote about two types of people: *homo civicus* and *homo politicus. Homo civicus,* or civic human, is not, by nature, a political animal.This type of person may become active in politics when he or she perceives danger, "but when the danger passes, *homo civicus* may usually be counted on to revert to his normal preoccupation with nonpolitical strategies for attaining his primary goals" (Dahl, p. 225). *Homo politicus,* or political human, on the other hand,"deliberately allocates a very sizable share of his resources to the process of gaining and maintaining control over the policies of government" (Dahl, p. 225). Why do most people turn into *homo civicus* and only a few into *homo politicus?* The best explanation Dahl provides is that "some individuals find that political action is a powerful source of gratification" (Dahl, p. 225). More-recent research, while not disputing this psychological approach, provides additional theories about why people do or do not get involved in politics.

Milbrath (1965) also classifies the American public according to three levels of participation: the apathetic, the spectator, and the gladiator.A large number (about 33%) of Americans are apathetic, but even this is a type of political activity.These people generally obey laws but otherwise do not expose themselves to political stimuli and are generally unaware of the political world.

The largest group (nearly 60%) is made up of spectators. These people participate in basic civic activities but do little else.They vote, they may initiate political discussions, and they sometimes try to sway the votes of family and friends. Spectators might also wear a political button or display a bumper sticker on their car.

A very small number (no more than 7%) of the American public are gladiators who live and breathe politics (Milbrath, 1965).Activities in which they participate include working on a political campaign, becoming an active party member, attending a caucus, soliciting political funds, and running for or holding public office, in addition to spectator activities. "A very small band of gladiators battle fiercely to please the spectators, who have the power to decide their fate" (Milbrath, p. 20).

Other political activities, such as contacting a public official, contributing money to a party or candidate, and attending a political meeting or rally, are transitional activities that spectators begin to engage in when their level of interest carries them toward becoming gladiators (Milbrath, 1965).

Four different factors lead to different levels of political behavior (Milbrath, 1965, p. 38). The first is the nature and level of the stimuli reaching the potential political actor. These stimuli can be thought of, first, as what is present in the environment; and second, as what stimuli actually reach the consciousness of the individual after passing through whatever perceptual screens are in place. Values are what allow political stimuli to reach an individual's consciousness and to activate his or her behavior. The second factor is the personal attributes of the individual, including attitudes, beliefs, knowledge, and personality traits. The third factor is the nature of the political system, which by its rules includes some and excludes others from participation. The final factor is the social position of the individual: age, sex, race, religion, socioeconomic status, and so on fit into this category. Given limitations on data and methodology and the purpose of his book, Milbrath does not seek to determine the relative importance of these factors.

Now, however, researchers have a better idea of the relative importance of various influences on political participation. One major theory, the resource model theory, was developed by Brady, Verba, and Schlozman (1995). This model stresses the importance of politically active people having resources in addition to interest: "motivations such as interest in politics are not enough to explain political participation. The resources of time, money, and skills are also powerful predictors of political participation in America" (Brady et al., p. 285).

Resources include not only money, but also skills derived from one's job or from holding organizational office in social or religious organizations. Another resource is large amounts of free time. The various types of political participation, such as voting, contributing funds, working in political campaigns, or attending protests, are dependent to different degrees on levels of free time, income, and number of civic skills (Brady et al., 1995). "To give a reductionist version of our findings—political interest is especially important for turnout; civic skills, for acts requiring an investment of time; and money, for acts involving an investment of money" (Brady et al., p. 285).

One variable, political interest, is important to understanding *all* of these types of political participation (Brady et al., 1995). Although level of education is an important predictor of political interest, a person's values are an important vehicle through which concern about current events can be molded into interest about politics. Remember, values are what allow political stimuli to reach an individual's consciousness and to activate his or her behavior (Milbrath, 1965).

Given the nature of the social work profession, with relatively high levels of education (undergraduate or graduate degrees), high levels of civic skills (public-speaking experience from classroom presentations, organizational skills from working in agencies, etc.), but not especially high incomes, we might wonder about the extent of social workers' involvement in the political process. The next section describes to what extent social workers, as a group, are politically active.

ARE SOCIAL WORKERS POLITICALLY ACTIVE?

There is considerable literature on the role of social workers in politics, with the contributions generally falling into one of two camps. Either the contribution is a description of the how-to of being active in politics (Albert, 1983; Dear & Patti, 1981; Ginsberg, 1988; Haynes & Mickelson, 2009; Mahaffey & Hanks, 1982; Richan, 1996; Salcido, 1984) or it examines whether or not social workers are politically involved (Ezell, 1993; Hoefer & Felderhoff, 2014; Mary et al., 1993; Pawlak & Flynn, 1990; Ritter, 2008).

The second of these categories is further divided into two types of writings: The first and earlier literature consists of exhortations directed at social workers to either increase their political efforts or to continue with the good things they are already doing (Amidei, 1987;

Cohen, 1966). These articles usually have little empirical basis, other than some appropriate anecdotes.

The second type is a look at actual behavior. Some empirical work has been conducted to answer the question of how active social workers are in politics (Ezell, 1993; Mary et al., 1993; Mathews, 1982; Pawlak & Flynn, 1990; Wolk, 1981). Data indicate that NASW members are more likely than the general population to report a party affiliation, with 74 percent associated with the Democratic Party. Much smaller numbers of social workers said that they are Republicans (12%) or independent of any party affiliation (12%). A few (2%) were connected with other parties (NASW, 1995). These percentages are quite different from those for the entire American population. According to unpublished Gallup poll data from nearly the same time as the NASW survey, the American population was 32 percent Democratic, 36 percent independent of party affiliation, and 32 percent Republican (Stanley & Niemi, 1995, p. 149). The NASW survey confirms other research that indicates "social workers tend to be more politically active than the general population" (p. 1).

Earlier studies of political participation documented a similar story. "Social workers *are* political members of society" (Wolk, 1981, p. 287). Social workers, according to Wolk's data, are as active as members of other professions and business executives. Ezell (1993, p. 92), in a study somewhat comparable to Wolk's, finds that there was "significant growth in the political involvement of social workers" between 1981 and 1989. More specifically, Ezell shows, "Social workers are politically active largely by writing letters to public officials but also by discussing political issues with friends, by belonging to politically active organizations, and by attending political meetings. In addition, substantial proportions of social workers make campaign contributions and get involved in candidate elections" (p. 92).

Recent research indicates similar findings. Ritter (2008) finds that fewer than half of the social workers in her study could be characterized as active or very active in the political arena, based on their activities. She finds that social workers were much more active (two to four times as active) as the public. Ritter (2007) found that social workers were more active by voting and encouraging others to vote than they were by any other form of participation.

Hoefer and Felderhoff (2014), surveying social workers in Texas, collected data on both what respondents thought social workers should do in the political arena and what they said they actually did. For many activities, there was a great deal of agreement between these two data points. Nearly three quarters (74%) stated that social workers should contact elected officials often or almost always, and 76 percent said they had done so within the past two years.

Other tasks were not matched as closely. More than two thirds (68%) said social workers should often or almost always engage in protests of social injustices, but only 39 percent had done so in the past two years. Interestingly, only 36 percent thought that social workers should often or almost always give money to political candidates, but nearly half (45%) claimed to have done so.

According to Hoefer and Felderhoff (2014), the percentage of social workers who voted ranged from 93 percent in the 2012 presidential election to 81 percent at the local level. This rate is much higher than the 58 percent of the American public who voted that year (Bipartisan Policy Center, 2012). In 2014, in a midterm election where turnout is usually lower than when a president is on the ballot, only 39 percent of eligible Americans voted (PBS NewsHour, 2014).

Social workers have historically been and still are more active than most Americans. The reasons behind this have not been explored in depth recently. Ezell (1993) examined why the social workers in his study were active: "The major reasons social workers are involved in advocacy are because of personal values, professional responsibility, and they like to see things change" (p. 89). These findings are probably still correct. According to Dickinson (2004), about 80 percent of social work students she surveyed agreed or strongly agreed with statements in the NASW Code of Ethics regarding political participation of social workers. Felderhoff et al. (2014) report that more than 80 percent of their Texas social work respondents were more likely or much more likely to join NASW because of its political advocacy efforts. On the flip side, more than four fifths of respondents believed that ending all political advocacy would make them less likely to join or rejoin, compared to only 3 percent for whom this action would increase their likelihood of joining or rejoining. This represents strong endorsement of NASW-based social advocacy.

To summarize the chapter so far, research indicates that certain personal values contribute to both a sense of professional responsibility to engage in and a higher level of interest in engaging in advocacy. Educational level also affects the amount of interest in and skills needed for advocacy that a person possesses. Educational level also has a direct impact on the amount of advocacy, micro or macro, in which a person will engage. Participation in other organizations affects a person's skill level and also has a direct impact on advocacy because it provides additional opportunities to become an advocate. Finally, there must be time available to conduct advocacy. The relationships between these factors are shown in figure 3.1.

INFLUENCING THE FACTORS THAT LEAD TO GETTING INVOLVED

Knowing the factors that influence participation and advocacy is important, because this information allows us to analyze incentives and barriers to getting involved, whether personally or when recruiting others to become more active in advocacy. The next several sections address each factor in figure 3.1 and present concrete steps to

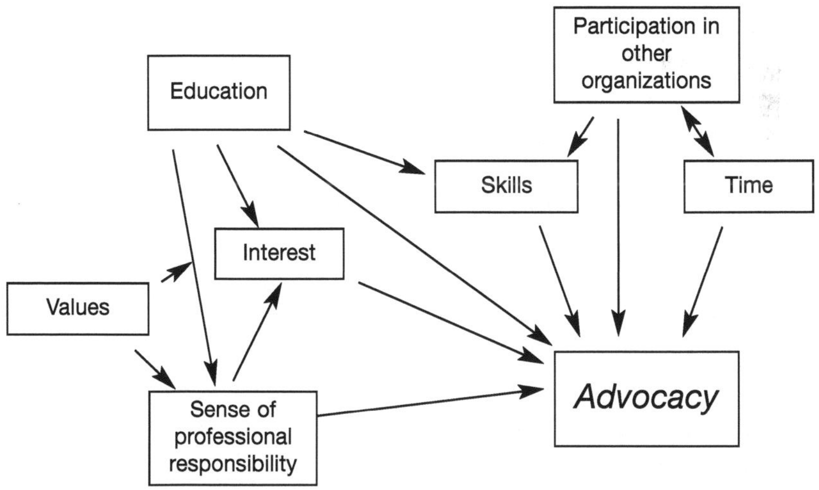

FIGURE 3.1   Factors Leading to Greater Use of Advocacy Practice

how to get involved. Table 3.1 shows how each factor may be affected by social work administrators wanting to increase advocacy levels in their organizations.

Education

Research indicates that people with higher levels of education tend to be more involved in political issues (Verba, Schlozman, & Brady, 1995). In the United States, higher education is strongly correlated with higher income. People with higher incomes tend to be active politically both because they can afford to do so and because they have more at stake in the system. Even in social work, higher education leads to higher income. So it is likely that higher levels of education also lead to higher levels of advocacy for social workers. Another reason that higher education may lead to higher levels of advocacy in the political world is that people with more education are more likely to become the executive directors of agencies and programs. Being in such a position requires a person to spend more time developing expertise to promote one's agency and to advocate in a macro arena for funding and on behalf of program clients (Ezell, 1991).

Although educational level is important in and of itself because of its impact on the ability to learn and analyze situations critically, and because of its correlation with income, the content of one's education is certainly important as well. A degree in social work should lead to greater use of advocacy than, say, a degree in German. A social work education involves learning skills that are vital to advocacy practice and also should spark an interest in advocacy at all levels.

There are several ways to affect a person's education level. Social work education programs are required by their accrediting body, the Council on Social Work Education (CSWE), to include information on policy making and other forms of advocacy. Students should graduate only after developing competencies in policy and advocacy practice. If a program does not provide such information to students, there is cause for concern. Social work students should know that such information is required and should make plans to advocate within their school so that they can be prepared to skillfully use advocacy in their professional lives.

TABLE 3.1 What Are the Factors of Getting Involved and How Can They Be Affected?

Advocacy "Getting Involved" Factor	How to Affect
Education	• Acquire information about advocacy through formal coursework • Provide in-service training • Provide continuing education unit–eligible workshops at conferences or local colleges and universities
Values	• Hire people into the organization with advocacy-oriented values, particularly people with a strong social work value orientation • Shape employee values toward advocacy by impacting organizational culture and reward structures
Sense of Professional Responsibility	• Hire people with a professional social work education, which includes exposure to and practice with social work advocacy
Interest	• Enhance hiring of social work–educated staff • Provide continuing education opportunities relating to advocacy • Expose staff members to advocacy opportunities and mentors • Show how advocacy efforts link to self-interest
Skills	• Create educational opportunities for learning advocacy skills • Provide opportunities to gain practical experience in advocacy, preferably under the guidance of talented mentors
Participation in Other Organizations	• Assign or allow employees to work with coalitions engaged in advocacy
Time	• Use job design principles such as flextime to provide productive time for advocacy efforts • Understand that some types of jobs (such as administrative ones) are naturally more related to advocacy than others, but do not allow this to be an excuse not to engage in advocacy at all for some

Agencies interested in higher levels of advocacy practice in their organization may want to increase the minimum level of social work education for the workers they hire and support the further education of non-MSW-level social work staff already employed. Having staff with higher levels of education should increase the amount of advocating, all other things being equal.

Social workers are also involved in continuing education or professional development efforts and can learn more about advocacy through in-service training, conference presentations, and other learning opportunities. It is helpful for agency trainers, conference organizers, and professional development course providers to plan for education in advocacy practice.

Values

Personal values are the touchstone for most of the actions people take, including whether to use advocacy practice skills in a particular situation. Organizational values can also affect the amount of advocacy workers conduct. Values related to working for social justice include a strong sense of fairness, the belief that people should try to make a difference in the world, and, often, a religious background that emphasizes the equality and importance of all persons.

It is common to hear that the world is not fair, and so we should stop complaining. Adults tell children this in order to justify decisions and situations that are not fair and to ease the anger and hurt children feel when they or others are treated unfairly. The result, after many repetitions, may be to blunt any desire the children might have to make the world more fair. After all, if the world is not fair now and never has been, what sense does it make to try to change it?

People who maintain their "childish" insistence that the world should be fair are likely to want to make a difference, whether or not they are social workers. Feeling angry at unfairness is often the precipitating factor for involvement.

Wanting the world to be fairer and actually deciding to try to do something about it can be separate issues. Sometimes people are overwhelmed with their situation and believe that they cannot reach out or extend themselves any farther in order to promote social justice.

Without the belief that they should try to make a difference, there is little impetus to take the extra steps required to get involved in advocacy.

The modern profession of social work is secular in nature, and most current aspects of social work training and education are nonreligious. Despite this fact, social work has religious roots, and many people who are outspoken social justice advocates for various populations are so because of their religious convictions. Not all religious backgrounds are equal in terms of their impact on advocacy, but most religions widely practiced in the United States agree that people are created equally in the eyes of God and deserve equal opportunities.

There are two principal paths for affecting the values of the workers in an organization: hiring people with the desired values, and shaping and maintaining employees' values once they are hired. The first approach seems the easiest, but it is often difficult to know fully the values and ideas of an interviewee. Also, organizations have to choose from among the people who apply for a job, so it is difficult to be certain that the perfect candidate with the desired job skills, attitudes, and values will be hired in every case. Thus, it is vital for all social work organizations to have a plan in place to affect their employees' values.

An important way to accomplish this task is to pay close attention to the organizational culture. Every organization has a particular culture that is passed from worker to worker, sometimes consciously, but more often unconsciously. Through this culture, workers come to learn the unwritten rules of the organization, which may or may not include an emphasis on advocating for clients. If an honest appraisal of the organization shows that frontline and other workers do not believe that advocacy is expected of them or that they can get in "a heap of trouble" for their advocacy efforts, the organization's culture might be getting in the way of a more-active focus on using advocacy.

In order to change culture in an organization, the leaders have to make it clear that they expect and support professional advocacy efforts on the part of workers for their clients. Even if agency leaders have a strong willingness to change the culture, it is important to realize that culture change is a long and difficult process. In order to achieve a shift in organizational culture, the top leaders of the organization must alter what they pay attention to and measure, model the new behaviors, and rework the criteria they use to allocate rewards and status (Schein, 1997).

Sense of Professional Responsibility

Values, as discussed above, are very influential in whether or not a social worker decides to act as an advocate. Specifically, values affect and to some extent determine a person's sense of professional responsibility. A person's educational level is also linked to his or her sense of professional responsibility. The more a person has been involved in a social work education, the greater is the likelihood that coursework has impressed on the student the idea that social workers should advocate on behalf of their clients. An examination of social work ethics is present in all coursework, so a higher level of social work education should lead to a greater sense of professional responsibility.

Although many types of classes can be useful for human service workers, no education is better for a professional social work job than a social work education. Social work students are brought face to face with key professional subjects that are not covered in other educational programs. Of these, one of the most important is the NASW Code of Ethics. Social work students are exposed to this material in many different ways and in many different settings so that the richness and vitality, as well as the ambiguities and weaknesses, of the code are infused in the educational process. This immersion can have a significant impact on a person's sense of responsibility.

Most states have requirements for licensed social workers to receive continuing education credits by attending workshops and seminars; some states, such as Texas, require that at least some of these credits are in the area of professional ethics. Thus, the best way to affect a person's sense of responsibility is to involve him or her in a thorough and ongoing social work education focused on what social workers should be doing, why they should be doing it, and how they should be doing it. One aspect of this education should emphasize the need for advocacy and the ethical and professional ways to conduct advocacy. The more that a person believes that advocacy is an integral part of a social worker's practice repertoire, the greater the amount of advocacy the person will engage in.

Interest

A person not interested in advocacy is less likely to engage in it. Interest in advocacy can be stimulated by a person's set of values, education, and sense of professional responsibility. Interest in advocacy can also be increased by performing advocacy.

Values guide much, if not all, of what we do on the job and off. If our values encourage us to look out for others, to work for social justice, to struggle against inequality, and so on, we tend to want to take action when we see those values being violated.

Education can affect interest as well. One of the important elements of professional social work education is to bring new ideas and information to students—including ideas and information about how laws and policies affect us all. As the saying goes in social work, "Policy affects practice, and practitioners affect policy." Many people have not learned how decisions of federal, state, and local politicians and appointed officials make a difference in the daily lives of social workers and clients. This lack of knowledge is why the CSWE requires that all schools of social work teach social policy.

Professional responsibility can lead to interest as well. Often a person considers a topic or duty uninteresting because he or she does not know much about it. Seeing how processes operate and observing their effects can open one's mind to topics formerly thought of as boring. Also, if some task, such as advocating for clients, has to be done, it may seem more interesting as the process unfolds, if only as the person attempts to prevent cognitive dissonance from setting in.

Examples of these processes abound among students and social workers in the field. One social worker found herself interested in the minute details of client eligibility determination after finding out that one of her clients had been turned down for a program despite meeting all the requirements. Another worker began to explore the intricacies of budget decision making at the county level when his program budget was threatened with a 20 percent reduction in funding. A school social worker decided that the process of assigning teachers of English as a second language (ESL) was an important topic after seeing a Vietnamese immigrant kindergartner crying at school and being unable to find anyone in the school who could communicate in that child's language.

Interest in advocacy and particular issues can also be linked directly to a person's self-interest. If an issue threatens one's family, livelihood, neighborhood, quality of life, religious center, or other cherished elements of living, the interest level in that issue shoots up immediately. As an example, I became very involved in planning and zoning issues, the hazards of underground gasoline storage containers, and the connection between convenience stores and crime when a developer proposed building a convenience store/gas station in my neighborhood. These were not issues that I had hitherto been interested in. I became enough of an expert, however, to present information to my city council and persuade at least one council member to vote against the zoning change because of safety issues.

Many people operate within a rather limited comfort zone made up of the daily tasks of helping one client at a time. Others, particularly those on an administrative level, may become disconnected from the recipients of services and forget that the reason for the agency is to promote client health, well-being, and quality of life. Advocacy can be such a powerful and life-changing experience that it can help move advocates beyond a small comfort zone. It can also remind us of the passion for improving the world and the condition of people in it that we had as we entered the profession. Thus, one of the key ways to promote an interest in advocacy is to model the behavior for others so that they, too, can see how it works and notice the results of the many small but necessary steps in the process. Even when advocacy is unsuccessful, the process of trying is an important way to kindle additional efforts that may be successful.

Another way to increase interest in advocacy is to show how it is in the person's self-interest to be an advocate. Advocacy may be tied to recognition, promotion, pay raises, greater status, or other extrinsic rewards. Naturally, there are intrinsic rewards as well, connected to a person's value system, sense of professional responsibility, and other individual characteristics.

An important element to remember when beginning an advocacy effort is that it can be started and completed by one person. A social worker can help a client navigate through rules that are hard to follow and needlessly bureaucratic without other people's involvement. Interest can be self-generated and then spread to others, as one candle can light another while still burning brightly itself.

Skills

One of the barriers to participating in advocacy practice is the sense that one does not have the skills needed to be effective. Social workers can see the need for increased services, greater funding, or more inclusive policy, yet still do little or nothing because they do not know what to do, who to see, or what can make a difference. This lack of skills may or may not be real, but the perception is what matters. This book, for example, is an effort to affect the level of skill that social workers have and the confidence they have in their skills.

The more educated a person is about advocacy—whether from classes in college or graduate school, from workshops at professional conferences, from having a mentor, or just from trial and error—the greater the likelihood that he or she will use advocacy in the future. Practice also is an important element in learning new skills, so an advocate's education should include ample opportunities to perform advocacy tasks.

Two elements are vital to increasing skills in advocacy, as in other areas of practice: education and experience. I addressed these elements earlier. A third aspect that can make a large difference is the presence of a mentor or guide. Having someone to learn from or to bounce ideas off can be one of the best ways to improve one's skills quickly. Learning from books and other literature is another way to increase skills. Trial and error can also work but is inefficient and can be more discouraging than necessary.

Agencies wanting to improve the advocacy skills of their staff can do so by making sure that experienced, competent advocates are already on staff and by providing them time to mentor and assist other workers with less-well-developed skills. Having books and other literature in the agency library is helpful, as is keeping an up-to-date list of useful Web sites for both skills enhancement and substantive content purposes.

Participation in Other Organizations

An element of the acquisition of advocacy skills that is often overlooked is the level of participation in other (nonjob) organizations. People who participate in different organizations learn things about how organizations work in general. They also pick up skills from being in leadership or supportive positions in those organizations. Being active in a church is one particularly common example. The list of possible volunteer positions in churches is long, and each position contributes to a participant's knowledge about how the world works. A participant in volunteer activities often can apply this knowledge and experience to understanding advocacy, and can feel more comfortable when speaking out on an issue or on behalf of a client. Activity in other organizations also provides access to larger numbers of contacts, all of whom a social worker can communicate with on behalf of an individual client or group of clients. A person can also learn how to influence policy making by seeing how others influence their organization's actions.

Much of the improvement in advocacy efforts related to increased participation comes from participation in organizations that are related to a person's private interests—an educational experience that comes free of charge because the person wants to attend a particular religious group, to be involved in a particular hobby or sport, or is interested in preserving the environment. These interests lead to organizational involvement and an increased understanding of the ways of the world.

An agency can foster a similar type of involvement by assigning or allowing employees to become active in coalitions that are working on issues such as homelessness, child health, or emergency social services, and in professional organizations such as NASW, or in organizations at the local, state, and/or national levels. Although over-involvement in outside organizations can happen, usually such added exposure of the employee and his or her agency is helpful to the organization and worth the time away from normal work duties. Not only do more people in the field know this particular employee, but also the exchange of information and skills across organizational boundaries can help the entire social services system, thus improving client outcomes. Having these types of connections is also a powerful asset when advocates can reach across agency walls for help with individual clients and policy issues.

Time

We would clearly expect people with more time to be able to advocate more. Time is, however, limited for everyone. Each of us has only twenty-four hours per day to sleep, eat, work, relax, and so on. How we allocate that time is the most important decision we make. And it is not always true that the people with the most free time are the most likely to be strong advocates: as the saying goes, "If you want something done, delegate it to a busy person." The ability to focus and to know what is important in our lives (i.e., what our values are) affects our perception of the availability of time for advocacy more than the actual amount of time in the day or the amount of time we work.

The way we allocate our twenty-four hours per day can be affected by design and expectations of our jobs. Job design is important because it affects workers' ability to use their time *productively*. Thus, even if all other aspects of life are equal, people with greater flexibility in their job schedules may be more likely to perform advocacy than people who have less flexibility, if only because flexibility allows a reallocation of time that maximizes productivity in other job elements. For example, some people have more defined times to work than others. A traditional job might start at 8:00 A.M. and end at 5:00 P.M. Another person might have flextime, which entails working the same number of hours but at different times. For example, a person might start work at 7:00 A.M. and end at 4:00 P.M. Another approach might be to work four days per week for ten hours each day. One way flexible work times could lead to greater use of advocacy is if a person who is able to function well early in the morning completes mandatory paperwork early in the day and thus has afternoon time (when decision makers may be more available and amenable to influence) for writing to, talking to, and visiting advocacy targets. Although flextime does not give a worker more time than another, job design can increase the amount of *productive* time during the same number of hours.

Also, different jobs have different levels of advocacy practice associated with them. Although advocacy is a part of all social workers' jobs, administrators typically use more of their workday for advocacy than do direct service workers (Ezell, 1994). Thus, the expectations of the administrators' jobs are more conducive to allocating time to advocacy.

Although social work administrators are expected to devote time to macrolevel advocacy, job requirements and expectations also are important for direct service workers. If organization supervisors' spoken or unspoken message is that "advocacy for our clients is part of the job" and they incorporate the message into formal and informal job performance ratings, staff will consider advocacy practice to be more important and will increase their advocacy work.

Wealth

While not depicted in figure 3.1, one might also add the variable of wealth. While we rarely think of social workers as being wealthy, if they have a steady job their incomes usually allow for at least limited wealth accumulation and discretionary spending. Potential advocates who have some wealth accumulation and funds for discretionary spending are probably more likely to engage in advocacy than are people with less wealth. A person who is more financially secure is able to donate more to political candidates; if supported candidates are elected, those candidates might consider the donor's views in making policy.

In addition, a family background of (relative) wealth is highly correlated with higher levels of education, and the ability to afford to enter a relatively low-paying profession such as social work. People with more to lose or gain from government policies tend to take a greater interest in advocacy, and so on.

Wealth, therefore, can be seen as an important element underlying many of the variables described earlier. As people consider whether to become advocates for social justice, their finances may influence them toward more or less activity. It is beyond the scope of most human service organizations to pay their employees so that they can become wealthy, but we do expect those organizations to pay living wages and better.

CONCLUSION

This chapter has laid out the first step in the advocacy practice process, getting involved. It discussed two main issues: the reasons why people are active in politics and the variables that influence people to use advocacy. These topics are vital to understanding both why a particular person may be involved in advocacy and how to influence others to get involved. After reading this information, you may have gained insight into why you are—or perhaps why you are *not*—interested in and active in politics. You may also have learned something about why you are or are not currently interested in advocacy at any level.

Many of the variables discussed are amenable to change—in you, in your colleagues, and even in clients. Education, values, and sense of professional responsibility are particularly important to stress in your own life and the lives of your social work colleagues. Learning about the other organizations that colleagues and clients participate in and the skills they have learned may allow you to discover people who are already involved and who may be excellent advocates and perhaps mentors for you.

Suggested Further Reading

Verba, S., Schlozman, K., & Brady, H. (1995). *Voice and equality: Civic voluntarism in American politics.* Cambridge, MA: Harvard University Press.

A modern classic of political science, these authors explore thoroughly how the American people make their voices heard in a democratic government. Based on surveys of and interviews with political activists and ordinary citizens, the authors develop and present a comprehensive model of political participation.

Discussion Questions and Exercises

1. In which areas discussed in this chapter are you already strong? In which areas are you not as strong? If you are a student now, how do you anticipate your strengths to change after you graduate?
2. Develop a plan to improve your advocacy abilities. How might you enlist your field agency or employer to assist you to develop your abilities in this way?
3. If you are currently a social work student, assess the extent to which your program currently supports students who want to develop skills in advocacy practice. What are the best aspects of the program right now? In what ways is the program not very supportive? What could the program do better? Discuss with other students, supportive faculty, and the program director or dean to make improvements.
4. If you are employed or in a field placement, what are the explicit and implicit messages about advocacy you are getting there? If you wanted to see stronger encouragement for advocacy practice, how would you approach the topic?

Chapter 4

Understanding the Issue

The small sign in the vacant lot was a bad omen. A local developer wanted to rezone the land to build a convenience store/gas station and strip mall right next to an older but well-maintained neighborhood, which was across the street from a large park. The public hearing was in one week. The one person who had noticed the sign was walking the streets of the neighborhood, collecting signatures on a petition, and making calls for action—"Let's write the members of the city council, call the newspaper, picket the developer's office. We have to do something, and we have to do it now!"

The person in the based-on-true-events vignette above is like many people are when first confronted with a situation that might call for advocacy. Once interest has been sparked, there is a desire to act. Time always seems short, and there is a natural desire not to allow a bad situation to continue any longer than necessary. Having an interest in the topic seems to instill potential advocates with an irresistible urge to get going and make a difference *right now.*

It is important to know that resistance to this urge is not futile—do not begin to take action just yet. Before *effective* action can begin, a potential advocate must first understand the issue. This chapter provides a way of making sure that the issue is understood: who benefits, who loses, and why. Without understanding the issue, the advocate is likely to make many mistakes and waste much time in trying to assist clients. In this chapter, I describe practical policy analysis tools.

Understanding usually comes in small stages, in which one piece of information fits into another and produces greater knowledge than either piece does on its own. Such synergy is the goal of the advocacy research process. Research, in this sense, may be very sophisticated, using statistical analysis and a thorough library search of relevant literature, but usually it is not. Usually, advocacy research is directed at answering one question, or a small number of questions, because it is believed that these answers will have an effect on decision makers. This process can be broken into five steps, as shown in figure 4.1.

STEP 1. DEFINE THE ISSUE

An often-overlooked step is defining the issue, as unambiguously as possible. Without being able to specify what the issue is, it will be

FIGURE 4.1   Steps to Understanding the Issue

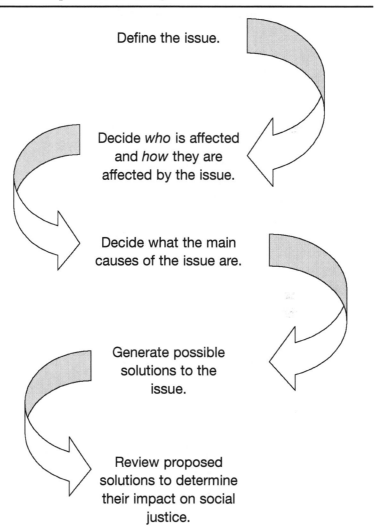

Define the issue.

Decide *who* is affected and *how* they are affected by the issue.

Decide what the main causes of the issue are.

Generate possible solutions to the issue.

Review proposed solutions to determine their impact on social justice.

impossible to understand it. Having a few facts at hand is not the same as defining an issue. A definition is important because "the same facts ... are often interpreted in markedly different ways. ... Hence, the same policy-relevant information can and often does result in conflicting definitions and explanations of a 'problem'" (Dunn, 1981, p. 97). It is also important to understand the difference between a problem and a condition: a condition is defined as a problem only after we decide something should be done about it (Kingdon, 1995, p. 109). Definitions are often shaped to a large extent by the values of the person doing the defining. These values are the lens through which the issue is categorized.

The way an issue is categorized has important implications for how it will be solved. For example, not too many years ago if a client came to a social worker with the presenting problem of spousal abuse (being hit), the issue would probably have been seen as a medical problem (if the physical harm was severe) and perhaps also as a marital problem (requiring counseling). It is far more likely nowadays that the social worker would see this as an issue of domestic violence and bring law enforcement officials into the picture to force the batterer to change, perhaps by giving him or her anger management training. The worker would also almost certainly refer the client to a local domestic violence shelter, if such a shelter is available. Thus, today the issue of spousal abuse is defined as a social problem more than as an individual problem, and is defined as the batterer's problem more than as the survivor's problem.

In another example of the importance of defining the issue, Kingdon (1995) describes the problem of transportation for people with handicaps as being a battle over the proper definition of the issue. If the situation is defined as a transportation issue, appropriate solutions are to provide subsidized taxi rides or dial-a-ride services. These services provide relatively inexpensive and convenient ways for people to travel to local destinations; by using these services, people with handicaps avoid being isolated from the rest of society. On the other hand, if the situation is defined as a civil rights issue, where separate accommodations are not equal, then proper solutions are to make public transportation accessible by installing elevators, lifts in buses, curb cuts for wheelchairs, and so on. In clinical work, the social worker sometimes calls this process framing the client's issue. Just as with clinical work, sometimes the role of the social worker is to reframe the issue if the current framing approach is not leading to successful intervention.

Problem Setting

Because the generalist model of social work is a rational, problem-solving approach to changing the world, we must deal with the topic of goal setting. Before we can set a goal (a process that we will examine in chapter 5), however, we must clearly articulate the problem. In some jobs, it is possible to envision a better future without reference to what is broken or untenable about today. In social work, though, we work with clients who experience hunger, psychic pain, and mental illness. Workers encounter situations of deprivation, discrimination, and desperation every day. Because we see so many problems, we cannot retreat to a fantasy world of perfection. Due to the many issues that we may attend to in our work, whether with one person or a community, it becomes vital for us to find a single problem to work on for each advocacy effort. This one problem may have many facets and several subsidiary problems, but we must find a way to encapsulate the issues into one problem statement. We do this in order to attain a focus for ourselves, our clients, decision makers, and others, such as potential allies (those who might be willing to try to change the current situation) or potential challengers (those trying to maintain the current situation) who may be interested.

A problem can be defined as a situation that should be changed and can be changed. Thus, biologically based situations such as being left-handed cannot be defined as problems because they cannot really be changed. A teacher's reaction to left-handed students may be a problem, however, because she may want to force the children to learn to write with their right hands. We might want to change this situation because research shows that forcing children who prefer their left hands for writing to use their right hands can damage them academically. And, we believe, the teacher may be open to changing her beliefs and behavior if she can be reached through advocacy by a school social worker. Thus, we can define the problem as the teacher's reaction to the situation, rather than as the left-handedness itself, which is merely a situation.

Practice looking at the world with this definition of a problem. You will quickly realize that many situations commonly called problems are not actually problems. It is not that these situations should not be changed, but rather that you believe they cannot or will not be changed. When encountering such a situation, the advocate's sense of social justice must take over and help him or her to find the part of the situation that can be changed. It is also possible to use reframing to keep the situation from leading to burnout. The following story about a girl and starfish illustrates this purpose for reframing:

> One bright morning a girl and her dad were walking along the beach near their home. Overnight, some freak occurrence of nature had stranded thousands of starfish on the beach. The girl was walking along, picking up as many of the dying creatures as possible, one by one, throwing them back to the salty, life-giving water. The dad praised his daughter for her efforts, but told her that she couldn't really make a significant impact on the overall situation. The girl looked thoughtfully at her father and said, "Dad, you may be right. But it makes a big difference to the ones I throw back!" (adapted from Eiseley, 1979)

No advocate can bring social justice to everyone. But by working carefully with their clients and others, advocates can make a big difference to the ones they do reach. You do not have to define the problem as thousands of people who lack food, live in inadequate housing, or are in danger of violence to be an advocate. You can define the problem as, "*This* man is hungry," "*This* family's home is falling down," "*This* child is in danger of being hit." Your efforts can make a world of difference to those individuals.

There are three possible approaches to problem (or issue, as we are using the term) definition: accepting the client's definition of the problem, using a pragmatic approach, and using the social-criterion approach (Patton & Sawicki, 2012).

Accepting the Client's Definition. Accepting the client's definition is an approach barely mentioned in Patton and Sawicki's (2012) policy analysis text, yet it is very important in the field of social work. It is part of the social work ethos of "starting where the client is." If a client indicates that she is having trouble getting her unemployment check and as a result is facing eviction, the social worker needs to look carefully at the issue the client is presenting for a solution. It may be that there is an underlying issue, such as the client not following through with paperwork or the client using rent money for other purposes, but the proper thing for a social work advocate to do may be to simply accept the client's definition as a starting point until he or she can collect additional information.

It can be fairly easy to get the client's view of the problem when working with clients in individual-level advocacy. The worker can consider the client to be the problem expert. What systemic barriers are getting in the way? What feelings are causing difficulty? What resources are lacking that would ease the situation? The client may be able to answer these questions readily. Significant others in the client's life may be able to provide additional, even if at times contradictory, insights into and views of the problem.

Social workers, with their training and professional expertise, also have much to contribute to the problem-setting process. It is possible that the client believes that society is to blame for the problem of his lack of success, while the social worker believes that society may be only part of the problem. Conversely, the client may want to take on full responsibility for a negative situation that can truly only be fully resolved at a community level. In either case, the analytical perspectives and techniques the social worker has learned can be of great value in helping the client focus, and thus they may be able to move quickly from here to there.

The process of problem setting is similar for a larger aggregation of people, such as an organization, a community group, or society, except that as the number of people increases, the chances of getting complete agreement on what *the* problem is diminishes rapidly. Still, the social worker's task in these circumstances is to work with a smaller group that can speak for the others. The task is then to get as much of a consensus as possible with this representative group.

A drawback in accepting a client definition is that the client and the professional social worker might view the issue differently, as was briefly mentioned above. For example, the client might view her issue as an individual failure while the worker believes it is more the result of systemic processes. Not being able to find a job in an area marked by high unemployment is one such situation. Alternatively, the client may want to blame others while the worker believes that the client can do something to fix his individual problem. An example of this might be that the client is not trying to stop using illegal drugs, saying that he is genetically predisposed to addiction. In both cases, the best approach in the short run may be to work toward a synthesis of the client's view and the social worker's view.

Another concern with using the client's definition of the problem is that it may be unclear who the client is, particularly with a macrolevel situation. In the case described at the beginning of this chapter, a community worker might immediately want to deny the zoning change request to prevent the construction of a convenience store/gas station and strip mall across the street from a large park and next to an established neighborhood. But it may be that some people living in the area would like to have such a close place to buy gas, and people who frequent the park might like to be able to buy cold drinks or ice on a hot day. Is the client the person who is leading the fight against the zoning change, the neighborhood as a whole (including both those who might be in favor and those who might be against it), or the city as a whole? Although the answer probably depends on who employs the potential advocate, we must answer the question if we are to accept the client's definition of the problem.

The Pragmatic Approach. If using a pragmatic approach, an advocate would be interested in understanding an issue only when there is disagreement about how the issue should be handled and when there are ways to handle the problem other than the one currently being used. In other words, if everyone agrees that there is nothing that can be done to change the situation or no one has a better idea, the pragmatically minded advocate would look for some other client to assist or some other issue to work on.

The danger of a pragmatic approach is that the social worker may become too cynical to seize the opportunities for change that exist, given the right approach. It is easy to say, even metaphorically, "You can't fight city hall" to mean that nothing can be done to alter the situation, whether one is dealing with an individual or community issue.

Often, however, more change can be made to happen than a quick look at the situation would suggest. It might take more than the usual amount of effort, but creative solutions can emerge that increase the range of possible options.

Social-Criterion Approach. An advocate using the social-criterion approach actively searches for issues and tries to define issues that should be solved. This approach involves an intricate calculation of whether an issue is an individual problem or a societal problem that requires intervention from others. The advocate usually chooses to work on problems that are both *widespread* (i.e., affecting large numbers of people) and *serious* (i.e., causing considerable distress to people who experience the problem). However, widespread problems may not be defined as serious problems, and serious problems may not be widespread enough for social intervention (Patton & Sawicki, 2012). If either is the case, it is less likely that there will be an advocate trying to solve the particular problem.

Two dangers are associated with using the social-criterion approach. First, the potential advocate may wrongly place the issue on the individual-societal continuum. One error entails defining the situation in such a way as to place blame on individuals for problems caused or exacerbated by social forces or institutions. Another error is deciding that the situation was social in nature when, in fact, it was unique to the individual client. Another danger of the social-criterion approach is that it may consume too much time in trying to be very inclusive of all issues in a community. It is also unrealistic to expect employees of agencies to be on the constant lookout for new issues to emerge—they generally have more than enough issues already vying for their attention.

An example may clarify the different approaches to defining an issue. The activist mentioned at the start of this chapter is concerned about a convenience store/gas station with an accompanying strip mall being proposed in his neighborhood. Using a client viewpoint–acceptance approach, a social worker in the city's community development office brought in for advice would just accept that building a convenience store/gas station and strip mall is a problem or that it may lead to a number of problems. Another social worker, using the pragmatic approach, might look at what else could be proposed for the land and how successful a challenge to the new zoning would be before deciding on a definition of the issue. If the zoning board and city council have already decided to support the proposal, the social worker advocate might decide to look for another way to use his or her time. However, if some disagreement exists among the members of the decision-making body, he or she would look at other ways to approach the use of that land. The social worker understands that how an issue is defined has an impact on how the issue is perceived and thus on which solution may be chosen. Finally, the social-criterion approach social worker would be out in the field on a regular basis, trying to find out what is going on in the community. This social worker might look at vacant land and monitor closely the rezoning applications that are submitted, and might believe that vigilance is needed to look proactively at land use decisions, particularly those that bring in low-end retail shopping. He will maintain ties with many people, always searching for land-use solutions that improve the distribution of life chances for residents of the neighborhood.

A good problem definition will put some parameters around the situation. It will describe a gap between what should be (based on a vision of social justice) and what is (the reality facing the social worker). It will be specific and, in and of itself, will be a call to action. The following are sample problem statements:

- Children are going to bed hungry in our city.
- I have a client whose bank loan application for home improvements has been denied because her neighborhood is redlined.
- Elementary school children in the local school district who speak only Vietnamese do not have access to anyone at school who speaks their language.
- Minority youth in our community are arrested more often and receive longer sentences than white kids who commit the same offenses.

Keep in mind that as you move through the steps of understanding an issue, you may want to change your definition of the issue. This change is acceptable, as it shows you have learned something important. A compelling definition of the issue is a necessary part of understanding an issue, but more information is needed before moving ahead to doing something.

STEP 2. DECIDE WHO IS AFFECTED AND HOW THEY ARE AFFECTED BY THE ISSUE

The second step to understanding the issue is to look at who is affected, both positively and negatively. Although it may seem odd to think about who benefits from a problem, this perspective helps us remember that laws, rules, conditions, and "the way things are" are not random circumstances. If negative situations occurred by chance, then the situations would most likely be altered quickly.

Depending on how you have defined the issue in the first step, you may be considering this as an issue affecting only one person or many. Let's take an example from the list provided earlier and say that we have a client who is unable to get a bank loan for home improvements. The client indicates that she has filed all the requested paperwork and has adequate income to repay the loan. Due to confidentiality requirements, the bank officials that the social worker has contacted for information are unwilling to talk without the client present. The social worker suspects that the client's neighborhood has been redlined—that is, banks have decided not to give loans to anyone who wants to improve property located in a certain area. The social worker and potential advocate asks the following question: Who is (or may be) affected by this situation and how?

A rough list of answers to this question includes the following:

1. The client who did not get the loan is negatively affected by a deteriorating physical environment.
2. Everyone else living in the neighborhood is negatively affected by a deteriorating physical environment.
3. Neighborhood institutions such as businesses, religious groups, and so on are negatively affected by a deteriorating physical environment.
4. The bank or banks involved (as institutions) are currently positively affected, because they have no risk of default if they do not make loans to people in a low-income neighborhood. In the future, they may be affected negatively, because redlining

(if that is what is happening) is not a legal practice. Even if the case is not proven in court, the bank or banks will suffer negative publicity if the charges are made public.

5. The bankers making loan decisions (as individuals) are probably affected in a positive way, as their job security may depend on keeping profits high. In the future, if someone brings this situation to court and proves that redlining is taking place, there could be negative effects, including fines and/or jail terms for those bankers.

6. Developers and property owners may be positively affected, as the value of homes that are not well maintained deteriorates and thus may be less expensive for developers and property owners of low-rent housing to purchase.

7. Businesses that supply home fix-up materials are negatively affected, as people wanting to fix up a deteriorating physical environment are denied funds, which prevents them from buying supplies at these businesses.

8. The community as a whole is negatively affected due to a physically deteriorating area of town. Such areas tend to continue to decline in value, bringing additional crime and violence to that neighborhood, which requires additional police resources. There may be a small short-term positive effect if the money that might be loaned to fix up deteriorating homes in one part of the city is used on other projects that are more economically profitable.

9. Banking regulatory officials, if redlining is occurring by the bank, can be negatively affected, because they may have to conduct an investigation.

10. Law enforcement officials, if a crime has been committed, might be negatively affected, because they may have to conduct an investigation.

Just this short list shows that many people and institutions are (or may be) affected, some negatively, some positively, while some, such as the community as a whole, may have some negative and some positive consequences. Laying out who is or may be affected and how they are affected allows the advocate to think about potential allies (those who might be willing to try to change the current situation) and potential challengers (those trying to maintain the current situation).

There are different ways of determining who is affected and how; these alternatives vary in their levels of sophistication (Patton & Sawicki, 2012). These are four back-of-the-envelope ways to determine the size of the population affected: *guess* the number, get *experts* to help you guess the number, look up the number in a *reference source,* and collect the number through a *systematic survey* or other investigation (Mosteller, 1977, pp. 163–164).

Each of these methods has advantages and disadvantages as a way of understanding the scope of the issue. The advantage of the guess is its ease of application: Anyone can come up with an educated or uneducated guess about the scope of an issue. All guesses should be defensible and based on other techniques, such as extrapolation and projection, but often they are not. Advocates for a particular issue who guess are often accused of lying with statistics about the size of a problem. For example, guesses at the size of the homeless population differ by several hundred percent; often the size of the guess is related to its purpose. People who want more funding for programs to assist the homeless favor a broad definition of homelessness, which results in many people being categorized as homeless. Government officials, or others who wish to minimize the size of the homeless population, move from the opposite position, and find that homelessness is less of an issue because of a stricter definition of homelessness. Without knowing the exact genesis of a social statistic, a potential user should approach it with caution (Best, 2012).

Many of the same caveats apply to the use of experts in the guessing process. Experts, by definition, know something about the issue in question, but experts are almost never neutral and may have ties to particular value stances that affect their estimates of the scope of an issue.

Many issues will not have accurate counts of the numbers of people affected, particularly in a small area, but one should not automatically assume this is true. Census Bureau data can be broken down into quite small areas called census tracts, so many local needs assessments can provide useful and accurate information that has already been collected. City and county planning departments and the United Way, or other private planning bodies, often sponsor surveys of various topics.

Systematic surveys or other research is the best way to have an accurate understanding of how many people and organizations are involved in an issue. If open-ended questions are included, very clear insights into how people and organizations are affected can be deduced. The disadvantages of this approach are its costs, difficulty, and need for expertise to have a truly valid and reliable survey.

STEP 3. DECIDE WHAT THE MAIN CAUSES OF THE ISSUE ARE

In any situation, one can identify proximate (or immediate) causes, even if it is difficult to locate true (or ultimate) causes of social issues. A search for ultimate causes generally ends up in a dispute over values and religious or philosophic views. For example, we may be able to trace many of the current problems of poverty to a history of an economically stratified and racist social structure in the United States, but what caused such a social structure? A selfish human nature might be called the ultimate cause, but what is the cause of that nature? At some point, then, it becomes useless to argue causes, particularly ultimate causes. Still, we must attempt an understanding of proximate causes.

Different definitions of the issue lead to different ideas about the proximate cause. For example, after interviewing our client who did not get a home improvement loan and the bank employee who processed the loan, we might find out that the client was not sure what all the terms on the application meant and did not have all the requested supporting documents. In this case, we might identify the proximate cause of the loan not being approved as problems with the application due to the applicant's lack of knowledge and preparation. On the other hand, we might suspect that the employee working on the loan application was not as helpful as he could have been and was looking for an excuse to turn down the application. Without additional information, we cannot really say what the cause of the issue is.

At this point, we have a useful definition of the problem and an analysis of who is affected and how. If we have determined that only a few people have had their applications denied and that all had prob-

74

lems understanding the application form, our interpretation of the issue's cause would likely be a lack of individual knowledge. If we have determined that more than a few people from different areas of town have been turned down and that they all report uncaring bank employees, we can believe that the cause of the issue has something to do with the selection and training of the bank staff. If we have found that many people living in one geographic area have had their applications turned down, we are more likely to believe that the bank is using a set of systematic and discriminatory guidelines. Once we have decided what is causing the problem, we are ready to devise ways of solving it.

STEP 4. GENERATE POSSIBLE SOLUTIONS TO THE ISSUE

One of the most difficult, yet most interesting, aspects of the advocacy process is generating possible solutions. Generation of solutions is difficult because after one or two solutions come to mind quickly, it can be more difficult to generate more-creative options. Generation of solutions is interesting, however, in that the ability to devise novel solutions is rewarding to the advocate if the solutions are adopted as being a better idea than current practice.

Although the phrase "think outside the box" has become a cliché, we should develop solutions that are not bound by currently perceived boundaries or structures. Four approaches to developing solutions are described next.

Brainstorming

Although one person could complete the following approaches, it is often useful to proceed with at least a small group in a brainstorming session. Brainstorming is a process of generating ideas without evaluating them along the way. It can be used as its own technique but is also often an integral part of other methods of idea generation as well. Because the term "brainstorming" is so common, most people have heard of it and even participated in what have been called brainstorming sessions. Still, a review of the basic principles of a brainstorming session is important, if only because untrained facilitators often violate the principles:

1. Have a leader and a recorder (one person may fulfill both roles).
2. Clearly define what the brainstorming session is about. Everyone involved should be working on the same issue.
3. Have rules to guide the process. The following are common rules: Everyone is allowed to participate. Comments about the ideas generated (if any) should be nonjudgmental. All ideas should be recorded unless they are a repeat of an earlier idea. A time limit should be set and adhered to.
4. If ideas seem lacking, sterile, or obvious, the leader can introduce random words to stimulate creativity. These words are best if they come from outside the main topic area and if they are tangible nouns rather than abstract ideas. The idea behind the use of random words is to spark creativity by injecting unusual images or ideas into the mix.
5. Evaluate the responses after the time limit for generating ideas is up. Evaluation includes grouping similar ideas, eliminating responses that do not apply or fit, and discussing the plusses and minuses of the remaining ideas as a group (Osborn, 1963).

The "George Costanza" Approach

This approach is named in honor of a fictional character on the television show *Seinfeld*. In one episode, George decides that his usual approach to dating and life in general is not having the desired effect. He therefore decides to consider what he would usually do, then do the opposite. In the episode, George immediately begins to experience success in every aspect of his life. To apply this approach in your work, think of the typical response by the client, worker, and/or agency. Given that there is a problem based on this typical response, what would the opposite response be? Is there more than one opposite response? What are they?

The "Win-Win" or "Super-Optimizing" Approach

This approach is based on the work of Stuart Nagel (2002), a prominent policy analysis scholar, and is outlined in his *Handbook of Public Policy Evaluation*. The basic idea of Nagel's win-win approach is to create an alternative policy that restructures the current situation to make it both more equitable and more efficient. Nagel outlines a number of basic approaches that have been successful (see table 4.1). Using this checklist, a social work advocate can develop alternative solutions for further consideration, whether the issue at hand is at a micro, mezzo, or macro level. By starting off asking, "What would happen if we ...?" and then adding each phrase in table 4.1, many ideas can be created that might not have been thought of without this set of prompts.

The "What Can Be Done?" Approach

An additional way to generate solutions to an issue is the "What Can Be Done?" approach (table 4.2), loosely based on the feasible-manipulations approach developed by May (1981). The focus of the "What Can Be Done?" approach is to look at important variables in the issue and develop alternatives that fall on a continuum of those that can be easily done to those that can be done only with difficulty. The first step in the process is to determine what elements of the situation are changeable—that is, What *can* and *should* we change about the situation or

---

TABLE 4.1   Developing Win-Win Policy Alternatives

---

1. Expand the resources.
2. Find a third party benefactor.
3. Set higher goals.
4. Minimize the causes of the problem.
5. Redefine the problem to emphasize goals rather than alternatives.
6. Increase the benefits and decrease the costs.
7. Socialize children in widely accepted values so the problem does not occur.
8. Find a new technology.
9. Contract out via an auction to multiple firms with societal strings attached.
10. Promote international economic communities.
11. Arrange for major benefits on one side and small costs on the other.
12. Fully combine alternatives that are not mutually exclusive.
13. Develop a multifaceted package.
14. Adopt the win-win solution in steps, in which the first step may be a traditional compromise.

Reprinted from Nagel, S. (2002). *Handbook of Public Policy Evaluation* (p. 6). Thousand Oaks, CA: Sage.

its causes? The analyst writes these in the left-hand column of a table, with one variable in each row. The analyst should also determine different actions that can be taken with regard to each variable; these actions should range from changes that are relatively easy to make to changes that are relatively difficult to make.

TABLE 4.2 "What Can Be Done?" Approach Example: Turned-Down Bank Loans

	Ease of Doing		
Variable	*Relatively Easy to Do*	*Moderately Easy to Do*	*Relatively Difficult to Do*
Applicant Knowledge	Develop materials to explain the loan process for in-person or Web exchange	Change when information can be transmitted via in-person classes; improve computer access to information on the Web	Increase applicants' free time to learn about home buying or the loan process
Bank Employee Selection	Increase/change places where loan application processor positions are advertised	Expand applicant pool to include more people of color and other minorities	Alter job requirements for loan application processor job
Bank Employee Training	Introduce basic "soft" skills into the training, such as a customer service philosophy	Provide/mandate ethnic and cultural sensitivity training	Change current procedures for becoming a loan application processor to require that most "hard" job skills (use of computers, ability to compute numbers, etc.) are already known
Possible Discriminatory Bank Practices	File complaint with banking regulatory bodies	File EEO case	File criminal case

As an example, we will look at the issue of bankers denying loans, as we have discussed earlier in the chapter. We have examined each of the identified variables—applicant knowledge, bank employee selection, bank employee training, and possible bank discriminatory practices. In table 4.2, for each variable there is at least one possible action that is relatively easy to do, one that is moderately easy to do, and one that is relatively difficult to do. The advocate, at this point, has a number of options from which to choose, any of which should improve the situation to some extent.

No matter which approach you use to generate alternative solutions (and it might be very useful for you to use more than one approach), you can evaluate the possible actions on the basis of their anticipated effect on social justice.

STEP 5. REVIEW PROPOSED SOLUTIONS TO DETERMINE THEIR IMPACT ON SOCIAL JUSTICE

The fifth step is to review the various solutions that are proposed and to determine how likely they are to lead to social justice. The basic approach to creating and looking at possible solutions is to ask, "What would be the results of adopting this solution? Who would be assisted? Who would be harmed? How would this solution act on people currently affected negatively by this issue? How would this solution act on people currently affected positively by this issue?" Rank proposed solutions leading to greater social justice higher than solutions that do not improve social justice as much. This part of the chapter examines a few quick ways to evaluate alternative solutions to the issue.

Six Thinking Hats

One approach to evaluating possible solutions is the six thinking hats approach (De Bono, 1999). The basic principle underlying this approach is that there is more than one thinking style, and each can contribute to a balanced evaluation of a proposed solution. Some of the conflict that arises in group discussions emanates from people using different thinking styles. By rotating among all six styles and having everyone use the same thinking style at the same time, all styles are given their proper due and better decisions can be made. This approach also works with just one person who rotates among the six styles, thereby moving beyond his or her usual and dominant thinking style. When combined with a clear focus on the goal of achieving greater social justice, use of the six thinking hats approach has the potential to improve the quality of the decision process and the development of more easily implemented and workable plans. I discuss the six hats (or thinking styles) next.

The *white hat* is the rational style: data analysis and historical interpolation are the key methods of understanding. The social worker identifies gaps in the data, as well as ways around those gaps.

The *red hat* is the intuitive style: emotion, subjectivity, and gut reactions are the key methods of understanding the situation. Trying to understand other people's emotional and gut reactions, not just one's own, is an important element in this style. With this hat, the social worker asks how people will react to the decision made, especially if those people do not know the reasons behind it.

The *black hat* is the negative style: the negatives of the situation or proposed solution are brought out. The social worker should ask the following questions: "What are the weaknesses of the proposal? How can it be shot down? What might go wrong? Can those possibilities be lessened?" By systematically focusing on problems with the potential solution, the decision is strengthened. By having everyone adopt the naysayer role, potential problems are brought into the open without anyone being unfairly labeled as unduly pessimistic. This protects lower-status group members from higher-status group members who might take criticism of their ideas personally.

The *yellow hat* is the optimistic style: the emphasis is on the possible benefits of the proposal and the value of the idea. When the proposal is in trouble or having difficulties, the ideas generated in the yellow hat stage are invaluable for maintaining momentum.

The *green hat* is the creative style: the emphasis is on seeing the situation in different ways. The social worker can use techniques such as brainstorming, random word seeding, use of analogies or similes, and so on, to see things in a different way.

The *blue hat* is the conductor's hat: the outcome of this type of thinking is to decide how the decision process for the meeting should be structured. A blue hat period is often at the beginning of a gathering, when the agenda is set, rules for the meeting are proposed and agreed to by participants, and other decisions are made about how to proceed. Unlike the other hats that move from person to person, one person, usually the group leader or meeting facilitator, keeps the blue hat on during the entire process. Others may also put on this hat to assist moving the discussion along, such as noting that someone is using the wrong hat for this point in the meeting. Blue hat thinking also summarizes discussions, provides overviews, and states conclusions. This can occur during the meeting as well as at its end.

Wearing one hat after another encourages a thorough examination of any proposed solution and, combined with a focus on social justice, may greatly improve the preliminary solution. This approach is also useful when comparing multiple possible solutions in that this multifaceted look at the different solutions to the same issue will bring out each alternative's strengths and weaknesses.

Social Justice Scorecard

There are many different variations of a scorecard approach (see, e.g., the description of approaches in Patton & Sawicki, 2012). The basic idea, however, is to compare alternatives without being able to reduce their characteristics to one number or score. Because the primary criterion for choosing a solution is to determine which solution most achieves social justice, Patton and Sawicki developed the Social Justice Scorecard, which uses four attributes of social justice from a social work perspective based on Abbott's (1988) work. Each alternative strategy is listed in a separate column and can be graded or rated on each of the social justice attributes. Social workers can make these rankings in either an absolute way (as shown in table 4.3) or in a relative way (worst, medium, best), using either numbers or a qualitative ordinal scale such as is shown. The Social Justice Scorecard should include a "Do nothing" option among the alternative strategies to make clear the rankings for maintaining the status quo. Workers can develop separate scorecards from different perspectives as well, such as viewing the situation from the client's perspective, the agency's perspective, or even a more global community perspective. Although the actual ratings may not change much between the different perspectives, it is possible that they will, and it is instructive to see where and to what extent they do.

TABLE 4.3   Social Justice Scorecard for Policy Alternatives:
Bank Loan Example

		Alternative Strategies	
Attributes of Social Justice	Do Nothing	Change Applicants' Knowledge of Banking Procedures	Change Bank Hiring and Training Practices
Respect for Basic Human Rights	Low	Medium	Medium
Promotion of Social Responsibility	Low	Medium	High
Commitment to Individual Freedom	Low	Medium	Low
Support for Self-Determination	Low	Medium	Low

In looking at the example in table 4.3, let's assume that we do not want to file any formal complaints with regulatory bodies or courts, preferring to first try to work with people in the community and the bank to improve the situation. We can hold the formal complaints and lawsuit option for later and use them as an implied threat if our initial efforts for improvement do not work. Thus, the three alternative strategies listed are do nothing, change applicants' knowledge of banking procedures, and change bank hiring and training practices.

In this example, we have assigned a ranking that shows the degree to which each alternative addresses each of the four attributes of social justice. We are using a community-wide perspective in this example. (Naturally, the ratings are subjective and others may rate them differently.)

We believe that the "do nothing" strategy does not do much to improve any of the four attributes of social justice. We rate the "change applicants' knowledge of banking procedures" strategy as having a medium level of support for all four of the attributes. The final strategy, "change bank hiring and training practices," is medium in affecting respect for basic human rights, high in supporting promotion of social responsibility, and low in both commitment to individual freedom and support for self-determination.

From this initial review, it is clear that doing nothing will not promote social justice as much as either of the other strategies. There is not an obvious choice between the other two strategies, as their scores seem fairly close. To ease comparison, we can assign a number to each qualitative score, such as 1 for low, 2 for medium, and 3 for high. Then the "do nothing" strategy receives a score of 4, the "change applicants' knowledge" strategy receives a score of 8, and the "change bank hiring and training practices" strategy receives a score of 7. Thus, the second strategy has a slight edge in terms of our belief about how well it promotes social justice.

In this case, because the two strategies are not mutually exclusive, we might think of implementing both strategies for a more comprehensive attack on the problem. This also has the advantage of improving social justice overall, as each of the two alternatives has one or more areas that are better than the other. Changing the hiring and training practices, for example, is better at promoting social responsibility for the issue, while changing applicants' knowledge of banking procedures is ranked higher for supporting self-determination.

Another option in using the Social Justice Scorecard is to assign weights to the different attributes. For example, if you believe that promotion of social responsibility is three times as important as each of the other attributes, then you would triple the score for that one attribute. In that case, the scores for each alternative strategy would be as follows: do nothing $(1 + 3 + 1 + 1 = 6)$, change applicants' knowledge $(2 + 6 + 2 + 2 = 12)$, and change bank hiring and training practices $(2 + 9 + 1 + 1 = 13)$.

In this case, while the scores are still close for the two strategies of action, the strategy of changing bank hiring and training practices now has the slight edge. In order to keep the weighting process honest, it is important to select the relative weights *before* you decide on the ratings.

CONCLUSION

This chapter has covered the important step of the advocacy practice process called understanding the issue. It is not wise to take action unless you understand the issue. This chapter has described a process of learning about and understanding the issue. The steps in the process are to define the issue, decide who is affected and how they are affected, decide what the main causes of the issue are, generate possible solutions to the issue, and review proposed solutions to determine their impact on social justice.

I have described several techniques to accomplish these steps, particularly techniques for generating possible solutions to the issue and for evaluating the alternatives that have been generated. The steps and techniques described are equally useful whether the focus of advocacy is at the individual, group, community, or societal level.

Once the issue is understood, the next step in the advocacy practice approach is to actually plan the advocacy effort. This step is the subject of the next chapter.

Suggested Further Reading

Best, J. (2012). *Damned lies and statistics: Untangling numbers from the media, politicians and activists* (2nd ed.). Berkeley: University of California Press.

In this era of statistically driven policy debates, we all must learn how to critically examine what we are told by people with vested interests in having us believe them. This book is both a catalog of inaccurate "facts" that seem reasonable but are not true, and a primer on how to spot such errors on our own. Best provides a number of techniques to help us independently verify what we are told.

De Bono, E. (1999). *Six thinking hats*. Boston: Little, Brown.

This slim book presents an approach to improving decision making that is easy to understand and implement. Using this approach also can eliminate some of the arguing that occurs in meetings when different people approach a situation without realizing they are wearing different hats. Although designed for groups, the approach also has application for individual problem solving and decision making.

Discussion Questions and Exercises

On your own or with a partner, choose an issue or problem that you would like to understand better. Follow the five steps as outlined in this chapter.

1. How challenging was it to develop a shared definition of the problem among the members of your group? What made it easy or challenging?
2. Who is most directly affected? Do you think you could get those people to work with you to advocate for change? Who most directly benefits from the current situation? How much would those people oppose efforts to alter the status quo?
3. How easily can you come to agreement regarding the proximate causes of the current situation that you want to change?
4. What are three possible solutions to this issue? Which one would lead to the highest level of social justice? Would you choose to work toward that solution, or would you choose to work toward one that achieves less social justice but might be more easily adopted or implemented?

Chapter 5

PLANNING IN ADVOCACY PRACTICE

The students went to speak to their professor about their group paper grade. Their assignment had been to organize an advocacy project designed to help solve a social problem. The group leader said, "This grade doesn't represent the amount of work and effort we put into this project. It just isn't fair." The professor, after teaching this course on advocacy all semester, was pleased that the students felt empowered enough to argue their grade, but he was sure that the grade was really fair, given the quality of the final product. "Okay," he said, "What do you want? What do you think a fair grade would be, and why?"

The students looked at one another in confusion. After some time, the leader finally mumbled, "Well, we want you to look it over again, I guess."

"That just proves you haven't learned much this semester," the professor declared. "You need to decide what you want from your advocacy effort and how to achieve it. Right now, you're just proving that the low grade is justified."

If you are in a situation where you are asking someone with decision-making authority for something and you cannot explain what you want, you are a victim of a self-inflicted wound—a lack of planning. This chapter will provide information about what planning is, how to conduct it, and how to know when it is time to move from plan to action. Premature action usually results in failure, while overly prolonged planning usually results in no change in the status quo. Both should be avoided.

The planning process is not something that you do on its own. It is predicated on the work that you have already done in getting involved, understanding the issue, developing possible solutions, and assessing those possible solutions. The planning process links together your previous work with a clearer focus on what outcomes you want to accomplish. After a full planning effort, you should be able to provide clear answers to these four questions: What do you want? Who can get you what you want? When can or should you act to get what you want? How can you act to get what you want?

Answering the first three questions provides the information needed to answer the last question. This chapter covers the first three questions, while chapters 6 and 7 answer the fourth question. First, though, we define what we mean by planning.

DEFINITION OF PLANNING

At its simplest level, planning is the process of deciding how to get from here to there. *Here* is the current situation, which we have already decided is inappropriate or unjust in some way and is certainly someplace we no longer want to be. *There,* on the other hand, is the future state of existence where the world will be improved, there will be more social justice, and at least one person will be better off. We use a map to help us move from one physical location to another. It is also helpful for us to use a planning tool when we employ advocacy to get from here to there.

After much experience in getting from here to there in a particular physical location, we can often discard the map we have been using: we know how to get to work, how to get to the theater, how to get to places we usually go. Planning, however, is a tool we should use every time we engage in advocacy, because the "there" of each situation is never the same; even after we become very adept at the process of advocacy, each new advocacy effort is leading us to a different "there" and into an unknown future. Thus, we need to retain the mapping process when we engage in advocacy.

WHAT DO YOU WANT? USING ADVOCACY MAPPING TO DESCRIBE YOUR AGENDA

Without a clear understanding of what you want to accomplish, it is unlikely that you will achieve what you thought you wanted. As a problem-solving strategy, planning in advocacy must set forth goals to accomplish.

A logic model—a tool derived from program planning and evaluation—is useful to the planning process (W. K. Kellogg Foundation, 2004). This model is an organized and succinct way to show the connections between what you plan to do and what you want to accomplish, including outcomes for the short, medium, and long terms. An advocacy map will assist you in connecting what you want to achieve by engaging in advocacy with the tasks that you will engage in for that advocacy effort.

The advocacy map has several different sections (see figure 5.1). Let's look at them one by one. The label on the second line is "Problem/Issue." It is important to have a clear idea of what you are working to fix before you go any farther. Considerable information was devoted to this topic in chapter 4, so it is now possible to fill in the problem/issue blank with what you have already decided.

The next line in an advocacy map is "Desired Outcome(s) for Client." This is what you would ideally like to see happen for the client. There are two important aspects about outcomes to which you must adhere: First, the outcome should indicate that the problem/issue has been resolved for the client. Second, but following from the first criterion, the outcome should be a change in the client's situation. This is your ideal, long-term outcome(s); it is not necessarily the one you believe is most likely or even likely at all, but rather is just the outcome(s) that would most improve the client's situation while being socially just. Be sure to write this as something positive and something that is a change in the client's situation.

Next, we look at some examples of how to fill in these two lines. The following is an example of a poor problem statement: "My fourteen-year-old female client is not in the afterschool class." The corresponding poor client outcome statement is as follows: "My client will be in the afterschool class." At first glance, these may not seem too bad. The outcome statement is the opposite of the problem statement, and being in a class is a change in the client's situation—she was not in the class, and now she is. So why are these poor statements for an advocacy map? The reason they are poor is that being in a class or not being in a class is usually not really the important aspect of a situation for a client—what *is* important is something that we can *know* is a negative thing. Being in a class may or may not be a negative thing. We do not

FIGURE 5.1 The Advocacy Map

DATE: _____

Problem/Issue: _____

Desired Outcome(s) for Client: _____

Ultimate Social Justice–Related Outcome(s) for Society: _____

Resources (col. 1)	Tasks (col. 2)	Short-term Outcomes (col. 3)	Medium-term Outcomes (col. 4)	Long-term Outcomes (col. 5)	Ultimate Social Justice–Related Outcomes for Society (col. 6)

really know why it is important for the student to be in the class, because we do not know what problem the client is facing. A better problem statement might be, "My client is engaging in risky behavior after school and before her mother gets home from work" (see figure 5.2). This behavior is definitely a negative that we want to correct. Perhaps instead the issue is something else entirely and is better stated, "Discrimination based on race or sex is limiting choices for minority and female students at my client's school, including my client." This statement, too, indicates a situation that is negative. A social worker might address either problem by getting his client into the afterschool class, but we can also think of other ways to address the problem as restated. If the problem statement remains, "My client is not in the afterschool class," the range of solutions is limited to getting her into the class.

The next line in the advocacy map is "Ultimate Social Justice-Related Outcome(s) for Society." This line is where you connect the desired outcome for the client you are working with now to a society-wide change that would assist individuals or is the result of all people having what you want for your current client. Using the above statements as examples, a corresponding ultimate social justice-related outcome for society might be, "All children will be in safe situations with nearby adult support." The other client outcome statement could lead to the following ultimate social justice-related outcome for society: "Discrimination based on race or sex will be eliminated."

The rest of the advocacy map is made up of six columns. Although the advocacy map reads from left to right—from the listing of resources to the listing of ultimate social justice-related outcomes— you can fill in the columns in any order that makes sense to you. We will fill it in, for the purpose of this example, from left to right, from "Resources" to "Ultimate Social Justice-Related Outcome(s) for Society."

It is often easy to list what resources are available. Column 1 is a listing of what is going to be used to solve the problem and address the issue. Resources include people (clients, their significant others, program staff, and volunteers), money, buildings, political support, other programs, and so on, that can be enlisted to achieve the advocacy

FIGURE 5.2 An Example Advocacy Map

DATE:

Problem/Issue: My client is engaging in risky behavior (unprotected sex and recreational use of marijuana) after school and before her mother gets home from work.

Desired Outcome(s) for Client: My client will not engage in risky behavior (unprotected sex and recreational use of marijuana) after school and before her mother gets home from work.

Ultimate Social Justice–Related Outcome(s) for Society: All children will be in safe situations with nearby adult support.

Resources (col. 1)	Tasks (col. 2)	Short-term Outcomes (col. 3)	Medium-term Outcomes (col. 4)	Long-term Outcomes (col. 5)	Ultimate Social Justice–Related Outcomes for Society (col. 6)
Student Client	• Search for acceptable alternative activities to the current risky behaviors. • Research potential consequences of engaging in unprotected sex and recreational use of marijuana. • Learn skills of advocacy for self and others.	• Student will engage in other activities that do not put her at risk. • Student will know negative potential consequences of unprotected sex, negative effects of pregnancy on student and her child in the future, and effects of marijuana on self and unborn child.	• This student will have no more (or at least reduced) engagement in risky behaviors such as unprotected sex and drug use.	• This student will not become pregnant and will discontinue use of all illegal drugs.	• All children will be in safe situations with nearby adult support.

91

Resources (col. 1)	Tasks (col. 2)	Short-term Outcomes (col. 3)	Medium-term Outcomes (col. 4)	Long-term Outcomes (col. 5)	Ultimate Social Justice-Related Outcomes for Society (col. 6)
Student Client's Parents	• Search for acceptable alternative activities to the current risky behaviors. • Try to arrange situation so that greater supervision of client can be done by a parent or other trusted adult. • If the afterschool program is considered the best spot for the child, advocate for her to be placed in an appropriate situation (either at school or elsewhere).	• Student will engage in other activities that do not put her at risk. • A parent or other trusted adult will be identified to supervise the student each day.	• This student will have no more (or at least reduced) engagement in risky behaviors such as unprotected sex and drug use.	• This student will not become pregnant and will discontinue use of all illegal drugs.	• All children will be in safe situations with nearby adult support.

Social Worker	• Search for acceptable alternative activities to the current risky behaviors. • If the afterschool program is considered the best spot for the client, advocate for client's inclusion in afterschool activities program.	• Student will engage in other activities that do not put her at risk. • Program staff will allow student into program.	• This student will have no more (or at least reduced) engagement in risky behaviors such as unprotected sex and drug use.	• This student will not become pregnant and will discontinue use of all illegal drugs.	• All children will be in safe situations with nearby adult support.
Staff running the afterschool activities program	• Allow this student into the program. • Expand size of program to include all students who would benefit from the program.	• Program staff will allow student into program. • Program staff will have resources to work with all students who would benefit from the program.	• This student will have no more (or at least reduced) engagement in risky behaviors such as unprotected sex and drug use.	• This student will not become pregnant and will discontinue use of all illegal drugs. • Female students in the program will not become pregnant and will not use illegal drugs.	• All children will be in safe situations with nearby adult support.

effort's desired outcomes. In the example advocacy map in figure 5.2, the resources listed are the client, the client's parents, the social worker handling the case, and the staff of the afterschool activities program.

Each of these resources should have at least one task assigned (column 2) to it. If there is no task to be done by a particular resource, there is no need for that particular resource in this advocacy effort. It should be noted that many of the resources may be assigned similar tasks, but because they come at the tasks from their different perspectives, the advocacy planner may need to coordinate efforts and mediate potential conflicts. If all goes well the individual efforts will lead to more-positive outcomes than what could be expected by any single resource's efforts.

An inanimate resource may have an important task, too. A resource such as a community center meeting room may have a task such as "provide a warm and inviting place for informal interaction among program staff and clients," although clearly a room by itself cannot do such a thing. This task would have to be combined with human resources.

In the example advocacy map in figure 5.2, almost every resource, including the client herself, the client's parents, and the social worker, are assigned the task of searching for acceptable alternative activities for the client to engage in. Although it appears at this early planning stage that the best solution for the client is the afterschool activities program at the school, this may not be true. The social worker might use some of the techniques in chapter 4 to generate additional solutions. Only if this initial judgment that the afterschool program would be beneficial is confirmed will additional efforts be made to enroll the girl in the program.

Each resource in this example also has at least one other task. The most common task is to learn to advocate or to actually advocate on behalf of the client.

Column 3, "Short-Term Outcomes," shows what the outcomes of the tasks should be in the near term. A short-term outcome is a change in a client's knowledge, attitudes, or behavior. There may not be a change in the client's objective, outward situation just yet, but we are planting the seeds for that to happen later. Short-term outcomes should happen shortly after the resource has completed the task.

"Middle-Term Outcomes" (column 4) are related to and follow directly from the short-term outcomes. They are often changes in behavior, though they may again be steps on the way to behavior change, such as changes in knowledge or attitude. The same middle-term outcome may have different short-term roots. In the example shown in figure 5.2, although there are many different short-term outcomes listed, all of them are thought to lead to the same middle-term outcome: reduction in or elimination of risky behavior by the client.

Column 5, "Long-Term Outcomes," continues the process of linking resources and their tasks to the accomplishment of getting to the desired "there" of the planning process. This column represents the stage where the problem/issue named at the beginning of the advocacy mapping process is fixed. This individual client, or this client group, is living in a different situation than before. The map shows the logical process of moving from the "here" to the "there" of successful advocacy.

Finally, we reach column 6, "Ultimate Social Justice–Related Outcome(s) for Society." This column represents moving from the single case or group advocacy to global cause advocacy. This statement is linked to all the other desired outcomes and calls for considerable movement toward achieving social justice. It can be a rather large leap of faith from solving the problem of one or a few clients to changing the world, but it is important to consider the next steps beyond our initial client and where they can lead. In the case of figure 5.2, the ultimate social justice–related outcome for society is that all children will be in safe situations with nearby adult support. This statement is the same one that was created earlier and written above the set of columns in the advocacy map.

Another example of a completed advocacy map is shown in figure 5.3. In this case, the problem/issue is that of a client and her family experiencing hunger at the end of the month. In addition to this problem, they are considered ineligible for food from the emergency food bank due to an agency rule that says you may use the food bank only three times per year. The desired outcome for the client of this advocacy effort will be for the client and her family to have adequate amounts of nutritious food throughout the month. Ultimately, the social justice–related outcome for society is that everyone has adequate amounts of nutritious foods.

FIGURE 5.3   Example Advocacy Map

DATE:

Problem/Issue: My client and her family experience hunger regularly at the end of the month when cash runs low, and they have been ruled ineligible for continued assistance because they have received groceries from the emergency food bank three times already this year.

Desired Outcome(s) for Client: My client and her family will have adequate amounts of nutritious food throughout the month.

Ultimate Social Justice–Related Outcome(s) for Society: A society where everyone has adequate amounts of nutritious food.

Resources (col. 1)	Tasks (col. 2)	Short-term Outcomes (col. 3)	Medium-term Outcomes (col. 4)	Long-term Outcomes (col. 5)	Ultimate Social Justice–Related Outcomes for Society (col. 6)
Client and family members	• Conduct research about other sources of resources. • Fill in other program applications.	• Are informed about other resources. • Complete applications.	• Clients are deemed eligible for food assistance.	• Receive adequate amounts of nutritious food. • Self-supporting, in terms of food.	• A society where everyone has adequate amounts of nutritious food.
Social worker	• Provides knowledge of programs to clients. • Assists client in program applications.	• Client learns about possible programs. • Social worker is aware of policies of program and the constraints of the agency.	• Clients make choices about how to overcome lack of food.	• Client has improved knowledge of system and how to access it appropriately.	• A society where everyone has adequate amounts of nutritious food.

	• Advocates to emergency relief program to see if family can receive additional food. • Pushes for more adequate funding for food programs.	• Social worker knows of need for more funding of program.	• Social worker tries to influence policies in other organizations and advocates for larger program budgets.	• Advocacy targets learn more about program needs. • Agencies receive additional resources for food aid programs.	• A society where everyone has adequate amounts of nutritious food.
Community programs, such as food banks	• Agencies disclose all rules and procedures for collecting and distributing food.	• Agencies agree to review rules and procedures to determine if they could be improved.	• Within agency constraints, benefits are increased—in any case, benefits are distributed as equitably as possible.	• Agencies self-monitor their policies and procedures, putting social justice at the fore.	• A society where everyone has adequate amounts of nutritious food.
Government programs, such as food stamps	• Advocates legislators and agency to examine laws, rules, and procedures for providing benefits.	• Legislators/program staff agree to review rules and procedures.	• Within agency constraints, benefits are increased—in any case, they are distributed as equitably as possible.	• Agencies self-monitor their policies and procedures, putting social justice at the fore.	• A society where everyone has adequate amounts of nutritious food.

Columns 1 through 6 are filled in, using the guidelines described earlier. Still, it seems clear that the entries are somewhat more macro focused than are the entries in figure 5.2. This difference is not a problem. The advocacy mapping process is flexible and has few hard-and-fast rules. The key aspect of the technique to focus on is to lay out a series of implicit if-then statements. For example, *if* the client searches for information on additional programs, *then* her knowledge of possible options will be greater. Another example of a possible if-then statement is, *If* the social worker provides information on the dangers of unprotected sex, *then* the client will not engage in unprotected sex. This may or may not be true, but it is what the developer of the model is asserting.

Naturally, not all of these if-then statements seem as strong or as likely as others, but the use of an advocacy map will make clear the strong and weak points of the planning logic. By laying out the desired resources, tasks, and expected outcomes, everyone involved in the planning process can better determine how strong the connections are and if they need to be strengthened further before proceeding.

Tips on Developing Advocacy Maps

Some wonder who should develop the advocacy map. It works best when as many as possible of the people you are counting on as resources can be involved. After all, most of us work more diligently and with more enthusiasm on a plan that we have been a part of developing. This level of involvement also fits in well with the social work value of client self-determination.

An issue to consider is the amount of detail to include, particularly in the outcomes columns. This will vary from one set of planners and from one set of circumstances to another. Outcomes, by their nature, however, are signposts or milestones on the way to a more distant goal. Although some specificity is needed to know if you have reached a desired point on the way from "here" to "there," those planning an advocacy effort must also leave room for unexpected detours and delays. Thus, advocacy maps are usually best seen as maps of major features along the way rather than detailed maps of every road and street. They are both strategic and tactical in nature, becoming more strategic the farther to the right on the page we go.

Another practical tip is to date each version of the advocacy map. Things will change as you move along, no matter how easy the project seems at its inception. Resources will appear and disappear, people will reevaluate what their contribution is going to be, and new conditions will emerge. To make sure you are working from the most current advocacy map, experience shows that it is very important to include a date on the page.

The advocacy mapping process forces the planners to determine what their desired outcomes are. What it does not do a good job of, however, is to set forth which of these outcomes is more important than others—that is, it does not prioritize among these outcomes. Those involved in the advocacy effort should engage in a discussion of the relative importance of the various outcomes. Everyone should agree on which of the desired outcomes can be jettisoned (if need be) to accomplish other, more-valuable, outcomes.

Prioritizing Outcomes

Your advocacy map contains a number of outcomes—short-term, medium-term, and long-term outcomes—for each of the resources you have identified. Although there is clearly overlap between these outcomes, they are not all the same. Thus, you must prioritize them. Some are more important than others. Some are less important, or merely instrumental—that is, they are important only because they lead to something else considered important. It is helpful to prioritize the outcomes within each column rather than between columns. In other words, rank all the outcomes at the short-term level against each other, rather than comparing a short-term outcome to a long-term outcome.

This step can be quite difficult, as the outcomes are all important, or they probably would not have been included in the advocacy map to begin with. The purpose of the prioritization is to make the advocate aware of where the most time and attention should be placed. Given limited resources for any advocacy effort, it makes sense to begin with trying to achieve the most important outcomes. In addition, an important part of the advocacy process is knowing that most advocates do not achieve everything that they would like to in any one effort. It may take several attempts to achieve even one or two of the desired outcomes. Thus, if it comes to having to trade off one potential outcome in order to achieve another one, it is vital to know which outcomes are more important.

After this process of figuring out what you want, you are ready to answer the second question of the planning process: Who can get you what you want?

WHO CAN GET YOU WHAT YOU WANT?
IDENTIFYING YOUR TARGET

Another element of the planning process that up to now has been more implicit than explicit is the identification of the target—that is, the person who can make the decision that the advocacy effort seeks. The target is the ultimate recipient of the advocacy effort, even if others are contacted as intermediaries in the advocacy process. As the advocacy map is developed, it often becomes clear who your target should be. If it is not clear, the planners will need to make this more explicit. It may take some time and effort to determine who, indeed, can make the desired decision. If you change your mind as to who this person is, be prepared to change the advocacy map as you go along. Like all planning documents, it presents the best plan at the time it is created. The map should not be considered unchangeable.

The choice of the target may not be as easy as it first seems. The following is a well-explained description of the situation: "In a complex, interrelated, urban society, it becomes increasingly difficult to single out who is to blame for any particular evil. There is a constant, and somewhat legitimate, passing of the buck. . . . One big problem is a constant shifting of responsibility from one jurisdiction to another—individuals and bureaus one after another disclaim responsibility for particular conditions, attributing the authority for any change to some other force" (Alinsky, 1972, pp. 130-131).

This shifting of blame can happen within an agency when an advocate tries to alter policy, and it certainly happens when larger-scale problems occur. Your supervisor cannot make the decision you want her to because it contradicts agency policy. The agency director points the finger at her board of directors for making poor policy choices but says her hands are tied. The board indicates that it is acting on legal advice related to local government edicts. Local officials blame state government for policy decisions they enforce; everyone complains about the federal government, claiming that the laws and rules that are handed down are out of touch with reality. Who, then, should be the target?

This is the time to return to your advocacy map to determine who, indeed, can get you what you want. Start with short-term objectives. Who can make the decision or start action on the outcomes that are the most immediately desired? Once these are accomplished, it may be possible to find the right target(s) for the medium-term and long-term outcomes.

At times, though, you may believe you are in the policy equivalent of a telephone answering system where you keep pushing buttons for other options and never are able to reach a human being who can take your call. In this case, Alinsky (1972) advises freezing the target—that is, picking one person and making him or her the personification of the issue. Given enough pressure, the person may be able to find a creative way to take effective action in order to get away from being the target. You must be careful, however, when trying to freeze the target within your own job setting, as it may cause problems for you in your work.

For many advocacy situations, however, finding one person to personify the issue may not be feasible because it will take a group of people (such as a city council or other legislative body) to make a collective decision if you are to get what you want. In this case, the legislature is your target. Still, you will need to convince only a majority of the legislature to adopt your viewpoint, not the entire organization. Because the legislature is made up of individuals, you must figure out how to reach these men and women—your targets—within the larger body.

Now that you know what you want and you think you know who can get you what you want, you must decide when to act.

WHEN CAN OR SHOULD YOU ACT TO GET WHAT YOU WANT?

Napoleon Bonaparte, emperor of France, once said, "Take time to deliberate, but when the time for action has arrived, stop thinking and go in." In most cases, no witching hour or magic time is going to happen. There is no perfect moment, that moment when victory is assured, for advocacy. When the planning is done to an adequate level to make it clear what resources are available, what tasks are to be done, what outcomes are to be achieved, and who can get you what you want, no reason for delay exists. The time to act is now.

Sometimes you cannot do what needs to be done immediately. You may have to schedule a meeting to talk with the target, or you many need to wait for a public hearing that is already scheduled before you can speak out. But there are, nonetheless, actions you can take today to prepare for what will come later.

Due to anxiety or fear, people often delay taking action to achieve the outcomes they have developed. It is natural to want to avoid taking steps that require you to move beyond your usual routine, even if you are a seasoned advocate. Focusing on the desired outcomes, however, moves your focus from you and your feelings to the better world waiting for your client and the increased realization of social justice that you can make happen. Reminding yourself of the larger goals of your planned advocacy effort often is enough to rekindle a desire to act and to act now.

CONCLUSION

This chapter has described the importance of planning in advocacy. I introduced advocacy maps as a tool for thinking about and communicating an advocacy effort. In an advocacy map, resources and tasks are linked to desired outcomes that will achieve a better situation for the immediate client and also for society at large, as we consider and work toward social justice goals.

Once the planning stage is completed, it is time to act. The next chapter provides information on how you can get what you want.

Suggested Further Reading

Knowlton, L., & Phillips, C. (2012). *The logic model guidebook: Better strategies for great results* (2nd ed.). Thousand Oaks, CA: Sage.

This book provides an in-depth treatment of creating logic models and applying them in many ways, although planning an advocacy campaign is not one of them. One of the book's strengths is that it provides abundant examples so that readers can grasp the basics of developing and refining logic models for program design, implementation, and evaluation.

Discussion Questions and Exercises

1. How is planning in advocacy similar to or different from planning in direct practice or community and administrative practice?

2. For the solution you developed after reading the previous chapter, develop an advocacy map. Discuss it with another person to receive feedback, then adjust your map as necessary.

3. Which parts of the process of developing an advocacy map are easier and which are harder? Why? What have you learned by doing it?

Chapter 6

ADVOCATING THROUGH EDUCATION, PERSUASION, AND NEGOTIATION

Never get angry. Never make a threat. Reason with people. "Don Corleone," M. Puzo, *The Godfather*

Advocating involves many skills, each coming together in pursuit of the desired outcomes designated on the advocacy map. So far in this book, I have covered skills such as analysis, planning, and idea generation. Still, no advocacy has yet occurred because you have not yet approached anyone with an idea that you want him or her to adopt. What will happen when you actually have a decision maker listening to you or reading your material? How can you make the most of the limited time you will have to make an impact?

Three of the most important skills at this stage of advocacy are education, persuasion, and negotiation. All rely on having appropriate information. This chapter covers education, persuasion, and negotiation, and also describes how an advocate must gather useful information and employ different approaches to education, persuasion, and negotiation, depending on the target of the advocacy. Without knowing how to educate, persuade, and negotiate, an advocate will find it difficult to make a difference.

EDUCATION

In clinical work, you might use the stages of change model (Prochaska, Norcross, & DiClemente, 1994) to get a client to think about changing a behavior that is a problem or potential problem. For example, while almost everyone knows that smoking is a dangerous habit, not all smokers are thinking about quitting. Someone trying to change a smoker's behavior has to introduce the idea of smoking cessation in a way that assists the smoker to consider stopping. The client is in what is known as the precontemplation stage, and the change agent wants to move the smoker to the next stage, called the contemplation stage, where he or she is actively considering a shift in thinking pattern or behavior. To move a client from one stage to the next requires overcoming his or her defenses.

How is this relevant to advocacy? There is a direct correspondence to an advocate bringing a new issue to the target. It is often the case that the target you have chosen is not informed about the issue that you are passionate about. The target may not ever have thought about the topic and so can be considered to be in the precontemplation stage in terms of being willing to act as you desire. You will need to overcome the target's defenses to obtain action.

Let's take a rather simple example of local advocacy. Suppose you purchase a new home and discover that the lamppost right next to your driveway is too bright for your comfort and is also an impediment to you getting in and out of your garage, due to the driveway's unusual shape. You know that the previous owner of the house once knocked the lamppost over when exiting the garage. So you want to have the city move the lamppost to another location. This will get it away from the house where it is too bright and also eliminate the danger of it being knocked down. You make an appointment to meet with your city council representative, Ms. Lovelace. When you present this problem to her, you may encounter the following reasons that she does not want to support your position:

- Denial and minimization: "I've never heard of anyone else having problems with a lamppost in their yard. It can't be that bad!"
- Rationalization: "City policy says the lampposts have to be placed just so. Moving that lamppost would be against regulations."
- Projection and displacement: "This is not the city's problem. Perhaps you really need better shades on your windows. And just be careful when backing out!"

- Internalization: "I'm sure this is a problem for you, but I just don't know what to do for you. Lamppost regulations are beyond me!"

Before you can get your preferred solution adopted, you need to move Ms. Lovelace from precontemplation to contemplation. Two empirically supported techniques to use in this process are consciousness raising and social liberation (Prochaska et al., 1994).

Consciousness Raising

Before being able to change, the precontemplator needs to realize the damage being done by current behavior or conditions. Sometimes this is simply a matter of not having accurate information, and all an advocate has to do is to present the information collected in earlier steps of the advocacy process. The information may be so compelling that the target quickly converts to wanting to take action. At other times, you must confront the defenses of denial and minimization, rationalization, projection and displacement, and internalization. If you do not remove the defenses, the target may not hear the information you are presenting.

The first step in the consciousness-raising process involves building a relationship with the target. Only then can you get beyond the defensive walls that block the information from getting through. Sometimes you can make a connection quickly, though developing a relationship may take longer. Important aspects of the advocate role in consciousness raising include the following:

- Don't push someone into action too soon. The target may seem to comply, but may also push back and refuse to engage in further discussion with you.
- Don't nag. Have other concerns to discuss and at least sometimes provide positive feedback on things you and your target agree on.
- Don't give up. Presenting accurate information over time, in different ways, and in different contexts can help get past defenses as the target learns more and sees your determination.

Social Liberation

Social liberation is a process of "creating more alternatives and choices for individuals, providing more information about problem behaviors, and offering public support for people who want to change" (Prochaska et al., 1994, p. 100). Examples of successful advocacy efforts revolving around social liberation include no-smoking sections in restaurants, wheelchair-accessible public facilities, and public awareness campaigns regarding drinking and driving or the dangers of using illegal drugs. Three techniques have been identified as being helpful in using the social liberation approach:

1. Ask, "Who is on the target's side and who is not?" In other words, who gains and who loses if the target supports the advocacy effort? What benefits accrue to the target?
2. Ask, "Whose side is the target on?" Is the target on the side of the problem and/or the side that benefits from people having the problem? Or is the target on the side of people wanting to improve the situation and make the world a better place?
3. Seek and welcome outside influences who already have the target's ear and who support the advocacy effort's desired outcomes.

The main objectives of education are to cause the target to be knowledgeable about the topic and to develop a relationship with you if you have not yet done so. You also want to move the target from not even thinking about the topic to wanting to take action.

Self-Interest: WII-FM

A speaker I heard once talked about how the most important job of a marketer was to be tuned into WII-FM because that is what the target of marketing is listening to most of the time. WII-FM is shorthand for "What's in it for me?," the default location of most of us even when we're working for the common good. One of the important approaches to an education approach in advocacy is ensuring that it is clear what is in it for the person you are requesting take action.

Many things might be "in it" for the listener—and it is up to you as the advocacy practitioner to figure out what these might be. Elected officials may be interested most in political support in an upcoming election, such as help getting the vote out, finding funding or volunteers for the next campaign, speaking to your members, and so on. Businesses might like positive publicity and a connection to your community.

Advocacy groups might also have negative consequences that they can impart to a target that does not work with them—people campaigning for an opponent, a boycott, publicity about the stances taken, and so on. Education could include information on the consequences of particular actions or lack of action. This may come across as threatening or, worse, extorting, but that is not the intent here. Just as there are natural and logical consequences to smoking or having unprotected sex, there are outcomes that your group will try to enforce and it is appropriate to let the target of your actions know what these are before the target makes a final decision.

To be clear—education along these lines should follow all social work ethical principles, including believing in the person's worth as a human and so on. But it should not be beyond an advocate's ability to work for social justice by clearly laying out what is "in it" for the target of the action.

If you are lucky, you may find your target is completely on board with what you are advocating for, simply after hearing the facts from you. Education as a strategy has the benefits of often not being confrontational; providing knowledge that the target was not aware of can be a very gentle process. Listing consequences may become tense if it is you or your organization that will inflict the consequences, but you can still do it in a nonconfrontational way. In other situations, you may need to engage in the processes of persuasion and/or negotiation.

PERSUASION

Although popular depictions of advocacy may involve people sitting around a table tossing proposals back and forth, arguing the final points in a negotiating session, persuasion is a more powerful method of advocacy than negotiation. In negotiation, you and the other party make a series of concessions, which implies that neither side gets what it really wants. In persuasion, however, you are able to get the other party to do what you want. (There are other ways of getting others to do what you want, such as coercion, but this book does not cover these other ways.) In persuasion, one party gets all of what it wants, and the other side, by agreeing to a new position, also gets what it wants. While we will cover negotiation later on in this chapter, we begin with education and persuasion because they frequently are seen as more in line with social work values and practices.

Research on persuasion treats it as a goal-oriented behavior (Burg, 2011; Gass & Seiter, 2013). A considerable amount is known about what is important when attempting to influence (Dillard & Shen, 2013). In every attempt at persuasion, four important variables are the context, the message, the sender, and the receiver (Wilson, 2002).

The Context

The context of the advocacy attempt determines most of the content used. How each actor views the situation establishes, to a large extent, his or her reaction to it. Various terms have been used to describe the process of getting a particular viewpoint accepted as the "right" way to see a situation. A term often used in the political world is "spin," a negative term that describes putting the best face on facts in order to reach a predetermined outcome. Another, less-loaded, term for the same process is "framing" (Rhoads, 1997). "A frame is a psychological device that offers a perspective and manipulates salience in order to influence subsequent judgment" (Rhoads). A frame thus provides a certain standpoint on how observers should interpret the facts, emphasizing some details and minimizing others in order to get the recipient to act a certain way. A frame highlights some information as being important to consider while filtering out other information that does not fit in. Framing occurs in policy arguments. For example, is domestic violence a personal problem or a community problem? Is poverty caused by flawed character or by restricted opportunities? (Schiller, 2007). Shifting images of issues actually lead to rapid changes in laws and regulations (Baumgartner & Jones, 1993). The ability to frame a debate advantageously is often enough to win it.

Framing a decision makes people more likely to act in a certain manner. People are much less willing to suffer a loss than they are to go for an equal gain (Kahneman & Tversky, 1990). There is evidence that the way choices are laid out, even if functionally the same, affects decisions (Kahneman & Tversky). Eating a hamburger that is 75 percent lean, for example, sounds more appealing than eating one that is 25 percent fat. Eating escargots is more alluring than eating snails. Shakespeare, it seems, was wrong—a rose by any other name probably would *not* smell as sweet.

There are several typical frames that advocates use to define an issue or proposal that are actually borrowed from Rosenthal (1993). Five of these frames are useful to kill an idea, and one is useful to promote an idea. I also list and explain three others that are likely to promote a good image for a proposal.

"It Isn't Fair." In the first frame, proposals are tagged unfair to one group or another. Almost any proposal an advocate comes up with—from helping one client more than others to economic policy that affects global trading—can be called unfair. A newspaper article describing views of tax policy shows how frequently this frame is put forward (Benson, 2004). In this article Grover Norquist, president of Americans for Tax Reform, is quoted: "Flat taxes treat everybody the same. If the government is going to want some of your dollars, it should take the same from everybody. It's a question of equity" (Benson, p. E4). In the same article, David Cay Johnston, author of *Perfectly Legal,* states, "We have a system in which some already wealthy people don't want to contribute to maintaining the society that has made their wealth possible. They want you to take on the burden for them, and they hire people to argue that what they want is good for you" (Benson, p. E4).

"It Won't Work." An alternative frame used to argue against a proposal is that whatever goal it is trying to achieve will not be reached. An idea you have, for example, to improve intake procedures at your organization could be met with responses such as, "We've tried that before. The problem is that clients are just too lazy to get all their paperwork together before coming in for their intake interview." Not only has your proposal been attacked, but an alternative frame has also been provided that blames clients for the problem. This frame is some-

times also presented with the following argument: "That sounds good in theory, but it just doesn't work like that in the real world."

"It Can Be Done in Other Ways." In arguing against a proposal, you may also say, "It can be done in other ways." This frame is similar to the previous one, although it presents an alternative to what it cuts down. This approach to attacking a proposal has a long history and is enshrined in Robert's Rules of Order (Robert, Evans, Honeman, & Balch, 2000) as a substitute motion, whereby one idea is totally eliminated in favor of another.

"It Costs Too Much." Another frame is to say, "It costs too much." If an advocate's idea is stuck with this rhetorical tag, the proposal is going to have a difficult and probably short life. Particularly in times of government cuts to existing programs, new ideas are tough to fund. But belt-tightening occurs in every organization, no matter its size, and there is always pressure to keep costs low. New ideas that have significant financial repercussions may not ever be seriously considered, much less adopted. Agency managers will say, "I think that sounds like a good idea; if only the budget could support it." Elected officials argue, "The days of big government are over" and want to reduce taxes. Sometimes advocates are challenged to come up with a way to pay for their idea. Even when advocates provide viable funding approaches, however, he or she frequently hears one of the other negative frames aimed at the idea.

"It Will Hurt the Public and/or Clients." Sometimes this frame is a variation of "It costs too much" or "It isn't fair." Often, however, it has a life of its own. When the Texas social work licensure board was threatened with elimination or consolidation with other professional licensure boards, the state chapter of NASW argued that, due to the unique nature of the social work profession, the lack of a licensure board just for social workers would potentially harm the public. When a neighborhood organization wanted to prevent rezoning that would put a convenience store/gas station in a residential and park-filled area, the advocates argued that changes to the environment, increases in crime and alcohol use, and decreased property value would hurt the public. This frame can be extended to intra-agency debates by arguing that a new idea or administrative rule will harm the organization's clients.

The above five frames are typical when trying to shoot down an idea. The following four frames (the first is from Rosenthal, 1993, p. 194; the rest are original) are used to support a proposal.

"It Will Help Consumers and/or Clients." Deregulation of the trucking and airline industries was promoted as a way to increase choice and lower prices. Many proposals are set forth with the idea that consumers will be offered more for less. At the agency level, many advocates focus on the benefits their suggestions will have for clients. After all, in the NASW Code of Ethics, the first value listed is service, and the first ethical principle is, "Social workers' primary goal is to help people in need and to address social problems" (NASW, 2008, Ethical Principles). If a plan is seen as beneficial to clients, it is difficult to derail it in a social service organization.

"The Benefits Outweigh the Costs." The cost of an idea is often cited as a reason not to adopt it. The seasoned advocate learns to expect such an attack and frequently counterattacks with this frame. In this context, advocates talk about the difference between short-term and long-term thinking and accounting. When legislators wanted to reduce the state budget in Texas, one program they targeted was the Children's Health Insurance Program (CHIP). Advocates who wanted to maintain the program's funding argued two main points: First, because the federal government provided three dollars for every dollar the state provided, cutting state expenditures on this program was a terrible way to save money. Second, the costs of not attending to children's health-care needs when they are young show up later in life and are then much more expensive to treat. Another example of the use of this frame is the following slogan: "If you think education is expensive, you should see how much ignorance costs."

"If It Saves the Life of One Child, It Will All Be Worth It." This frame unashamedly pulls at heartstrings. It says that costs might be high, but challenges anyone to say that life, particularly an innocent

child's life, is less precious than gold. Will it be expensive to install a school crossing sign, put up chain-link fencing around the perimeter, and provide a school crossing guard every day? Perhaps. But what is more important than the safety of our children?

"After What They've Gone Through, They Deserve It." The argument here acknowledges that the outcomes of the idea might not be fair in some sense because some people will get more than others. Yet there is an element of fairness involved, because the people who are getting more (money, services, opportunities) have also earned it by what they have gone through. This frame is a strong argument for some groups of people, like those who have served in the armed forces and have clearly put themselves at risk for the benefit of all. Other groups who might be labeled, generically, as victims may also be able to use this advocacy approach, particularly if they are seen as not contributing to their own situation. Widows, orphans, crime victims, people who have nature to blame for a calamity, and others who have had ill luck may find this approach to be a powerful frame. This frame is sometimes called the equality of outcome (everyone ends up similarly in the end) versus equity (people get what they deserve) debate and is based on different approaches to what is considered fair.

The importance of framing in advocacy cannot be overstated. In order for you to have a chance at being persuasive, the target must accept your framing of the issue. If your frame differs from the target's, you should spend a great deal of effort in getting the target to alter his or her view of the issue. Similarly, you must be careful not to uncritically accept someone else's view of a situation. Implicit assumptions regarding your clients' deservedness or different views on social justice may be influencing your target to see the situation you are advocating about in a very different way than you do. Make sure to understand what frame your target is using when listening to what he or she states and proposes.

The Message

The message the advocate sends to the target is the information designed to be persuasive. Here we look at the characteristics rather than the content of the message. Nonverbal as well as verbal signals are part of the message, but those will be covered in the next section, which describes the sender. The content of the message is also clearly important, but that is covered in chapter 7.

Six general principles of persuasive messages are discussed in this section: intent, organization, sidedness, repetition and redundancy, rhetorical questions, and fear appeals. Advocates who understand how to use these principles can expect to craft messages that are powerful and persuasive.

Intent. In most cases it is counterproductive to announce your intent—that is, to say you are going to try to influence someone. The moment the target hears your intent, he or she starts to put up defensive walls and to mentally rehearse justifications for past behavior. It is better to begin the persuasion effort without forewarning the person whose mind you want to change. There are two important exceptions to this general guideline, however. The first is when you want to ask for only small changes, knowing that those receiving the message already agree with most of what you are about to say. Thus, by saying that you want to ask for only incremental change, you lower any resistance. The target feels safer, knowing that you do not want to shake things up too much.

The second exception is when your target already expects you to attempt persuasion. Thus, in most structured office visits or telephone conversations with elected officials, it does not hurt to say you are going to try to influence their opinion, because they know that is why you have come in or called. Admitting the purpose of the conversation recognizes the intelligence of the target and lets the advocate seem more honest.

Organization. Well-organized messages are more persuasive than are poorly organized messages. This point seems too obvious to mention, yet there is always a temptation for advocates to hurry up and get going, neglecting the preparation and organizing phase of the message. It is worth taking the time to make key points more salient and to ensure a logical consistency in the material. If the message is not perfectly organized, however, all is not lost. Minor discrepancies generally do not cause targets to have much trouble comprehending or being persuaded by messages.

Sidedness. The next principle to consider is sidedness. When should advocates present both sides of an issue, and when should they present only their side? The research shows that two-sided messages (those that present the position advocated and the opposing view) are more persuasive if they do two things: they must defend the desired position *and* they must attack the other position. If the other position is mentioned but not attacked, there is no advantage to the two-sided presentation as compared to a one-sided presentation (Cialdini, 2008).

The reason for these results is that a two-sided message appears more fair and balanced. Because most people do not think deeply about most issues, presenting the other side makes the advocate seem more credible. Even if the target is thinking deeply about the issue being presented, the combination of defense and attack gets that person thinking even more about the issue. The attack on the other side and the defense of the advocate's position can leave a lasting impression of having explored the issue completely. If the reasons provided are strongly in favor of your position, you may be successful in your persuasion effort.

Repetition and Redundancy. Repetition and redundancy are different, though they are closely related. *Repetition* refers to communicating the same thing over and over. *Redundancy*, on the other hand, refers to having multiple ways of communicating similar information. A redundant message repeats the major theme of other messages but does it in a different way. Think of a redundant message as a back-up plan: if the first message did not get the target's attention, maybe the next one will.

A little repetition adds a lot of persuasion power because it can take several communication attempts for information to sink in. You cannot assume that your target will hear all the information you are trying to push the first time. After some time, however, simple repetition of a message creates frustration on the part of the target, causing him to think, "Oh, no—I'm going to hear all about her pet project again!" You, as the advocate, must sense when this frustration effect begins to interfere with your being heard. At that point, you should switch to a redundant message, which presents the original (or slightly altered) message in a new package.

Rhetorical Questions. The use of rhetorical questions is very effective, isn't it? Advocates who understand the science of persuasion achieve more results, don't they? Rhetorical questions are disguised statements—they stake out a position without appearing to do so. At the same time, the advocate can back away from the position if opposition emerges. Research shows that the use of rhetorical questions can change how people think (Cialdini, 2008). Rhetorical questions can catch people off guard if they are not paying full attention and pull them back to awareness of what you are saying. If you use rhetorical questions late in a presentation, targets often understand them as a persuasion cue, indicating a correct position.

This effect is particularly strong if the topic is not of great interest or importance to the target. In these conditions, targets assume that evidence has already been presented that show these statements to be true and that they just missed the evidence.

Fear Appeals. A fear appeal is a message that focuses on the bad things that will happen if the target does or does not do something. The message indicates that the target had better do whatever it is that the advocate is suggesting in order to avoid some sort of catastrophe. You are probably familiar with advertising that uses this technique:

- Buy our life insurance or your loved ones will live in desperate poverty when you die!
- Don't drink and drive or you may end up in a fiery, burning car wreck, killing yourself or someone else!
- Use our shampoo or people will shun you for having dandruff!

An advocate can use the same kind of appeal:

- If you do not pass this bill, millions of children will be without health insurance, leading to huge financial burdens placed on local charitable hospitals!
- If the board makes that decision, we may be liable in court for large sums of money!
- If a gasoline station is built near a river supplying water to the town, a gas spill could pollute millions of gallons of water, making it unsafe for human consumption!

It is thought that the reason fear appeals are effective is that they motivate greater thinking about the topic. When a situation is described in a way that increases fear, a natural reaction is to want to take action to protect oneself against that threat. In order to work, however, not only must a person have a realistic and personal fear of negative consequences, but the appeal must also provide information about a feasible action the target can take to avoid those consequences. In other words, you cannot just scare people into action, but you must also guide them to safety.

This section has covered ways to shape the advocate's message so that it is more persuasive. There are also principles that apply to the message's sender, or the advocate. I cover them next.

The Sender

No matter how you shape your message using the ideas from the previous section, a considerable amount of your ability to be persuasive is dependent on aspects of you, the advocate, and how your audience perceives you. This section emphasizes the role of credibility. To be persuasive, you must be believable. Without credibility, an advocate is not going to persuade anyone. Credibility, however, is a multidimensional concept comprising three factors: expertise, trustworthiness, and likeability.

Having expertise about the issue for which you are advocating is important to be persuasive, but it is not enough by itself. In fact, if the target already has a strong position on an issue or is distracted from the expert's presentation, all the expertise in the world will do little good. The testimony of an expert is most effective when the target does not care too much about the issue or does not have the capacity to counter argue, such as from a lack of sleep or because the topic is complex and the listener is overwhelmed. In either condition, the target uses the expert's ideas as a shortcut to thinking for himself (Perloff, 1993).

There are several ways to improve your perceived expertise. One is to have a title associated with expertise: professors and doctors immediately have more expertise than ordinary people do. If the person has been awarded a prestigious honor such as the Nobel Prize, a halo effect is created. For example, Linus Pauling, 1954 Nobel Prize laureate in chemistry and 1962 Nobel Peace Prize laureate, is perhaps most well remembered today for his efforts to promote the use of megadoses of vitamin C. Pauling's advocacy of vitamin C has been accepted based on his endorsement. People assumed that, because he had two Nobel Prizes, he must know what he was talking about. Pauling preached that large amounts of vitamin C helped to prevent colds and other illnesses (including cancer), despite a lack of scientific evidence to support this idea. The outcome of Pauling's halo effect has been dramatic: "Thanks largely to Pauling's prestige, annual vitamin C sales in the United States have been in the hundreds of millions of dollars for many years. The physical damage to people he led astray cannot be measured" (Barrett, 2001).

Many professionals hang their diplomas, licenses, or other credentials in their offices to promote their expertise. People without such credentials may offer other proofs of expertise, such as testimonial letters.

Another way to demonstrate expertise is to talk like an expert. Using the language of a field is an important element of being an expert. You have to be able to talk the talk, which means you must know the jargon. One study even showed that an expert was seen as more credible when speaking in complex, difficult-to-understand terms than when conveying the same content using ordinary language (Cooper, Bennett, & Sukel, 1996). This research indicates, "Acknowledged experts may be most persuasive when nonexperts can't understand the details of what they are saying" (Rhoads & Cialdini, 2002, p. 516). Although this is an empirically validated way to be persuasive, it runs counter to social work ethics. Still, it is important to know that this technique works in order to guard against it.

The difference between expertise and trustworthiness is important, but both are vital to being an effective advocate. Whereas expertise indicates that you know what you are talking about, trustworthiness indicates that you are honest and lack bias (Rhoads & Cialdini, 2002). Because of the central role of trustworthiness in establishing credibility, it is a key duty of advocates to develop an image of trustworthiness in the eyes of their targets.

Trust can be developed over time as the result of many interactions with a target. This development of trust is the reason that advocates should meet with elected officials and their staffs in order to develop connections and establish a relationship *before* a legislative session (Ezell, 2001; Hoefer, 2001; Richan, 1996; Schneider & Lester, 2001). Developing trust early will make the advocate's job much easier later on, when, in the midst of voting, no time is available to make a persuasive pitch on a bill or issue.

As the advocate, you may also enhance trustworthiness if you counteract two particular types of bias that your audience may infer about you: knowledge bias and reporting bias (Perloff, 1993).

Audiences often attribute a bias to speakers and other persuaders. If, for example, you are a social worker, most listeners will expect you to be in favor of more spending on social services. If you are a minority female, most will expect you to be in favor of affirmative action and equal pay for women. Knowledge bias is when the audience "assumes that [the speakers'] background (gender, ethnicity, age) and knowledge about the topic [prevent] them from looking objectively at the various sides of the issue" (Perloff, 1993, p. 143). It is difficult to be persuasive in these circumstances if you fulfill your audience's preconceptions. If, on the other hand, you speak against the expected bias, you have increased trustworthiness. You have become a convert communicator (Levine & Valle, 1975). Just as Richard Nixon, the hardline anti-Communist president, was able to open diplomatic doors to Red China and not be accused of being soft on Communism, people who take the side of an argument that is the opposite of what is expected gain credibility. They are presumed to have overcome their natural biases in order to look at the situation objectively. It is important that these views appear to be voluntarily expressed rather than coerced. Statements by American prisoners of war that are negative about the United States, for example, are not given much credence.

A reporting bias is the audience's assumption that situational pressures sometimes force a speaker to compromise her willingness to be open and honest (Perloff, 1993). People also assume that speakers say what the audience wants to hear—so if a political candidate promises the AARP that he is in favor of increased Social Security benefits, his statement is discounted and disbelieved. On the other hand, if a speaker tells an audience something it likely does not want to hear, the speaker's credibility is increased, even if his popularity is not. Credibility increases even more with third-party observers who later hear about the content of the statements and contrast them with the makeup of the audience.

Trustworthiness can also be reflected in what speakers wear, how they speak, and how they use body language. Clothing, of course, can be used to show authority. Almost all male politicians and businesspersons use a so-called power suit of dark blue cloth, a red tie, and black shoes to show they are serious and wise. Women's dress-for-success clothing styles change frequently but exist as well. Because authority can be used to impel change, most traditional persuaders use some variation of power outfits in formal settings. Clothing, however, can be used to promote a feeling of similarity rather than authority. Advocates may purposely dress differently when going to the office than when entering a community group composed of lower-income or blue-collar workers. In this case, it is important not to wear formal attire that may send a message of different class or social separateness.

The way one speaks can also have an impact on how trustworthy one appears to be. It is useful to "control your tone of voice, speed of delivery, pitch, and volume to project confidence and authority" (Mills, 2000, p. 70). Pausing in the right spot also increases the impact of what you say next (Mills).

Body language is another powerful nonverbal cue and a way to increase your influence. Mirroring your target's posture, if not overdone, creates a connection and improves your target's perception of your trustworthiness (Mills, 2000). Direct practice social workers are taught to mirror posture to improve rapport with clients—it has the same impact on influence targets.

Likeability, although perhaps not as important as expertise and trustworthiness, nonetheless influences your persuasiveness. Roger Ailes, who has advised U.S. presidents on successful presentation of their messages, gives the following advice: "If you could master one element of personal communications that is more powerful than anything we've discussed, it is the quality of being likeable. I call it the magic bullet, because if your audience likes you, they'll forgive just about everything else you do wrong. If they don't like you, you can hit every rule right on target and it doesn't matter" (Ailes, 1988, p. 69).

Likeability has four dimensions: similarity, physical attractiveness, praise, and cooperation. Each of these contributes to your ability to persuade, but each of these dimensions, on its own, also has considerable limitations.

People are more persuaded by those who are similar to them than by those who are different, in most cases (Perloff, 1993). Similarity can occur across four dimensions: attitude, morality, background, and appearance, although the first two, attitude and morality, appear to be most important. When solicitors for a charity on a college campus added the phrase "I'm a student, too" to their requests, donations more than doubled (Aune & Basil, 1994). Relevance and the factual basis of the decision modify the importance of similarity, however.

If a similarity is relevant to the decision, it is more likely to increase the advocate's credibility. Knowing that you are a college graduate who grew up in an impoverished neighborhood might make an audience in a low-income area pay close attention to your ideas about the ability of poor children to succeed in college. This same similarity would probably have little effect in persuading people to buy a shirt of a certain color. In the first case, your similarity is highly relevant; in the second case, it is irrelevant.

The type of decision that the audience has to make can also undermine the importance of similarity. When the decision relies on facts, an audience may believe that agreeing with someone who is dissimilar shows more credibility, as it reinforces that "facts are facts." If the decision is based more on emotions, however, more similarity is seen as desirable for maximum persuasion potential (Perloff, 1993). Thus, the advocate's decision to emphasize expertise or similarity depends on "the context, the persuader's goals, and a message recipient's attitudes about the issue" (Perloff, p. 149).

Most evidence supports the view that physically attractive people are more persuasive than average-looking or below-average-looking people (Perloff, 1993). For example, in a research study, good-looking fund-raisers for the American Heart Association generated nearly twice as many donations as did other fund-raisers (Reingen & Kernan, 1993). Still, there are important conditions that limit this conclusion. This type of persuasion tends to be short-lived and irrelevant to the purpose of the persuasion attempt. Good-looking people are more likely to persuade you to buy a different brand of shampoo, for example, than they are to affect your views on social justice. Also, people tend not to be perceived as attractive or unattractive at all times. One study concluded that slight changes in hairstyle, weight, and clothing would be enough to make an unattractive person attractive, and vice versa (Webster & Driskell, 1983). Although the transformation may not be as complete or dramatic as in movies, where a relatively unattractive person can, by unpinning a bun in her hair, suddenly be beautiful, most people can make changes in how they are perceived without much trouble. This would include wearing a flattering hairstyle, maintaining a healthy weight, and purchasing high-quality clothing.

People are persuaded by people who praise them. And, according to some research, the praise does not even have to be true to generate higher levels of likeability (Cialdini, 2001). To put it bluntly, flattery increases your likeability.

It is easier to like someone who is cooperative than it is to like someone who seems primarily uncooperative. Too many people trying to sell something, whether a product or an idea, increase rather than reduce their target's anxieties (Bedell, 2002). Following the principles of persuasion correctly will reduce your targets' anxieties about doing as you ask (Bedell). A cooperative approach makes it easy for the audience to accept your offer. For example, offer to help solve problems, and do not mention the problems without also giving your ideas for solving them. You can offer to assist the decision maker to explore options or research new ideas. Have an upbeat attitude. Do what you can to be a positive influence on people rather than having a negative or even neutral effect. All of these steps will affect your likeability.

In summary, the most important attribute that a message sender must have to be persuasive is credibility. Credibility comprises several components: expertise, trustworthiness, and likeability. Likeability, in turn, comprises similarity, physical attractiveness, praise, and cooperation. An advocate can alter each of these factors or dimensions to at least some degree, and can thus affect his or her persuasiveness.

The Receiver

The receiver is the last of the four main variables in determining the approach and success of any persuasion effort. Successful advocacy requires different approaches to different types of audiences. The bottom line of persuasion is a bit counterintuitive, however—you, the advocate, do not persuade the target. The only way a target can be convinced to adopt a view or take an action is if the target convinces him- or herself to do so. Your job as an advocate is to understand the target well enough that you assist in this process. Thus, it is vitally important for you to both gather as much information about the target as you can before the persuasion attempt and to be able to change tactics on the fly if your efforts are not working. The only way to truly get what you want from people is for them to believe it is in their best interest to agree with you. "People will do what you ask only if they believe they'll fulfill their own personal needs by doing so" (Bedell, 2002, p. 22).

Three personal needs stand out: the need to win, the need for security, and the need for acceptance (Bedell, 2002, p. 25). The first step in persuasion is to use your social work skills to decide which of these needs seems most important to the target. The next step is to frame your communications to allow the target to persuade her- or himself that this need is being met. With politicians, the need to win is usually very strong—they are, after all, always in contests where there are winners and losers. If their need to win were not strong, they probably would be in a different line of work. Still, we should not rule out the personal need for security and acceptance in any particular circumstance.

These personal needs are strongly influenced by another characteristic of the target: how much he or she cares about this particular issue. Targets who are not particularly interested in the issue may employ heuristic thought. This type of thought is a state of mind that is not very alert, where the target is not paying much attention to the situation (Chaiken, Liberman, & Eagly, 1989). If your target is in this mode of thought, it is easier to convince him or her of your position. It is not necessarily the best argument that wins or convinces, but rather the personal characteristics of the sender. Easy-to-digest information that looks good and comes from a nice-looking, pleasant person can be convincing if the target does not care much and pays relatively little attention to the presentation.

Although it might seem easy to overturn a decision based on such a presentation, once a commitment is made to support a position (yours or your opponent's), it can be difficult to get decision makers to flip-flop on the issue, as they prize being able to show a consistent pattern of support either for or against a policy position.

The other type of thinking, called "systematic thinking," is employed when a person finds the topic interesting, understands what is at stake, and/or has a strong personal stake in the outcome of the decision (Chaiken et al., 1989). In systematic thinking, the mind is alert and carefully examines the issue. The best way to deal with a systematic thinker is with strong facts and logical arguments.

If you find yourself trying to persuade someone who uses heuristic thinking, you can use cues, such as "Everybody else is doing it," "Authorities say it is the best idea," and "It's the same thing you did before." The other approach is to try to shift the heuristic thinker into systematic thinking by finding a way to show how the topic is interesting or how it will affect him or her. The advocate trying to shift the receiver's thinking mode can also make sure that the information presented is understandable.

Research indicates that if the persuader uses arguments with someone who is thinking heuristically, the process is bound to fail. Similarly, using cues with someone who is thinking systematically is also ineffective. Thus, an advocate must match the style of persuasion with the characteristics of the receiver. Although we would like to believe that decision makers give all issues considerable attention and always apply systematic thought, experience teaches us otherwise. An underappreciated reason for this seeming negligence is that, with many issues, there are good arguments on both sides. Thus, a decision maker might not be using heuristic thinking because he or she is lazy, but rather because he or she is a victim of information overload and is seeking a way out of a situation in which systematic thinking will not yield a clear answer. A fully prepared advocate realizes this fact and can make the necessary shifts in persuasion tactics quickly.

The receiver can also be categorized as the active ally, the committed opponent, the uninvolved, or the ambivalent (Richan, 1996). Each category requires a different approach.

Although the advocate does not need to persuade the active ally of the merits of the position, the advocate does need to keep the ally active and try to prevent other issues from taking a higher place in the ally's mind. Advocates also need to keep their allies supplied with the latest information to support the cause and to respond to and counter attacks.

Committed opponents are unlikely to change their minds, no matter what you do. The usual approach is to leave them alone, because you do not want to stir them to any more action than they are already taking. When an advocate debates or otherwise encounters opponents in a public setting, the goal is not to alter the opponent's position, but rather to convince people in the audience. These people may be either uninvolved or ambivalent, so use tactics appropriate for them, as discussed next.

People who are uninvolved usually see no relationship between the issue and themselves. Thus, the most important way to get someone involved is to show how the decision at hand will affect him or her. If an advocate can link the issue to a strong interest or personal need of the uninvolved person, then the advocate has created a foundation that he or she can build on. A novel presentation of the "same old" information can also lead to involvement. We have all heard, for example, that the destruction of the rain forest is bad for the environment, but it is hard to get many people worked up about an issue happening far away with very gradual consequences. A demonstration of how much oxygen a typical tree in a rain forest creates in one day (by showing a room with the same number of cubic feet of space that the oxygen from one tree occupies) might make it more real to an uninvolved person. (Chapter 3 includes many ideas about how to change a person's involvement.) As with the other types of receivers, the advocate must try to understand an ambivalent receiver's beliefs and feelings, or what is keeping the person from taking a stand. There are five questions people ask themselves as they come close to making a decision:

1. But what about the options I'm giving up?
2. Am I making a mistake by agreeing with you?
3. How will I explain my decision to others?
4. Am I going to come out of this a loser?
5. Is this going to cost too much? (Bedell, 2002, p. 80)

These questions reflect reluctance to agree with someone that people believe is trying to sell them something. Furthermore, each of these questions relates to one of the three personal needs discussed earlier: the need to win, the need for security, and the need for acceptance. If you can diagnose which questions are not yet answered to the receiver's satisfaction, you may be able to get the ambivalent person off the fence and onto your team.

NEGOTIATION

Negotiation is a "process between two or more parties (each with its own aims, needs, and viewpoints) seeking to discover a common ground and reach an agreement or settle a matter of mutual concern or resolve a conflict" (Business Dictionary.com, 2014).

Advocacy is, by its nature, also negotiation. Negotiation frequently takes place as a conversation of sorts, in which participants state their positions in order to find a position that all participants can accept. Simple advocacy negotiations can involve two busy people discussing when to set up a meeting; more-complex negotiations involve many coalition partners deciding what should be included in a piece of legislation. This section describes some of the key elements of negotiation.

One of the first rules in any negotiation is that you are unlikely to get everything that you want. That is one reason that prioritization (discussed in chapter 5) is so important. Knowing what is more important and what is less important in your advocacy effort means that it is easier to choose which outcomes to give up in order to achieve the more important ones. When prioritizing outcomes, negotiators develop their limit, their initial positions, and their fallback positions.

Limit

A limit is the worst possible offer by the other side that is still acceptable. When the other side in a negotiation offers less than your limit and sticks to that as the final offer, it is better to walk away than to accept the offer. The benefit of deciding your limit before starting negotiations is that you will not have to make such a weighty decision while bargaining. Deciding what you cannot accept while you have time to consider issues in an unpressured environment will lead to better decision making later on. Naturally, you hope to achieve a result that is better than your limit.

Initial Positions

Initial positions are the first thing you say when you are asked what you want. Initial positions ask for more than what you expect to get, but they are presented to provide a starting point and some room to negotiate. An initial position should be reasonably ambitious, but not so outlandish that the person on the other side of the deliberations believes it is ridiculous. In general, negotiators prefer to get the other side to reveal its opening position first. If the other side opens with an offer that is better than you thought you could achieve, you have the upper hand and can probably walk away from the negotiation session very pleased. Even if that ideal situation does not occur, some people believe that whoever talks first loses by revealing his opening position. Naturally, however, someone has to go first. Others believe that the side that opens sets the terms of the negotiation (anchors the discussion) and is thus in a stronger position. Differences in negotiation ability make a difference here, but it is useful to know that you can do well with either strategy.

The best negotiators ask a lot of questions to gain information from the other person (Bedell, 2002). The most obvious way to invite the other person to begin is to ask what she hopes to attain in the negotiation. Sometimes this is too broad a question, so you can provide additional information about what type of answer you are looking for. This process, called signaling (Bedell), requires that you narrow the question.

Imagine you are working with a coalition partner, putting together an agenda for the upcoming legislative session. Instead of asking, for example, "What would you like to attain in this negotiation?" you could ask, "Given that we are trying to determine the legislative priorities for the coalition, what are three points that are very important to you?" (It is better to say "very important" rather than "most important" because it keeps the other person from being locked into particular points being *most* important. If points are *most* important, then they have to be included in the bill or your counterpart may think he has lost something in the negotiations and then seek to undermine the outcome.) This question cues an appropriate answer and allows for a meaningful beginning to negotiations. You could find already existing areas of agreement between your positions and use them to work for further agreement.

Another tactic is bat listening, or echolocation (Bedell, 2002). With this tactic, if you do not receive enough information from your negotiating partner, you send out a signal and listen closely to what comes back in order to determine your next move. Suppose you are working with your son's teacher to improve your son's school performance. You know you do not want him to be labeled as learning disabled, and you want him to either be held back a year or to have extra assistance from the school counselor. You do not know what the teacher is going to recommend, but you suspect that she does not want to spend extra time on your child, given her other duties and the large number of children in her class who might also need extra attention. If the teacher seems adamant about putting the onus on you to start the ball rolling, you might say, "Putting extra effort into helping a student takes time away from your other duties, doesn't it?" This leading statement allows her to vent her anxieties about what you might want from her. You can then discuss your ideas with a better sense of her concerns. If she does not respond much, you can try again, looking for an issue that will start her talking. This type of interaction is one most social workers are good at and have been trained to do.

An advantage of this process is that it also allows people to talk about their personal needs (which are always important, whether or not they mention them) rather than their official needs. In this case, the official need is for your son to do better in school. Although that need is undoubtedly important to the teacher, she may feel even more strongly that she does not want a personal need violated, namely, the need to accomplish all her other duties in a timely way, which is how the principal is going to judge her performance.

A third approach is called looking forward. This approach brings out what the result of the negotiation should be. For example, you might say, "Let's project into the future. What do you visualize as the ideal outcome? How would things work? How would things work if you could write the script and everything went as you'd like it to go?" (Bedell, 2002, p. 66).

A fourth technique reverses looking forward to looking back. In this approach, the questions that are asked bring out what the other person does not like about the current or past situation. An example of using this technique is if you were working with members of a community group who are reluctant to attend a meeting at city hall to present testimony to the city council: Members of the group went once and did not care for the experience. Before you can convince them to do something that you believe is essential to the advocacy effort, you need to know what they did not like and what changes they would like to see.

The final way to address the dilemma of getting the other side to go first is to ignore the rule, at least partially. This approach is called "What do you think of that?" (Bedell, 2002). You begin by stating one of the parts of your opening position (assuming you have more than one part) and allowing the other person to react to it. You can actually use the question, "What do you think of that?" The other person usually will counter with an initial position that is less than you want. And so the negotiation game starts in earnest. Of course, you should try to persuade your target of the validity of your position. After all, you have not adopted an initial position that is wholly unreasonable. Your initial position should have a basis in reality, even if it represents a better-than-expected result for the negotiation. Do not be too quick to abandon it.

Once that point has been discussed, even if you have not reached a firm agreement, you can ask the other person to lay out her side's other desires. If she is reluctant, you can point out that you got the ball rolling on the previous point, and so it is only fair for her to take the lead on this topic. You can also use the "What do you think of that?" technique again, if all else fails.

One of the important elements of negotiation is that we often have to negotiate with our friends. Advocacy is not just about facing opponents—oftentimes advocates must negotiate agreements with people who are basically on their side but perhaps do not see things in exactly the same way.

Fallback Positions

Fallback positions are also standard in any negotiation. They are concessions that you make in order to keep the negotiation moving. Fallback positions get you less than the initial position but still represent an acceptable result for the advocacy effort. Your target, if well prepared, also has a set of concessions. Sometimes in the negotiation process you link keeping something you want with letting the target get something. Some of your fallback positions should be the outcomes in your advocacy map. You should also have one or more fallback positions that are less desired than the outcomes on your advocacy map if such results would, nonetheless, represent acceptable progress.

Only you can determine how quickly to move from your initial position to one of your fallback positions. If you cave immediately, you run the risk of seeming to be either a weak negotiator or unprepared. If you hold out too long, however, you run the risk of blocking progress as the target also hardens his or her stance. The best results can often be achieved by making a minor concession on one of your lower-priority points and then taking cues from your target's behavior about how quickly to make or to demand future concessions.

At some point, you may run out of concessions you are willing to make. This means you have reached your limit—the point at which not continuing to negotiate, and achieving no agreement at all, is preferable to agreeing to the target's offer. Your limit can be determined by only you and others involved in the advocacy effort. If the proposal on the table worsens matters for your client, if it means that your long-term efforts toward social justice are harmed, or if it does not achieve anything worthwhile for the investment of time and energy you have made, it may be time to walk away. Sometimes just the act of preparing to walk away loosens the target up to more concessions. But you cannot count on that: if you indicate that you have reached your limit, you *must* be willing to end negotiations if no concessions are forthcoming.

Using the techniques covered under the sections on education and persuasion will help you be a better negotiator. Preparation (including practice) helps you work in the actual negotiation sessions. Wheeler (2013) believes that one of the skills needed to be a master negotiator is that of improvisation—the ability to shift techniques, ideas, and positions quickly while still arriving where you want to go. He cautions against sticking to your plans so closely that you miss opportunities for even better outcomes. As he puts it, "We can't script the process. Whoever sits across the table from us may be just as smart, determined and fallible as we are. . . . Adaptability is imperative in negotiation from start to finish. . . . We have to make the best of whatever unfolds" (Wheeler, 2013, p. 2).

CONCLUSION

In this chapter I have described the basics of education, persuasion, and negotiation, along with implications for their practical use by advocates working at all levels. Armed with this theoretical knowledge, along with the advocacy map created earlier in the planning process, you as an advocate are now prepared for actual contact with a target. Presenting information is the topic of the next chapter.

Suggested Further Reading

Cialdini, R. (2008). *Influence: Science and practice* (5th ed.). Boston: Allyn & Bacon.

The study of what motivates people to do something that is not their idea has progressed greatly. This book presents what researchers and professional persuaders (such as salespeople, fund-raisers, and advertisers) know will increase the odds of getting people to be influenced. This book is comprehensive in covering the literature yet also has enough anecdotes applying the material that the reading is not too heavy. Advocates for social justice will find a great wealth of detail on how to negotiate with and persuade decision makers to adopt their positions.

Wheeler, M. (2013). *The art of negotiation: How to improvise agreement in a chaotic world.* New York: Simon & Schuster.

Once you have learned the basics of negotiation as described in this chapter, you may be ready for a look at the nuances of using education, persuasion, and negotiation techniques. The unique value of this work is the emphasis on finding even better solutions while working through the process. These techniques and ideas should be familiar to most social workers who have ever been involved in direct practice work to change patterns of thought and behavior. The application of skills such as maintaining presence of mind and situational awareness to negotiation will make this topic seem like an extension of already-established abilities.

Discussion Questions and Exercises

1. What are your frames and other advocacy strategies at this point?

2. Compare the advantages and disadvantages of the processes of education, persuasion, and negotiation, as methods of advocacy in your situation. Be specific.

3. What are your current strengths and weaknesses as an educator? Persuader? Negotiator? What can you do to improve?

4. What are your current strengths and weaknesses as an educator? Persuader? Negotiator? Why?

Chapter 7

PRESENTING YOUR INFORMATION EFFECTIVELY

Grasp the subject, the words will follow. Cato the Elder

The title of this chapter uses three key words: "presenting," "information," and "effectively." Advocacy occurs at the point when you present information. The purpose of this chapter is to help you learn to effectively present information. Up to now, the information in this book has been about understanding and planning for advocacy practice, but not really about *doing* advocacy. Without a doubt, all that has come before is needed to advocate effectively. Still, at this point you should be chomping at the bit to actually *do* something and make a difference. This chapter describes the types of information to present and the most effective ways to present it.

INFORMATION

If you have been following the advocacy practice model developed in this book so far, you have gathered a considerable amount of information that seems germane to your advocacy effort. The information may be as simple as stories about how an agency policy affects clients or as complex as a community needs assessment. You have looked at other actors in the situation and, either formally or informally, reviewed their stances on the subject. Now you must categorize all this information and present it in the most effective way to persuade your target to make the decision or decisions you want. This process of categorization will also help you spot gaps in the information. Before discussing types of information, I want to remind you that you need useful information to present, and not just a random collection of facts.

In the vocabulary of advocacy, "useful information" is information that helps make your case persuasive to the target. It can be difficult to determine what makes the information persuasive. As noted in the previous chapter, different people have different cognitive styles and thus view the same information in different ways. Also, people may or may not have opinions and values about what to do in cases like the one you are presenting. These factors affect their willingness to negotiate and to be persuaded.

The information that you present, in order to be useful in persuasion and negotiation, can be either substantive or contextual. Substantive information is the set of facts on which you base your arguments. Contextual information relates to how the situation appears to interested (or potentially interested) others—it is political information, if you will.

Substantive Information

Substantive information relates to what most people would call the facts of the case. Substantive information can range from singular, compelling anecdotes that are representative of the issue, to results of rigorous empirical research. In the middle of that range is mid-quality substantive information, which can come from official documents, statistical data (such as data from the U.S. Census Bureau), testimony from individuals; newspapers, popular magazines, television, and radio; and public meetings (Richan, 1996). We can rate the quality of these different sources of information as we do in academic research, but for advocacy purposes the best information is the information that is most persuasive to the target. Thus, stories of individuals, particularly when self-told, are often the most persuasive information because they have an emotional impact. If an advocate tells a legislative panel how many people in the panel's state do not have health insurance and that those people worry because of this lack, the legislators will probably listen politely. If a person who works full-time and does not have health insurance describes the same situation from his or her own experience, the legislators are more likely to pay close attention. Someone in such a situation who plays by the rules by working and paying taxes has a better chance of capturing attention than does an advocate speaking about the problem from a once-removed status (i.e., the advocate works with people without insurance but has it him- or herself).

Despite the obvious tendency for an individual's story to be emotionally involving, an advocate should have more than stories to tell. Although a story may be compelling, evidence on the extent and depth of a problem is also extremely important. A few isolated incidents do not necessarily lead to policy change. A mix of information types is the best approach, because there are people who are convinced by statistics and others who are convinced by testimony. A mix of information will help everyone find reason for action in the direction you are advocating. The key is to have what is needed for the target to be convinced and for the convinced target to be able to convince others, if needed.

Contextual Information

Information about the context of a decision can be important to a target. An elected official, for example, may not be persuaded to side with your advocacy effort until you point out that your organization has several hundred loyal members in his district who tend to be single-issue voters on the issue you are advocating. Even if that one bit of information is not enough to convince the official, it will be enough to pique his or her interest. Contextual information in an agency setting may relate to the way other staff members view the situation or how the issue is being discussed informally, around the water cooler.

One of the advocate's roles is to look for potential allies. Coalition building is an important aspect of an advocate's job. If an advocate can threaten to expand the scope of conflict by bringing in currently uninvolved people and groups, it is possible that the target will find it preferable to go along with the advocate's position. One way to expand the scope of conflict is to expose the situation and the target's lack of adequate response to the media. Just the threat of such publicity can sometimes result in negotiation efforts and results.

PRESENTING THE INFORMATION

Once you have gathered the information, you must decide how to present it to the identified target. The method of presentation is related to the type of advocacy being conducted and the relationship to the target. If you are advocating within your organization for a new approach to helping an individual client, your target is probably your supervisor, and a five-minute, informal conversation with him or her may be all you need. If you are seeking a change in legislation and have never operated in the legislative arena before and do not know any legislators or their staffs personally, you will probably need another approach. Even if your situation is like the first example, follow the steps of the planning process and be prepared. What seems like a simple request to you may contain surprises because there are issues you have not considered. Also, remember that presenting your information to an assistant or an aide is often as good as speaking directly with the ultimate target. If you convince the aide, you have a full-time helper on your side, someone who is with the target much more frequently than you are.

The decision regarding presentation of your information has two key elements. The first relates to the manner of the information and the second to the format of the presentation.

Manner of Presenting the Information

The important elements to considering the manner of presentation are accuracy, brevity, message style, content, and clarity.

Accuracy means that you have carefully checked the information in your presentation and that it is fully reliable. Although you do not have to present all your sources to your target immediately, you must be able to document your facts if they are challenged. Without a firm commitment to accuracy, you will develop a reputation for not being credible. As we saw in chapter 6, if people do not trust you, you will not be an effective advocate. Be sure to document your source(s) for each fact you present.

The second important element is that brevity is usually beneficial. Five minutes of your target's full attention may be all you get, regardless of whether you are meeting in person, making a phone call, or presenting written information. You must present the key points in this amount of time. If the target grants more time to you, of course you should be able to expand on the topic. If you have not captured the target's attention and kept it in the first five minutes, however, the odds of you getting more time at that time are not good.

You should choose a message style after analyzing the receiver to whom you will present. If the receiver is one person, analysis is a relatively easy task, assuming you are familiar with that person. In cases of larger audiences (such as at a rally), printed information going to many people, or debate settings, you still need to analyze the audience, but realize that there may be more than one type of receiver. Thus, you may need several different message styles within the same setting in order to reach people where they are. I will discuss five message styles: cues versus arguments, positive versus negative, one-shot versus repetitive exposure, private versus public, and collaborative versus confrontational.

In the first message style, cues versus arguments, you should decide if you are going to assume the person or people in your audience are thinking heuristically or systematically (see chapter 6 to review these thinking styles). Use cues if you believe heuristic thinking will be predominant, and use arguments if you believe systematic thinking will be more common in your audience.

With the positive versus negative style, you should decide if you are going to emphasize positive or negative appeals. In this context, a positive message means to stress the good things that will result from taking the action the advocate is pushing. A negative message means to call attention to the bad things that will ensue if the desired action is *not* done. Some research suggests that people are more likely to protect themselves from negative events than to push for positive outcomes (Cialdini, 2008). If this research is true, then a negative message is more persuasive than a positive one.

With the one-shot versus repetitive exposure style, you should decide the frequency with which you will communicate your message. One-shot efforts are less likely to be effective than repeated ones, but they can still be delivered in more-effective or less-effective ways. Similarly, although persistent and repetitive messages are usually more effective, they can be more or less effectively done, depending on the content and the layout of the information. Time constraints play a role in this decision: the amount of time left before a decision is made is crucial to whether you will have an opportunity to be repetitive or must rely on giving it your best shot all at once.

With the fourth message style, private versus public, you must remember that information can be delivered in private or small-group meetings or communications (via individual or small-group conversations or written material such as letters or briefing papers), or it can be presented in a mass appeal (via large meetings, media exposure, or mass mailings). Research indicates that having a personal, private relationship with decision makers (an inside strategy) is more effective than working to influence decision makers indirectly through the use of mass media and other public approaches (Hoefer, 2001). Still, each situation requires a separate decision, because the circumstances are different.

The final style choice is collaborative versus confrontational. Although the popular vision of advocacy may include protest marches, picketing, angry words shouted at public hearings, and other in-your-face tactics, advocacy is more often part of a collaborative process than such open confrontations. If advocacy is frequently part of your social work practice, you can see that using confrontational tactics at every opportunity could quickly burn bridges with decision makers whose support you need to achieve your goals. At times, however, confrontation may be required to obtain any movement in the target's position. Remember that confrontation exists on a continuum, with gentle, as well as more-forceful, confrontation possible. Forceful confrontation should not be the first choice, but when it is needed the advocate should know how to use such a tactic to achieve the maximum effect, while keeping social work ethics in mind. Forceful confrontation, such as picketing and protests, may be needed when the target is unwilling to listen to your position, has employed delaying tactics to keep you from taking action, or has been dishonest. Although sometimes effective in the short run, forceful confrontation also runs the risk of making future contacts and influence much more difficult. Thus, it should be used sparingly and usually with the intent of changing who the decision makers involved are.

A general template for the content of any advocacy message has two elements: describing the problem (including how serious it is) and telling what can be done to solve the problem. The content of the message should, of course, be in line with the message style. Try different frames (discussed in chapter 6), and decide which evokes the best response. Do not settle for the first approach that you put together; test the message frame, style, and content before deciding on your approach. Be ready to switch to another message style and use different content if one effort begins to lose its punch. Try, however, to keep the same frame: reframing an issue is a long-term process that needs consistency over time in order to be effective.

The degree of content detail you can put into your presentation (whether in person, on the telephone, or in writing) will vary in strict correlation with the amount of time you have to present. In a meeting of five or more minutes, you can probably do a thorough job if you are well prepared. However, in a very brief meeting (e.g., going up three floors in an elevator), you may have only one or two sentences for each of these points or you may have to combine important points in one sentence. Here is what you might be able to present in a thirty-second encounter, using a negative message style (emphasizing the negatives of not doing what the advocate wants): "Working families without health insurance are in danger of being driven into poverty by one bad break. More than 180,000 Texas children have lost their CHIP health insurance due to state budget cuts in the past year. Their care will move from being preventive to emergency in nature and cost millions more to taxpayers in the next two years. Vote to restore CHIP funding by voting 'yes' on House Bill 124."

If you wanted to take a positive message style (emphasizing the benefits of doing what the advocate wants) and had only five seconds, you might be able to communicate only the solution and action step: "Vote for health care for children. Vote 'yes' on House Bill 124."

You should be prepared to get your point across in whatever amount of time is available. The construction of the content should not change—just the amount of detail.

The sad truth is that advocacy messages often are unclear. In order to communicate a message clearly, you must deliver the information in language the target can understand; after receiving the message, the target must know what you want done. Your audience may not agree with you or comply with your wishes, but advocacy will not be effective if the decision maker does not know what you said or what you want him or her to do. Compare the following two messages. Which one is clearer? Could you do even better?

Message A. "Our program's current policy allows children without tutors to move ahead of others on the waiting list to receive a tutor if they receive failing grades. Our policy thus penalizes students who keep struggling and avoid an 'F.' It rewards students who make no effort to keep up in their studies. This has happened twenty-four times in the first two six-week periods. We should reexamine this issue and come up with alternative procedures in the next month."

Message B. "Currently, according to the program policy handbook, Section 4(a)(3), a waiting list is required when sufficient tutors are not available, unless the student on the waiting list has a failing grade. While on the face of it there is some merit in the current policy, which has been approved by the ADOPR Commission, a certain amount of injustice also emerges, as many times the child who does not receive a failing grade seems to be trying harder than the student who is jumped to the top of the waiting list. This effort is what enables the student to not get a failing grade, yet, paradoxically, no reward for such effort is evidenced on behalf of the program. All in all, two dozen children have been given priority based on getting a failing grade in the first and second six-week grading periods. Don't you think we need to do something to fix this problem?"

Message A is intentionally written to be clearer than message B. The problem statement in Message A is sharper and leaves out unnecessary detail. Message A also has a more forceful statement of what should be done and by when. A clear advocacy message tells what is wrong and what can be done to make the situation better.

Format of the Presentation

There are three main formats in which to present information. It can be presented in person (such as at a one-on-one meeting with the target, at a small-group meeting with the target, or at a public hearing), via a telephone call, or in writing (letter, fax, or e-mail). Each of these options has advantages and disadvantages. You should make the choice based on which approach will be most convincing to the target and practical for you. Still, within each format there are more-effective and less-effective ways of presenting the information.

The in-person format is generally considered the most powerful, because there is an immediacy and power in personal communication where feedback can be seen and heard instantaneously, even if such feedback is nonverbal. An in-person advocacy effort also shows the most commitment, because it is the most trouble for the advocate to do.

In-person advocacy can be broken into two types: the first is when you present the information to one or a few people, and the second is when you address a larger audience. While some considerations are applicable in both situations, others are not.

In-person visits (either one on one with the target or as a small group visiting the target) tend to have the most impact. The advocate(s) and target are able to exchange information and positions, engage in negotiations, and reach agreement more easily and naturally. A person who is experienced, self-confident, and well prepared can usually be effective in a one-on-one meeting. Meeting by oneself with the target may prove daunting, however, if you lack even one of these attributes.

A group visit can be advantageous because it shows that more than one person is involved in the advocacy effort. In addition, members of the group can lend support to each other. The information to be presented can be spread out among the group members, easing the preparation burden on each member of the group. Group members must be able to back each other up, however, if someone misses the meeting or forgets some of the points to be made. The disadvantage of a group meeting with the target is the need for greater coordination of the visit. One person, usually the most experienced advocate in the group, should be designated as the leader or stage manager for the visit; this person brings consistency to dealing with the unexpected.

Examples of unexpected occurrences during an in-person visit include the target agreeing with your position almost immediately, meaning that the job of convincing can be eliminated and the visit can move to other aspects of the issue; the target shifting attention to a person other than the group leader; the meeting being cut short; the target extending the meeting because of his or her interest; someone who holds a different opinion joining the meeting; and the target asking questions that the group members are unprepared to answer.

While the in-person format can be powerful, it holds certain dangers. One major problem is getting off point. The immediacy and fluidity of the situation allows for the advocate or target to go off on tangents. It is possible to engage in a fascinating conversation with the target and never get around to actually delivering your message. In a more public setting, questions may be raised that are purposely misleading or provocative. The remedy for these situations is to have a plan and to stick to it in a flexible manner. In other words, the advocate cannot come across like a single-minded robot, but neither can he or she afford to be distracted from the purpose of the presentation.

Besides losing track of the purpose of the visit or testimony, an even greater danger is saying something regrettable. Even when provoked, people giving information in an in-person format *must* stay in control of their emotions. Particularly when conflict is expected, only advocates who can keep their cool should be allowed to represent the organization or present its views. These high-pressure situations may require special training and experience. Advocates must keep their guard up, even when the target seems to be genuinely friendly and interested, as such a situation might lead to the advocate revealing too much information about negotiating plans and positions.

Advocacy situations in which there are many recipients and one or a few advocates can occur at a public hearing or in an even more formal presentation where the advocate is in front of five to 5,000 or more people. You still have the advantage of being in person and of reaching many people and addressing their concerns all at once. But these advantages are also joined with the stress of public speaking and the dangers of erring in front of so many people. The formality of the situation can stifle true dialogue between advocate and target, even if questions and answers are allowed.

It is often necessary to advocate at a public hearing. Most city and county governments have meetings where testimony on important issues, ranging from budget issues to zoning cases, is heard. Frequently, three to five minutes are all that are allowed for the advocate to present a case. To an inexperienced speaker, this may seem a long time, but under pressure to talk and be coherent, the time may seem to fly by. Agency boards may also have staff or other advocates present information to them. Depending on the board, this may be a formal presentation or a more-informal consideration of a proposal given by the advocate. The key to performing well in any public hearing, however, is to have a clear message and to practice many times.

Books on giving an effective presentation are plentiful. Here are a few tips to remember:

1. Vary the pace of your words, using pauses to add dramatic effect and power to what comes next.
2. Stand or sit tall but not rigidly—your posture communicates your level of confidence.
3. Gesture to add emphasis to your words but do not get carried away with it.
4. Visual aids or props can add punch to your presentation.
5. Practice, practice, practice! Do not read from a written document verbatim unless you have a very special quote or figure that you need to get exactly right.
6. Have an excellent beginning and an excellent call to action at the end.
7. Do not exceed your time limit. Present only as much information as you have time for. If you have practiced well, you should be able to speak in a natural voice and manner, present the planned information, and stick to the allotted time. If you go over time in practice, cut details out.
8. Practice answering questions, including both easy questions that you may have planted before the presentation and difficult ones that you would rather not have to answer. Find answers that are positive for your position.
9. Always leave behind written material that reinforces the points you made, and provide your or another spokesperson's contact information so the audience can follow up.

In many cases, presentations are accompanied by a computer-based set of slides, using a program such as PowerPoint. PowerPoint presentations are ideal when used to help structure the information visually; to present data or other information in charts, graphs, and animation; and to appeal to people with visual learning styles.

Although the advantages of such a program are many, the advocate must remember several things when developing slides. First, the speaker must use the presentation and not be captured by it. Too often, presenters turn to the screen and read what is there with their backs to the audience. Another common error is to put too much information on each slide. The most important lesson when putting slides together is that the limited amount of information on each slide should be simple, big, and legible. Each slide should make only one point. The point can have an example, a visual, or data to support it, but you should stick to one main idea per slide. Any visuals you use should support the major idea of the slide. Font size on a slide should be at least 24 point for the text and 36 for the title. The typeface should be simple, and the font color should contrast well against the background. Everything on each slide should be large enough to be comprehensible to the person in the back of the room where you are presenting. Remember, each PowerPoint slide is free—you are not being charged by the slide, so you do not have to worry about how many slides are in your presentation. Be sure, however, that each slide conveys an important and necessary element to your advocacy effort.

Two last points regarding PowerPoint presentations: First, do not use clip art images—at this point, they make users seem amateurish. Second, the best PowerPoint slide deck may be none. Alternatives such as Prezi exist but just speaking with knowledge and from the heart may be the best approach by far.

If you use a PowerPoint presentation, printouts of the slides should be available to the audience during or after the presentation. Some prefer to hand them out at the same time as the presentation so that audience members can write on them, while others like to have the audience's attention during the presentation and to be able to control the flow of information. This decision is more a personal preference than something that has been shown to be more or less effective.

A telephone call may also carry considerable weight with elected officials and other potential targets, particularly if it would be very difficult for you to make an in-person visit. A telephone call can convey a lot of nonverbal information—including the intensity of your beliefs, the degree of confidence you have in yourself and your material, and the depth of your knowledge, since the person you are talking with can ask you questions and receive immediate answers. A telephone call does not convey as much information about body language as an in-person visit, but some things, such as how relaxed a person is (you or your target) can be determined accurately by voice tone, breathing rate, and other audible clues. (Video teleconference users have more ability to see body language and other visual cues, but often advocates use traditional phones in making their calls.)

To have a substantive discussion in a telephone call, it is best to set up a specific time and person with whom to talk. The advocate must carefully plan a telephone call, as much as or more so than he does for an in-person visit. Unless the target has been told the timing and nature of the call, he will probably not be well informed about the topic and may not budget time for anything other than a short conversation. When dealing with elected officials, it is likely that you will have to speak with an aide, which, as noted before, is a perfectly acceptable alternative. A telephone call made via an appointment is much like an office visit and should be treated with the same amount of preparation. (In such a situation, be prepared to hear the person on the other end of the phone line typing on a keyboard. More and more, telephone calls are logged into a computer system during the conversation so the office can track constituent opinions.)

Of course, when you are working with someone with whom you have a long-standing relationship or with whom you work closely, more informality is acceptable, and it is more likely that you will not be rushed off the phone.

A telephone call to an elected official's office can also be very brief, particularly if all you want to do is ask the elected official to vote a certain way on a specific piece of legislation. In that case, the conversation may be as follows:

ELECTED OFFICIAL'S AIDE: This is Senator Jones's office.
ADVOCATE: I'd like the Senator to vote "Yes" on SB 104.
ELECTED OFFICIAL'S AIDE: Thank you. I'll make a note of that. Is there anything else I can do for you?
ADVOCATE: No, thank you.
ELECTED OFFICIAL'S AIDE: Thank you. Have a nice day.
ADVOCATE: You, too. Bye.

In this type of situation, your phone call will likely result in a pencil line on a piece of paper under the "Vote Yes" column heading. It is not likely to be the make-or-break bit of information in a hotly contested legislative battle, but the legislator will look at it as part of the larger picture. It is much better than nothing and, because it is not difficult or costly to do, can be used to activate others who have not yet been involved in the advocacy effort.

The written document is also a powerful tool for advocates. Information on paper, such as a letter or fax, often carries more weight simply because the target can pick it up. It may be shredded at the end of the day, but there is a chance that it will stick around and be picked up and read again. If additional information is attached to a short letter, that information may find its way into relevant official documents and speeches. An example of a letter to a legislator is shown in figure 7.1.

It is worth repeating that brevity is important in any written document that you hope your target will read. While additional information can be attached or included, the cover letter for such material must be short and to the point. Use your leanest writing style, stating plainly what the situation is and what you would like to see happen, all in the first or second paragraph. Many busy people find themselves looking for the meat of the document immediately; help them out by being as clear and concise as possible. If your primary document is more than two pages long, it is too long, and even two pages can be stretching your target's attention span.

Letters, faxes, and e-mails should always be personalized and customized for the particular individual or group target. Find and use the proper address and salutation for the decision maker, such as a local, state, or federal official. If the recipient is not an elected official but rather a member of the civil service, on a board or commission, or an employee or owner of a business, it is even more important to use the proper street address and salutation. In every case, it is helpful to know the person's views, positions, and/or past actions and to refer to them in order to let the recipient know that you have done your homework. This knowledge increases your credibility with that person immediately. Letters also must be timely and call for specific action on the part of the target.

Letters to state and local officials are often delivered in a few days, and a reply letter can arrive quickly. Letters to federal officials are currently being irradiated and scanned for security reasons and so may not get to the officials in a timely manner. As a result, faxes and e-mail are being used more often to communicate with federal officials.

FIGURE 7.1   Letter to a Legislator

January 2, 20XX

The Honorable John Cornyn
517 Hart Senate Office Building
Washington, D.C. 20510

Dear Senator Cornyn:

Thank you for your work as a member of the Senate Republican Task Force on Health Care Costs and the Uninsured. It is heartening to know that you are interested in one of the most important domestic issues facing America today. I could not agree with you more when you say, ". . . there are many. . .Americans who are uninsured not out of choice, but because they lack the economic means." It is important to ensure adequate health care for all.

The plan put forward by your task force has some good points, but I must take issue with the recommendation to make drugs more affordable only by "extending the federal 340B discount pricing program to additional providers, and freeing eligible providers to use multiple pharmacies." I would like to ask you to consider lowering the cost of prescription drugs by allowing people to buy from the least expensive sources—which are often in Canada. Canadians have a strong interest in keeping their prescription drugs safe, just as we do. It is difficult to accept the FDA's assertion that Canadian drugs are not safe.

My mother-in-law, as an example, has priced drugs that she needs to take monthly at about 40 percent less if she ordered them from a Canadian mail order sales outlet. She does not buy them, however, as she is concerned about violating the law. She is not the only person in Texas and across the country incurring substantial costs each month that could be alleviated by making this one change.

Thank you for your consideration.

Sincerely,

[YOUR SIGNATURE]

[YOUR PRINTED NAME]

[STREET ADDRESS, CITY, ZIP—THIS IS REQUIRED]

Faxes are used less frequently now that e-mail is universally available, but they still have their own advantages. First, because a fax is essentially a letter transmitted over a phone line, anything that could be in a letter can be in a fax. Thus, it is possible to employ more-impressive visuals than with e-mail. Although e-mail can have attached documents containing visuals, most e-mail writers avoid unsolicited attachments, because they know that many recipients will not open attachments for fear that they might contain a computer virus. The main difficulty with faxes is that one must be able to connect one phone line to another, and fax machine phone lines may frequently be busy.

Some research suggests that e-mail does not currently receive the same weight as do other forms of communication from constituents. Elected officials apparently believe that sending an e-mail is not as valid a showing of interest and concern about an issue as are visits, phone calls, letters, and faxes.

E-mail is easy to send, and every government official has an e-mail address that you can access. If you do not know the e-mail address you want at a state level, the Web site "State and Local Government" (http://www.statelocalgov.net/) has links to almost 10,000 government Web sites at the state and local levels. For the U.S. Senate, you can locate an e-mail address as well as links to contact forms for individual senators at http://www.senate.gov/general/contact_information/senators_cfm.cfm. The same is true at the House of Representatives' Web site (http://www.house.gov/representatives/). Company and nonprofit Web sites often have e-mail addresses listed so that anyone can contact them. Despite the ease of sending e-mail, any e-mail that you send should be as carefully composed and rechecked as a letter or prepared presentation.

No matter what type of written document you use, it is also vital to include your contact information so the target can respond. Envelopes and fax cover sheets are frequently discarded, so advocates should remember to place their full name, address, phone number, and/or e-mail address at the end of every written communication, even e-mail. If the comments and information have struck the target's nerve and he or she wants to respond, it should be easy for him or her to contact the advocate. More than one advocate has been asked to serve on a commission or advisory group after writing a letter about an issue. Be prepared to follow up on your own suggestions.

You should check and recheck all letters and other written documents for correct spelling, proper grammar, and clear writing. It is beneficial if more than one person looks over the document. Several drafts may be required before the wording is just right.

The advocate should always leave a written document behind when making an in-person visit to elected officials and should write a thank-you letter after the visit. This letter is another opportunity to present your case. In more-informal settings, such as dealing with your colleagues or supervisor, a follow-up e-mail describing your view of the meeting's outcomes can be substituted.

There are many other ways to use the written word in advocacy. Foremost among these are sending letters to the editor, writing editorials, and collecting signatures on a petition. None of these tasks is particularly difficult to do but can require time and practice.

Most newspapers select a number of letters sent to them by ordinary citizens to publish. More letters are posted online than are printed. These letters are short (50 to 250 words) and express opinions about current events. Some also respond to other letters that have been published, supporting or refuting others' ideas. If a newspaper receives many letters on the same topic, it is more likely to print at least one of the letters. Thus, organizing a campaign to write letters to the local newspaper can increase the chances of a particular viewpoint being printed. Including controversy or humor in the letter also increases its odds of being selected. With letters to the editor, perseverance is important. An advocate may have to write many letters before one is selected and printed. Smaller newspapers tend to print a greater percentage of the letters they receive than do major newspapers, which receive dozens or hundreds of letters each day. Letters to the editor must be signed. If a letter is written on behalf of an organization or coalition, the opinions presented should be stated as the official position of the group.

Editorials are another way to see your position printed in a local newspaper. Most papers offer an opportunity for community or organizational leaders to explain their positions on current issues. If unsolicited by the paper, these writings are much less likely to be printed than are letters to the editor, but editorials provide more space to explain why a position has been taken. Most editorials are fairly short, only 500 to 750 words long. They require careful thought and many drafts before you submit them for publication. Advocates with contacts among the newspaper staff may be able to use them to get feedback on their initial writing efforts.

One additional type of document used in advocacy is a petition (these can be physical or virtual [online]). A petition is a document that presents information on a certain condition and requests the petition recipients to take some action. Organizers of the petition ask people who agree to sign the petition to provide their address to show that they are constituents. At some point, someone will present the petitions to decision makers. Petitions not only are valuable in their own right as a way for citizens to express their sentiments, but in addition petition drive organizers can take the names and addresses provided on the petition and add them to a database of likely supporters of similar future efforts. When writing a petition, organizers should keep the message short, simple, and direct.

It can take a long time to collect names on physical and online petitions. Many volunteers are needed to have a substantial number of names on a physical petition. Online petitions and physical petitions require different strategies, but both need considerable effort to collect names. There is some doubt that elected officials take petitioners very seriously because they believe that you can get people to sign nearly anything if you are a persuasive person. Still, the effort may be worthwhile if advocates get many names for future advocacy and if the process increases the level of attention paid to the topic by members of the public, the press, or elected officials.

In the end, the format chosen depends greatly on the way that the target is most easily persuaded. Each format, however, has advantages and disadvantages, and so, if not all are used, the format must be chosen only after careful thought.

WORKING WITH THE MEDIA

There are differences among communicating one on one, in small groups, or even from yourself to a large audience. These are all types of personal communication. When one moves from this type of communication to working with nonpersonal approaches, such as from you or your organization to others through a media campaign composed of newspaper editorials, letters to the editor, radio or television interviews, and social media outlets, certain elements remain the same, but other elements are different. This section discusses what additional steps you will need to think about as you branch out from individual communications to mass communications.

The Role of the Media

The importance of the media is hard to overstate. Most people get almost all the information they have about issues from the media, traditional and electronic. As the use of the Internet has spread, people have less reliance on the traditional media of newspapers, magazines, radio, and television, and more reliance on the Internet versions of these media. Now, blogs, uploaded videos, and other sources of information are available on the Web, but these outlets are usually barely noticed until their postings have been spread in other ways. (More information on electronic forms of advocacy and using social media is presented in chapter 8.)

One way of looking at the role of the media is to look at this diagram:

Information → Media → Public opinion → Decision makers

First, information exists. It comes from the real world of events, crime, sports, weather, and so on. But, just as we can ask, "If a tree falls in the forest and no one hears it, did it make a sound?," we can ask, "If something happens that the media outlets do not report, did it really happen?"

For most of the world, the answer is no. If a protest happened at a speech by the president and it was not reported on, then did the protest really occur? Yes, it happened, but it will not be a factor in molding public opinion. This is where alternative media and, especially, online media can make a difference. Citizen journalism, consisting of ordinary people's ideas, writings, photos, and videos, can have an important role in detailing what is happening in a particular location or time.

Once something is reported, it can affect public opinion, and public opinion, when communicated, can have an impact on decision makers.

While it is common to think of the media as those reporting what has happened, reporters are by no means passive disseminators. They help shape the messages that are sent through six different processes (Rubin, 2000):

1. Selecting: They choose what to cover.
2. Editing: They decide how to cover, who to talk to, and what to select.
3. Highlighting: They determine the importance, how often to cover, and where to report it.
4. Analyzing and interpreting issues: They place things in context relating to other events and issues.
5. Opining on issues: They supplement the news with opinions.
6. Providing a forum for discussion: They publish letters to the editor and other material on the op-ed page.

The power of the media often comes from shining a light on activities that policy makers prefer to keep hidden. Often, instead of explaining decisions, policy makers will change the decision once the information is public.

The purpose of a newspaper, news magazine, radio station, or television channel is not to report the news—the purpose of these outlets is to make money. All traditional media are businesses. If they do not make a profit, at some point they will cease to exist. Content (the news) is provided so that people pay attention to the advertisements that also exist in the same space. This is true for Internet news outlets as well. Google, for example, though well known as a search engine, sells space to advertisers on its search results pages. Other search engines are similar. YouTube and Facebook also generate advertising revenue to pay for the content that they host.

Let's start with the most traditional medium—the newspaper—and dissect its various parts to illuminate how advocates can frame their issues and presentation in many ways to appeal to different parts of the readership. Let's use health-care reform as an example and apply it to each section of the paper:

National News. Obviously, the debate over health-care reform in 2010 was national news, appearing on the front page and elsewhere in the first section of the paper. Both proponents and opponents of the proposed legislation were quoted in such stories, including people from advocacy organizations such as NASW and the American Medical Association, as well as leading Republicans and Democrats.

Local Stories. Local stories are often paired with national stories on the same topic. Adjacent to an article on national changes in health care, one might see a local tie-in that quoted local experts or advocates, tried to understand how the changes might affect a local physician, hospital, low-income worker, business owner, and so on. The newspaper will try whatever it can to bring the story closer to home.

Lifestyle. The lifestyle section often covers topics of interest such as advice columns, fashion, and feature stories on so-called soft or relationship issues. One way that health-care reform might get covered in this section is to have a feature story on one or more families' probable experiences under different types of health-care changes. There might be a story about someone with a preexisting condition who is not able to find insurance, or parents who were going to be able to retain insurance for their daughter until she became twenty-six years old.

Business. Considerable information on topics important to social work is in the business section. This is where reports on poverty, unemployment, work-life issues, and so on are often reported, as well as the profits and losses of various businesses and the stock market tables. One element of health-care reform that was found in the business section is the effect of various provisions on local businesses' bottom line.

If a particular element of any bill seemed to be hurting a business's ability to make a profit, this alone may bring public opinion against the reform effort.

Sports. This might be a longer stretch, but it is possible that some current or former athletes in the area had health-care issues as they were growing up. A feature story on such athletes could bring home the issue of making health care a right and how proper treatment provided at the correct time saved a future athlete's career chances.

Arts and Culture. One could put on an art show created by people who have been or are in a health-care crisis. If this were to be covered, it could lead to interesting interviews of how life experiences have affected the artists' works.

Editorials, Op-Eds, Columns, Editorial Cartoons, Letters to the Editor. These pages are devoted to opinions and what people think about issues. It would be very natural to have material on health-care reform, pro and con, in this section of the paper.

Interesting the Media in What You Have

Given considerable decreases in the size of news staff, it may be difficult to get a newspaper or other media source to pay attention to your event or story. You must strategize, therefore, to maximize the odds of being the event that is chosen to be covered. The following list of elements that will increase your chances is based on Rubin (2000). The examples of how advocacy could be built around the element is provided to make the ideas clearer.

Controversy or Conflict. Organizations that held health-care reform debates by prominent speakers might have had an easy time getting coverage.

Injustice. Advocacy groups in favor of health-care reform could have press conferences with people who could tell their own stories relating to denial of coverage for preexisting conditions, or the organization could showcase young adults without insurance because their employer did not offer the option, who were then in medical emergencies and unable to pay. Groups who were against health-care reform could have interviews available with owners of small businesses who might be forced to drop all insurance because they could not afford to offer health insurance anymore, or who might be forced out of business because of the high cost of providing health insurance under the provisions of the new law.

Irony. The United States has higher costs than almost all other industrialized nations, yet has worse health-care outcomes in many areas, such as infant mortality, than countries paying far less per capita for health-care costs.

Celebrities. Both sides of the health-care reform debate sought to enlist celebrities to make statements in support of their side.

Milestone Events. Advocates could look at events that mark the thousandth local person who signed a petition in favor of health-care reform, or the hundredth day after a budget cut was put into place.

Large Numbers. The Million Man March on Washington was held in 1995 to support renewed interest in civil rights legislation; more-recent events have attempted to regain the power of such a large number of people advocating on behalf of a single topic.

"Est"—Biggest, Smallest, Newest, Oldest, and So On. Advocates in favor of no reform often said that the United States had the world's best health-care system. Advocates who desired reform argued that the United States had the most expensive system, with the worst return on investment.

Focus on People. Anecdotes about real people are always good; several examples of this strategy have been provided already.

If you are able to stress one or more of these elements as you plan your advocacy media campaign, you will be ahead of the game and increase the probability of having your event and ideas in the paper, on radio, and on television.

Be sure to understand the differences between the different traditional media as you plan your advocacy campaign and seek to include all of them. For example, if you want to be heard on the radio, it helps to have an articulate spokesperson who can answer questions without stammering or appearing to be unprepared. If you want to be seen on television, it helps to have interesting or alarming visuals to be able to present, as well as an articulate spokesperson. Finally, if you want to have an impact on people through print media, you need to assist the reporters in developing your story—What's the hook? Why should people care?

It is very helpful to establish a media kit with background infor-mation to make it easier for any reporter to understand your informa-tion and point of view. The backbone of this is the news release that includes the who, what, when, where, why, and how of your event, accomplishment, or report. Reporters who have something to start from are more likely to finish writing the article quickly and accurately, compared to those who must do all the work themselves. In addition, as newsroom staff sizes are decreased, a well-written news release may be printed verbatim as it is received, especially in smaller outlets.

Possible Frames in an Advocacy Campaign

Recall the idea of framing that we discussed earlier. The advocacy cam-paign should choose one or a few frames to tell your story. Here are some frames that are positive that you might like to embed in your information:

- Freedom
- Justice
- Security
- Family
- Health
- Fairness
- Opportunity
- Choice
- Community
- Caring

On the other hand, do not associate yourself with the next list. You may find that others try to paint your side as being related to these words. You must try to create the frame by which the public sees your efforts, and not allow the other side to create that image for you.

- Unfairness
- Oppression
- Harm
- Deceit
- Greed

- Favoritism
- Dependency

Setting Up a Media Campaign

Most of us in industrialized countries receive hundreds, if not thousands of communications every day, ranging from television and radio commercials, billboards, advertisements in the newspaper, mailings from organizations, e-mails, Facebook status updates, tweets, and other messages targeted more or less directly at us. A well-constructed media campaign can potentially break through this clutter to inspire action. It is beyond the scope of this book to detail how to do this precisely, but this section will give an overview of the basics you need to know in order to understand what needs to be done.

According to Day (2000), communications or media campaigns are "varied, multifaceted, highly planned, and strategically assembled media symphonies designed to increase awareness, inform, or change behavior in target audiences" (p. 79). They can consist of paid or unpaid advertising, media releases or events to "make news," and entertainment products or celebrity endorsements. Day indicates that all media campaigns should have four stages: In the first stage, formative research helps define the goals and the target audiences, as well as the media diets of the audiences. In the second stage, the campaign strategy is developed, and messages are developed and pretested. Third, the campaign is implemented. Finally, the results are evaluated and used to further refine the strategy (Day, p. 81).

Stage 1: Developing the Goals and Target Audiences

In stage 1, Day indicates that goals and audience are selected. In addition, the advocate must determine if and how the audience is exposed to various media. This latter point is important so that appropriate message vehicles can be chosen strategically. It would make little sense, for example, to use newspapers to carry a message if few people in the target audience read a newspaper. Another aspect of stage 1 is to understand the audience in enough detail to know whether some members of the target audience already know, believe, and act in the ways the advocacy group desires. If so, what are the differences between the converted and the nonconverted? Finally, resources must be gathered and budgeted among the various possibilities. Resources include money, personnel (staff and volunteers), time, and goodwill. Part of the strategy developed should specify who will do what, when, where, and how often.

Stage 2: Developing the Strategy and Pretesting the Message

In this stage, the message is delineated, preferably by having experts regarding the content work alongside experts in graphic arts and message delivery. This set of people, working with the results of the information gathered in stage 1 and bound by resource constraints, develops the information and physical products that convey the message to the target audience. Day (2000, pp. 81–82) specifically admonishes advocates to pretest the message and delivery strategies before releasing that message in order to avoid potentially embarrassing and expensive problems of misunderstanding the needs, wants, and habits of the target audience. If the message is provided to people of different cultures or languages, the pretesting should be completed for each segment of the audience separately. This can be expanded to include people of different age groups or genders, who may effectively have different media habits, abilities, and interests.

Stage 3: Implementing the Campaign

In this stage, the campaign is implemented. The better the work done in stages 1 and 2, the easier it will be to follow the plan and deliver the message to the target audience in a convincing manner.

Stage 4: Monitoring Results and Refining the Strategy

From the start, the campaign should be monitored to ensure that the message is being delivered appropriately to the target audience in the planned ways and frequency. Evaluation should also happen from the beginning so that changes in the campaign can be implemented if the desired results are not happening.

CONCLUSION

This chapter has provided information on the best ways to communicate useful information to decision makers. By giving clear messages with up-to-date and powerful information, the ability of advocates to prevail is greatly increased. Advocates should pay attention to the trade-offs that need to be made, the methods selected, and the ways in which advocacy is conducted. This is the aspect of advocacy practice that is so exciting—win or lose. By following the information in this chapter, you can be more likely to be in the winners' column.

Suggested Further Reading

Richan, W. (1996). *Lobbying for social change*. New York: Haworth.
This book, while somewhat dated, has extensive material on all aspects of the lobbying process but is especially strong in analyzing an audience. Readers will find more detail on reading the audience and reacting in the most effective ways than in other materials on advocacy.

Nash, R., Johnson III, R., & Murray, M. (2012). *Teaching college students communication strategies for effective social justice advocacy.* New York: Peter Lang.
While the authors are not social workers, their interest in social justice is strong. Their book helps students understand different communication strategies that they can use in pursuing whatever social justice efforts they are interested in.

Discussion Questions and Exercises

1. Discuss how to set up a social media campaign to promote your advocacy goals. Which tools will you use (including tools not mentioned in the chapter)? Why?
2. What are some of the important differences between one-on-one communication strategies that you plan to use (see the previous chapter) and broader strategies such as a social media campaign? How do they fit together?
3. If your advocacy effort does not plan to use social media or the Internet, what is this decision based on? Be sure to explain why you are choosing this approach.
4. Start and use a Facebook page, a Twitter account, or a YouTube channel for a social justice purpose, even if it is not related to your current class project (if you are doing a class project). Discuss your experiences.

Chapter 8

ELECTRONIC ADVOCACY

Over the past decade, a sea change in electronic and social media occurred, which continues to bring sweeping transformation to advocacy practice around the world. L. Goldkind, "E-Advocacy in Human Services"

More than anything else, the infusion of electronic tools into advocacy practice challenges social workers to stay current. It is certain that at least some of the software, apps, and hardware that will seem obvious and mandatory in a decade have yet to be created. Conversely, some tools that we cannot do without today will go the way of the IBM Selectric typewriter. The shift from Web 1.0, a one-way means of transmitting information via a fairly static Web site, to Web 2.0 (and beyond) with social media capabilities, has already occurred for all but the most stodgy organizations. For that reason, this chapter will focus more on the principles of electronic advocacy, than on specific applications of current methods. We begin with the belief that electronic advocacy is the application of new tools to the processes of education, persuasion, and negotiation, and not a new approach to advocacy itself.

WHAT IS ELECTRONIC ADVOCACY?

A succinct and useful definition of this new approach to advocacy was provided nearly two decades ago by Fitzgerald and McNutt (1997). It is "the use of technologically intensive media as a means to influence stakeholders to effect policy change" (p. 3). At the time of this definition, the Internet as we use it today did not yet exist. Most organizations did not yet have a Web site and there was skepticism that there was much benefit in learning the arcane coding languages required or in paying someone to create one. Computers that were hooked up to reach beyond office walls used noisy, squawking modems over phone lines to reach the Internet. IBM ran a television ad that had a business-man say, "The newspaper says the Internet is the future of business," but the speaker was unsure why or how (thus implying the need to call in IBM for help). (See the advertisement at http://youtu.be /IvDCk3pY4qo.)

The current situation for nonprofit organizations and individuals alike is that a knowledge of advocacy practice as discussed in this book is vital to be effective but it is no longer sufficient—organizations and individuals must also understand how to engage with and effectively implement tactics of education, persuasion, negotiation, information-sharing, and mobilization using digital approaches and tools. Web sites are important but advocates need to be able to use social media plat-forms such as Facebook and YouTube, as well as other communication applications.

Researchers and others have engaged in serious thinking about the realms and purposes of electronic advocacy since the mid-1990s (Bonchek, 1995; Browning, 1996; Schwartz, 1996). The techniques that were once cutting edge (e-mail, teleconferences, and online surveys, for example) are now incorporated into everyday organizational life. One of the shortcomings of the early research was that it tended to simply count what was being done. It was only later that the idea of linking technique to organizational advocacy purposes became prominent.

McNutt and Menon (2008) discuss three spheres within which these activities have emerged: as adjuncts to traditional advocacy, as aids for transnational advocacy, and as a means of activism in virtual communities. Those authors lay out two main purposes for electronic advocacy: One is to organize more supporters over a larger area at a lower cost. The second is to create information and resources to influ-ence decision makers more effectively.

A somewhat different picture is painted by Guo and Saxton (2014). Based on their analysis of tweets sent out by organizations, they find that social media are used for three purposes: reaching out to people, keeping the flame alive, and stepping up to action (p. 70). Because people are continually coming into contact with advocacy groups for the first time, organizations must do all three steps, all the time. Content relating to recruitment, retention, and calls to action alternate in the Twitter feed. This approach is named "mobilization-driven relationship-building" (Guo & Saxton, 2014, p. 71). Most advocacy-related tweets are designed to share information about a current issue, a smaller number sustain community and retain interested people, while the fewest seek to mobilize active participation. The implications of Guo and Saxton's research is that advocates should choose electronic advocacy tools that are appropriate for their tasks and goals.

ORGANIZATIONAL ATTRIBUTES OF THE USE OF ELECTRONIC ADVOCACY

Just as chapter 3 discusses the attributes of individuals who are more likely to become advocates, this section delves into the research relating to the attributes of organizations that are more likely to use electronic means of advocacy. While electronic advocacy is not a new idea, it is important to understand which organizations are more likely to adopt new tools and techniques as they become available. Research tells us that organizational innovation is associated with being a larger organization, having a more tightly connected structure, being led by people with more-entrepreneurial personalities, possessing more resources (such as time and funding) that are not being used at their maximal capacity, possessing appropriate technological knowledge, and being situated in an open environment where ideas can flow easily from one organization to another (Rogers, 2003).

In addition, the diffusion of innovation process usually follows a process of knowledge of the innovation, persuasion or pressure to try it, a decision to adopt it, implementation of the innovation, and confirmation of the pilot project (Rogers, 2003). Thus, with any new electronic advocacy effort, the instigator can expect to need appropriate knowledge, power, or persuasion skills to get a decision to try it out, and a way to keep it going.

Besides these organizational and innovator attributes, aspects of the potential innovation affect whether or not they are tried, and the extent to which they stick and become part of the organization's playbook. Innovations that are proven to work (at least somewhere), are in line with the organization's values and situation, can be tried out as a pilot effort without too much trouble, and have an effective advocate supporting them are more likely to be given a chance (Rogers, 2003).

Building on prior research exploring characteristics of organizations that conduct advocacy in general, Goldkind (2014) tests whether organizational age, level of resources, structural supports for advocacy efforts, and organizational culture supporting advocacy efforts are linked to higher levels of electronic advocacy. Her results indicate several direct effects: older organizations are less likely to use electronic advocacy, organizations with larger budgets are more likely to use electronic advocacy, and organizations with a higher level of advocacy culture are also more likely to use electronic advocacy. Organizations with a higher level of structural support do not have a higher level of electronic advocacy but this variable is associated with a higher level of advocacy culture, thus having an indirect effect on electronic advocacy use.

The reason to delve into this theoretical material is to help you, the advocate, who wants to enlarge the use of electronic tools in your organization, and to understand what you are up against. You need to be able to lay out a plan to add particular advocacy tools to the organizational repertoire—in fact, you can rightfully consider this as an advocacy effort in its own right!

THE GROWING INFLUENCE OF THE INFORMATION AGE

Living in an information society means that you have some great advantages compared to advocates in earlier periods. The foremost advantage is that you have easy access to the Internet and all the benefits and tools associated with it. In a few minutes of artful searching, you can find information that could have taken weeks or months to find looking through paper records in a large library or government repository. Huge volumes of government documents and the latest in scientific research are, literally, at your fingertips. You can search for, find, and download news reports, historical information, and the opinions of large numbers of other people within seconds, perhaps giving you just the bit of information or compelling story that can drive your point home as you advocate for social justice.

The Internet is also changing the way that people are learning about and paying attention to political behavior. The rate of Internet use to get political news and information continues to increase. As recently as 2006, one research report was titled "The Internet and Politics: No Revolution, Yet" (Cornfield & Rainie, 2006). Just a few years later, the data show a very different reality.

To illustrate the magnitude of change, let's examine some data from the presidential election year of 2004. At that time, nearly one third of the public and over half of Internet users said they used the Internet to get news or information about the election, up from 18 percent and 33 percent (respectively) in 2000, just four years earlier. People below the age of fifty were more likely to use the Internet (more than half), while those fifty years old and above were less likely to use it (Rainie, Cornfield, & Horrigan, 2005). The corresponding information for 2012 shows that more than half (52%) of the public uses the Internet at least sometimes. Adults below the age of fifty were still more likely to turn to the Internet compared to those above that age (Pew Research Center, 2012a). Other means of political education than referring to a Web site came to the fore in 2012. For example, 38 percent used social networking sites such as Twitter to show support or educate others on political or social issues. Nearly that many (35%) encouraged others to vote via a social networking site and 34 percent used such sites to post their own political thoughts. More importantly for activists to know is that one fourth of social network site users became more active politically after their exposure to information there, and 16 percent changed their minds on a topic (Pew Research Center, 2012b). The percent of people using their cell phones to access political information more than doubled between 2010 and 2014 (13% vs. 28%, respectively) (Smith, 2014).

A second benefit the Web brings to you is the ability to easily connect with like-minded individuals from around the world. One group, the Doe Network, for example, uses its members' Web savvy to "give the nameless back their names and return the missing to their families" (Doe Network, 2008). They do this by "giving the cases exposure on our Web site, by having our volunteers search for clues on these cases as well as making possible matches between missing and unidentified persons, and lastly through attempting to get media exposure for these cases that need and deserve it" (Doe Network). The Doe Network is made up entirely of volunteers, many of whom had previously worked on their own to identify the unidentified deceased people of their community. Through the power of the Web, however, not only can Doe Network volunteers find otherwise obscure information that might lead to an identification years after a person's death, but they can also share tips, provide encouragement, and celebrate successes as part of a community of interested advocates for a forgotten group.

Political advocates used the power of Web-based organizing tools to run the revolutions of the Arab Spring starting in late 2010 that resulted in the overthrow of many established leaders, including those in Libya, Tunisia, Egypt, and Yemen (Lindsey, 2013; O'Donnell, 2011). A Google executive in Egypt, Wael Ghonim, is cited as "the anonymous administrator of the Facebook page that sparked the unrest in Egypt"—a powerful example of the ability of social networking sites to inspire action ("Ghonim Invigorates Crowd," 2011, p. 8).

In the United States, social media have been invaluable to both Tea Party conservatives (Crabtree, 2014) and the Occupy Wall Street progressives (Comart, 2011). Skillful use has enabled both movements to survive and to move beyond a few key initial supporters. Countless successful local-level uses of social media are available to examine as well.

A third benefit of the Web is the ability to garner publicity in ways that are otherwise beyond the scope of most individuals or small groups. A strategically promoted, entertaining YouTube video may be the start of an advocacy campaign that shakes the foundations of a corporate giant. Friedman (2007a) discusses how the plans of TXU, a huge supplier of energy and electricity in Texas, to build eleven new coal-fired, carbon-dioxide-spewing power plants were drastically altered due to the intervention of environmental activists who developed a Web-based plan to stop TXU. The Natural Resources Defense Council (NRDC) created a dedicated Web site; and wrote regular e-mail alerts to a wide audience of policy makers, mainstream journalists and editorialists, environmentalists, and others in a successful effort to change the terms of the debate. In the end, TXU was purchased by another company but only on the condition that the NRDC approved of the plans for expanded production of electricity. Among other concessions that NRDC received before giving its approval were a cut in "the number of new TXU coal plants from eleven to three," support for "a federal cap on carbon emissions," a commitment by TXU for "plowing $400 million into energy-efficiency programs," and "doubling its purchase of wind power" (Friedman, p. 491).

Friedman (2007b) summarizes this episode in an op-ed piece in *The New York Times*: "Message to young activists: if you do your homework, have your facts right and the merits on your side, and then build a constituency for your ideals through the Internet, you, too, can be at the table of the biggest deal in history. Or as Mr. Krupp puts it: the TXU example shows that truth plus passion plus the Internet 'can create an irresistible tide for change.'"

It is important to think about the differences between one-way communication (advocate to public via Web site) and two-way communication (advocate to public and public to advocate) using Web 2.0 features or social media. Millions of Americans (particularly those under the age of fifty) use social media to be involved in political activities (Smith, 2014). "These platforms are now utilized by politically active individuals of all ages and ideologies to get news, connect with others, and offer their thoughts on the issues that are important to them" (Smith, 2011, p. 1). It is the social nature of social media that builds interest in a topic and creates a sense of community among interested people that may lead to action in the future. Among the Internet-savvy, politically participating population, tools that allow users of the Web the ability to respond, leave comments on blogs or videos, take polls, and so on, are now expected. These tools need to be as accessible and user-friendly on cell phones and tablets as they are on a traditional desktop computer, or they risk not being used much at all.

The challenge for advocates in an information age is to understand and use the Internet-based tools (old and new) available to make their most persuasive case, promote their views to opinion leaders, interested stakeholders, and the public, and to gain access to the correct target. Just as there are generally accepted approaches with traditional media, advocates developing social media campaigns need to keep some basic elements in mind during their efforts.

USING THE WEB AND SOCIAL MEDIA IN AN ADVOCACY CAMPAIGN

Social media campaigns are ways to use the Internet and its associated tools and techniques to spread and receive information. According to Christakis and Fowler (2011), connected networks have considerably more effect on the world than do uncoordinated efforts of similar numbers of people. The value for advocates of using the Web and, in particular, social media, is the ability to create networks of like-minded individuals who, working in tandem, can effect change. In addition, these authors describe how information that is introduced into a social network often travels far beyond the initial contacts and so can have ripple effects across the social network and over time.

The costs of a social media campaign do not have to be high. Many of the basic tools, such as a blog, Facebook page, Twitter account, and social bookmarking accounts are free. Web sites do have costs associated with the registration of the domain name and hosting of the accounts. Of course, there are resources consumed to create content and moderate comments or other interactive features. Thus, as part of the decision to create a social media campaign, resources must be consciously allocated and maintained.

The danger in writing this section is that it will be out of date before publication. Many of the mainstream techniques of Internet-based campaigns were in their infancy, at best, only a few years ago when the first edition of this book was written. Rather than providing many specific examples, then, this section presents a few key concepts that apply regardless of the specific tactics that can be used to include social media and the Internet in a media campaign.

Concept 1: Incorporate at Least the Barest Minimums for Your Web-Based Campaign

Oddly enough, the first decision to be made is whether to have a Web-based campaign. If your target audience does not use the Web, there is little point in heading down this path. However, as the influence and reach of the Internet has expanded, even groups that traditionally did not use it, such as senior citizens, now flock to it for information and companionship. Still, some segments of the population have less access than others, and advocates need to take this fact into account.

Once the decision is made to have an online presence, here are some of the minimum elements to include:

- Content that is unique, interesting, and relevant to the target audience and that is updated regularly
- Consistency in tone of writing and other communications
- A way for interested readers to receive new posts through an RSS (Really Simple Syndication) feed
- The ability for advocates to track metrics related to the goals of the campaign, such as page views, time spent on pages, numbers of comments, page rankings, and so on
- The ability to gather e-mail addresses from interested readers who wish to have further communication

Concept 2: Create Goals for Your Social Media Campaign

Just as in a traditional campaign, you need to think through what you want to accomplish and how you can measure whether you have achieved your goals. Following are examples of goals that you may wish to attain:

- A certain number of friends or fans on Facebook pages
- A specified number of online mentions
- A definite quantity of comments on your blog site
- A particular page ranking on Google, Bing, or Yahoo
- A certain number of back-links produced (e.g., the reproduction of your campaign's Web address or URL on another Web site)

Concept 3: Incorporate Interactive Elements into Your Campaign

Your Web site should make it possible to interact with the people you are trying to influence. Web sites are not restricted to a one-way communication pattern of delivering information to readers. The specific elements may change, but currently a social media campaign should have the following:

- The campaign should have a place for readers to leave comments or even videos. These can be moderated, or screened, so that nothing offensive is published on your Web site.
- There should be social bookmarking options to sites such as Digg, Reddit, Del.icio.us, and StumbleUpon.
- The campaign should include options to forward the information and Web site address to others quickly and easily.
- Potentially, there should be contests and surveys that generate interest and a reason to follow the content on the site.
- Facebook, LinkedIn, and Twitter are additional ways to spread messages and information and can be integrated to easily and automatically receive Web site and blog updates.

Concept 4: Always Include a Call to Action with Each Communication

Advocates use social media campaigns to achieve social justice. But just providing information will not be enough for most people to know what would be helpful. Thus, just as advertisers encourage people to buy their product, in their communications advocates should encourage people to take action to fulfill the goals of the advocacy effort, whether it is to contact decision makers, contribute time or money to the cause, attend a rally or protest, or whatever is the appropriate action.

Concept 5: Be Open to New or Improved Technologies

The Internet is the best source of new Internet and social marketing ideas. Mobile marketing, the use of cell phone technologies for spreading information and coordinating activism, is in constant flux.

Improved capabilities increase the options available to advocates: anyone can use a cell phone to text to large numbers of people, take and upload photos and videos within minutes, and update Internet sites quickly with new information and ideas. Advocates should think strategically about what methods may work with their organization and target audiences.

In closing this section, one element that media and social media campaigns should strive to achieve is an increase in engagement on the part of the receivers of its efforts. Kanter and Fine (2010) discuss five levels of engagement as steps on a ladder. On the bottom rung, with the least amount of engagement, are the happy bystanders who read blogs, are friends on Facebook pages, and so on. They are, in essence, passive viewers who are similar to Milbrath's spectators as discussed in chapter 3. The next rung is occupied by spreaders who share information, perhaps using social networking tools or talking with their friends and coworkers. On the third rung are donors, the financial contributors to a cause.

The two highest levels of the ladder are the evangelists, who actively seek to link members of their social networks to the cause, such as by soliciting contributions of time and money, and the instigators, who create their own activities that go beyond what the originators of the campaign have begun.

Advocates should use social media tools for advocacy not for personal gain or public glory, but to ensure social justice. When information age social workers do this, they join the distinguished history of the profession and provide future examples for the next generation to follow. The next pages provide specifics on using Web sites, e-mail, and the most popular (at the time of this writing) social media platforms for advocacy. Twitter, Facebook, and YouTube are the three social media platforms we will examine, though others, such as Pinterest, LinkedIn, Tumblr, and many more, are being used by limited numbers of advocates.

Web Sites

People and organizations primarily use Web sites to provide information, and the number of sites continues to grow daily. According to a Pew Research Center report, the Internet first became an essential part of politics in 2004, with millions of Americans turning to the Web to gather information on candidates and their positions, to read endorsements of candidates by organizations, and to join political discussions and chat groups (Rainie et al., 2005). Perhaps the most important lesson is that every advocacy effort or organization should have a Web site that is frequently updated. Web sites provide information to supporters and people who are curious about the topic. Reporters and others in the media may turn to such sites for background information on an issue. Some advocacy organizations think of their Web site as a library where important background information and links to other organizations are stored for easy access at any time. It is possible to have some parts of the Web site password protected so that only authorized members can see what is there. A basic assumption at this time is that every advocacy organization will have a Web site that interested people can turn to for information about the topic and organization. The process of setting up a Web site has become much easier than it was even five years ago and prices are minimal—sometimes even free.

The first step is to obtain a Web site address (its URL, for uniform or universal resource locator, meaning its location on the Internet). The first step is to create an account at a domain registrar, such as GoDaddy.com, BlueHost.com, or HostGator.com (there are dozens, but these three are well known and generally reliable). You choose a name, and an extension (the most common are .com, .org, or .net, though many new extensions, such as .ninja, .me, and .info now exist). If possible, choose a .com domain extension because that is what many people automatically expect, making the name easier for them to remember. You register your Web address for a limited time, starting with a one-year contract. If you do not renew your registration, you lose the right to use it and anyone else may then use the site address. You will need to have a hosting company as well as the domain; different hosting companies charge different amounts for their service.

In the not very distant past, Web sites were created using coding that took a while to learn. Now it is relatively simple to get your Web site up once you have a domain registered and hosted. YouTube videos show you step by step how to do this using templates and short-cuts. Use Google or go straight to YouTube.com and search for "How to set up a Web site."

One popular solution to having a Web site is to use a blogging software shell. The most popular is called WordPress.com; you can get a rudimentary blog site for free at www.wordpress.com. (If you have your own Web site and hosting, you should look at www.wordpress.org.) Other free blogging sites are available through www.blogger.com and www.weebly.com. Simple and free can be wonderful ways to begin, but if your effort is sustained, it may be worth the effort to use resources that cost something to allow you to have greater control over the outcomes.

It can be a burden to put together all the information that could be on your advocacy group's Web site and it is not always clear what to include. Box 8.1 lists six basic elements that need to be on every advocacy organization's Web site. Exact instructions for adding an opt-in form and donation button can be obtained from the vendors of contact management software (e.g., aweber.com) and payment services (such as PayPal.com). You must develop and implement a plan to keep the Web site updated or else it will lose value. If there are places on the Web site for visitors to leave comments or start a discussion, you need to monitor those places so that people have a reason to post. Also, you can remove offensive posts, but first you need to check for them.

BOX 8.1. What Should Be on Your Advocacy
Organization's Web Site?

These six elements should be on your advocacy Web site. Many of them will involve extra work or cost beyond a simple starter Word-Press.com blog site. It is perfectly acceptable to start with the basics and then build up as your effort becomes more sophisticated. Here are the five most important elements:

1. Organization name
2. Way to contact the site owner
3. Information about the advocacy effort or area
4. E-mail opt-in box (a way to get the visitor's e-mail address; requires extra expense for an autoresponder service to send out e-mails)
5. Way to accept donations (PayPal account or other options)
6. Method(s) to elicit conversation, sharing of thoughts, feedback, and community building

---

E-mail

Beyond a Web site, e-mail is the basic building block of electronic advocacy, which is why one of the most important elements of an advocacy organization's Web site is a way to capture visitors' e-mail addresses. Using an autoresponder such as MailChimp or AWeber, advocates can send e-mails to everyone who has opted to be on their mailing list. E-mail lists can also be segmented to provide greater selectivity in which subscribers receive which messages. You will need to connect in different ways with more-active supporters (e.g., those who have donated money) than you do with people who have just signed up. A wonderful aspect of an autoresponder program is that you can preload a set of e-mails that will be sent out on certain days (say, three days next week), or at certain intervals (twice a week for ten weeks after a person signs up to be on the list).

Sharing information is a wonderful way to maintain connection with supporters and those interested in knowing more about your organization and the issues it works on. When communicating via e-mail, advocates should strive to be conversational, and to write e-mails that they would be willing to read. If an e-mail is too long, few will read it to the end, so a journalistic style of putting the most important information in the first paragraph is a good starting point. An e-mail can also start with information and then link to the organization's Web site for additional information.

E-mails should contain a call to action—a specific request for the reader to do something, even if it is as commonplace as clicking a link for more information or forwarding the message to colleagues and friends, or if it is as involved as donating funds for a current campaign. Each of these calls to action can be tracked to see the proportion of your list that opens the e-mail and how many of those click on links. If the call to action is a request for money, it is easy to track results. You can even send different e-mails to different parts of your list to see which wording or example is more effective at motivating action on the part of your list.

Facebook

Started in 2004, Facebook has become as much a requirement for advocacy organizations as a Web site, and in some cases has allowed organizers to skip having a Web site altogether (although this is not recommended). Facebook has enormous penetration of the population: as of March 2015 it has 1.44 billion monthly active users, and 936 million daily active users (Facebook, n.d.). While most people have personal pages, groups can use open group pages that are accessible to anyone or create secret groups that only members may see or post to.

The benefits of a group page for advocacy include the fact that it is simple to post information that can be seen by anyone with a Facebook account. No one has to have access to an e-mail account or clog up their account with multiple messages from different people. Because so many people can look at the Facebook site on their smartphones, and because they can check their site so often, it does not take long for information to spread. Because it is free to set up and maintain, low cost is another benefit. Users are usually well versed on the basics of communicating their ideas and sharing information. Thus, the ease of adoption is high.

Concerns about Facebook exist as well. First, because Facebook can change its policies at any time, a Facebook user or group can be suspended with no warning or recourse. This could undo a lot of effort by an organization. Another concern about Facebook is that its record in terms of privacy is spotty. Users can set privacy settings at different levels, but the default settings often allow a wider distribution of content than the person posting intended.

Specific recommendations for using Facebook are these:

- Keep posts short and conversational. If you want to go into more detail, have the longer content on a Web page on your Web site, and use Facebook to get people to your Web site. People look at and share posts that include a photo more often than posts without.
- Post at least once per day, and encourage others to share your content.
- Create events in Facebook that can act as community-building face-to-face interactions.
- Plan who will keep the Facebook page monitored for comments and engagement.

Twitter

Twitter is a microblogging platform: blogging in that you can write whatever you wish and micro because you can use only 140 characters. Images do not count against this total and help people notice your tweet amongst the dozens they may receive each hour. Users often use Twitter to link to longer posts on Web sites; it is very useful to share information and share links. The use of hashtags (#) ensures that your tweet can be categorized with other people's tweets about the same topic. Thus, if you want to gather more attention, include a hash-tagged topic such as #TXSB12015, standing for Texas Senate Bill 1 in the 2015 legislative session. If others use this same hash-tagged term, anyone can search through Twitter to use information on this bill.

Twitter has been researched more than other advocacy tools simply because it is so easy to scrape data from the Twitter feed using the hashtag convention. One can quickly count the number of tweets on topics and download them. You can then study these data for theme or content. Understanding how to use the hashtag to categorize tweets is the key to following other people with your interests and finding others to follow. The National Alliance on Mental Illness (NAMI), has the user name @namicommunicate (all user names begin with the @ symbol) and often uses the hashtag #mentalhealth to let others interested in the topic find their tweets about mental health and their advocacy efforts. One of their tweets was this: "NAMI Maine Challenges Asks for Moratorium on Proposed Cuts http://bit.ly/6eB3Zr." The Web site URL is automatically shortened to help a tweet fit into the 140-character limit.

Tweeting your own information is important but people often will retweet information from others. This helps them spread their own information and helps you develop new connections and followers.

YouTube

YouTube is the second-largest search engine in the world, with hours of material added every minute. A video that goes viral (that gets shared many thousands of times) can lead to large numbers of people becoming aware of an issue and searching your Web site for additional information. This may lead to a huge increase in donations as well. Two examples bring this point home.

In March 2012 a thirty-minute video was uploaded by an advocacy organization, Invisible Children. The purpose was to bring awareness to the world of a brutal Ugandan war criminal,

Joseph Kony, and to bring pressure on governments to arrest him. The video, entitled *Kony 2012,* immediately went viral, and two and a half years later, in November 2014, had had nearly 100 million views on YouTube. The page for the video has a direct link to a donations page as well as the organization's Web site.

During the summer of 2014 a challenge became extremely popular. The ALS (Amyotrophic Lateral Sclerosis) Association was the beneficiary of "the ice-bucket challenge," whereby people would dump a bucket of ice water on their own heads and then challenge others to do the same. At first, this was in lieu of donating to the ALS Association, but soon people were donating, dumping water on their heads, and then challenging their friends to do the same. By the end of the summer, more than $115 million had been raised through this method. This amount was greater than the $64 million in revenues the ALS Association had brought in the year before (Silverman, 2014).

Of course, most videos that are uploaded do not achieve anywhere near that level of impact. That is not necessary, however, for any advocacy effort to consider developing a video to explain its cause and the reasons behind its efforts. Professional video production can cost many thousands of dollars. But videos can be made on the smallest of shoestring budgets with a smartphone and uploaded directly to YouTube. Editing software can be acquired at low cost and used for a version that has more visual appeal, but this is not a requirement. Over time, these videos can be watched more often than one might expect. One five-minute video on making better decisions that I put on YouTube in 2010, without promoting it at all, has been seen nearly 15,000 times as of this writing (Hoefer, 2010). (If you'd like to watch it, too, go to http://youtu.be/8ptq1SR0wok.)

Even a second-rate video is likely to get more attention than a boring looking Web site or e-mail. The choice of images is important, but even a talking-head video that is done energetically is more enticing than a page of text on a Web site. When thinking about creating videos, there are many different approaches to use. The basic talking head shows a single person talking. Another approach is to have a series of images (these can be put into a PowerPoint-type presentation) with an audio track of narration going along with it. You can record interviews that include different voices and information, and you can put a mixture of these into one video. Videos can branch out to include how-to information, such as how to call your representatives, how to approach people to get them to sign a petition, and whatever else your advocacy campaign might need. A video can be a better and faster way to communicate information, as compared to a written handout. The key is to make the video more interesting than a written document.

In order to upload your video to YouTube, you will need to create an account. At first there will be limitations on the length of the videos you can post, but this is probably a good thing. It is better to have five three-minute videos that are highly targeted than one fifteen-minute video that covers five topics. People's attention span is very short so you need to practice getting a cogent message across. Of course, some excellent videos are longer, but when you are starting out, you may not be able to achieve that level of result.

A good strategy to get your videos well ranked (and thus seen more often when people search for the information you want to share) is to choose the title carefully. Your title should include the key words that you want people to search for. For example, if you want to provide information on a problem with the school district in Dallas, Texas, your video might be titled, "Dallas Independent School District (DISD) Manipulates Test Scores." Someone searching for information about the Dallas school district may find it from the longer name and the abbreviation. She might also be looking for information about the test scores in the district. This highly targeted video can be linked to other videos titled "Dallas Independent School District (DISD) Ignores Homeless Children" and "Dallas Independent School District (DISD) Harasses Minority Teachers," and so forth. It would be ideal to have a similar format for each video with a branded look (including the same fifteen-second introduction with music) to build credibility and organizational status. If you have several videos, you will more likely fill the first page of results and thus get your positions across by being the major voice within YouTube about the topics of concern to your organization.

Another useful strategy to get more attention for your videos is to create a group of videos called a playlist that aggregates several videos on a single topic. If you search for the most popular video on the topic you want to be known for, and include your video in a playlist with it, your video will be seen by more viewers than if you put your video out there by itself. That is because people searching will be more likely to choose a group of videos to watch than to blindly go one by one.

CONCLUSION

This chapter has covered the ever-changing territory of electronic advocacy using the Internet and social media. We made a quick dive into how the tools found there can be added to the arsenals of advocacy organizations working for social justice. Many of these tools are those that individuals use for their own purposes. Thus, the innovation is not so much to find users of the tools, but rather to understand how working with Web sites, e-mail, Facebook, Twitter, and YouTube for an advocacy organization is different. The most important difference is that you will want to work diligently to have your information found on the Internet and among other individuals who are interested in helping you achieve your social justice goals. Including interesting information and calls to action in each communication is important to your success as an advocate for social justice.

Suggested Further Reading

Kanter, B., & Fine, A. (2010). *The networked nonprofit: Connecting with social media to drive change*. San Francisco: Jossey-Bass.

Advocacy is increasingly connected to the use of social media. Research shows that connected members of the public are also more likely to donate to the organization. This book provides a thorough explanation of how nonprofits can use social media to keep connected to interested people. Networked nonprofits, using social media, improve their ability to maximize their impact.

Kapin, A., & Ward, A. S. (2013). *Social change: Any time, every where. How to implement online multichannel strategies to spark advocacy, raise money and engage your community*. San Francisco: Jossey-Bass.

Kapin and Ward are enthusiastic and knowledgeable guides to the world of social media and advocacy. They also deal with fund-raising and community-building using the tools of social media. Their practical and action-oriented book is a helpful primer for the newbie nonprofit social media practitioner.

Discussion Questions and Exercises

1. Discuss how to set up a social media campaign to promote your advocacy goals. Which tools will you use (including ones not mentioned in the chapter)? Why?

2. What are some of the important differences between one-on-one communication strategies that you plan to use (see chapter 7) and broader strategies such as a social media campaign? How do these strategies fit together?

3. If your advocacy effort does not plan to use social media or the Internet, what is this decision based on? Be sure to explain why you are choosing this approach.

4. Start and use a Facebook page, a Twitter account, or a YouTube channel for a social justice purpose, even if it is not related to your current class project (if you are doing a class project). Discuss your experiences in doing so.

Chapter 9

EVALUATING ADVOCACY

If advocacy for social transformation values both process and outcomes, there must be spaces structured throughout the advocacy to think about and define what success is and how it will be measured in an iterative way. Evaluation, like other moments in advocacy strategies, is an opportunity to generate an empowering process and build capacities. C. Clark, *Making Change Happen*

You have done it! The advocacy effort that you envisioned, planned for, and implemented is over. Perhaps you met with your supervisor about a client's unmet needs. Maybe you told the board of directors at an agency how the agency's policy was negatively affecting clients and offered ideas for improvement. You might have testified to a legislative aide about changes to a bill that could benefit many citizens of your state. Whatever your advocacy effort, you have done it, and you are alive to tell the tale.

But a question still looms: To what extent did you achieve what you wanted to accomplish when you planned the effort? Sometimes your advocacy effort achieves everything you hoped for. Sometimes it seems to achieve nothing tangible. Most efforts fall somewhere between these two extremes. This chapter presents a way to systematically evaluate your accomplishments, which will show you how far you came and enable you to learn from your efforts.

Evaluation of advocacy efforts is important for one main reason: it allows advocates to judge whether their actions have accomplished anything worthwhile. In addition, a thorough evaluation documents what was done and links what was done to what was accomplished. Although every advocacy effort is different in nature and execution, you can draw lessons from each attempt. Synthesizing information from each effort can lead to more-effective action in the future. When data demonstrate that change has happened, morale improves and people are more likely to want to advocate in the future. This effect applies to staff and to others who might have been involved in an advocacy effort, such as clients or volunteers.

An additional reason for evaluation applies when the advocacy effort is underwritten by an outside source. The funder wants to know what was done and with what results. Conducting an evaluation allows the person reporting to the funder to provide credible and systematic information. Otherwise, the best information that can be reported is anecdotal and limited. A lack of credible evaluation may jeopardize future funding opportunities from that donor.

Knowing the importance of evaluating advocacy efforts, let's now turn to understanding how to conduct an evaluation. Evaluation of an advocacy effort is divided into two phases that can be called observation and judgment. We will cover each phase separately, though the judgment phase can occur only after the observation phase.

Before exploring these aspects of evaluation further, we must have a short discussion about terminology. The field of evaluation has a large number of terms that overlap in meaning. For example, some program evaluation authors use the term "formative evaluation" (which is designed to help shape the way a program is designed or administered), while others use the term "process evaluation" when discussing the same idea. The term "implementation monitoring" encompasses parts of what is meant by the terms "formative evaluation" and "process evaluation," though implementation monitoring has a somewhat more narrow meaning. All of these can be considered a part of the observation phase of an advocacy evaluation. Similarly, various terms exist (such as "summative evaluation," "outcome evaluation," "impact assessment," etc.) that all relate to the "judgment phase" of evaluation, as we use that term here. It is important to be familiar with all the terms that might be used, as different authors prefer one label over another, but it is even more important to know where these terms fit into the two primary functions of the evaluation process: observing the effort and judging the results. Examples of useful evaluation texts include McDavid, Huse, and Hawthorne (2013) and Mertens and Wilson (2012).

OBSERVATION PHASE

The purpose of the observation phase of the evaluation is to determine what was done, by whom, for whom, and when. This information is crucial. Without knowing what was actually done during the advocacy effort, it is nearly impossible to say with any degree of credibility that the effort was responsible for any of the outcomes. One of the first issues in the observation phase is to determine what one should be looking at or measuring in order to assess the level of plan completion.

Observation Using the Advocacy Map

The observation phase of evaluation is predicated on having a clear picture of what you wanted to do to achieve your desired outcomes. This picture is formed by developing an advocacy map (as described in chapter 5) or another set of goals and objectives, though I will assume that you have created an advocacy map as explained in chapter 5. (The two example advocacy maps from chapter 5, figures 5.2 and 5.3, are reprinted in this chapter as figures 9.1 and 9.2.) Recall that an advocacy map lists the resources available, the tasks to be completed, and what you want to achieve in the short, medium, and long term from an advocacy effort. Also included on the advocacy map is an ultimate social justice–related outcome for society.

Participants should be able to document the efforts made to accomplish the tasks assigned to them during the implementation of the advocacy plan. Was research conducted? Were applications completed? Was testimony provided? How often, or to what extent?

Because advocacy efforts must stay flexible and respond to changing conditions and needs, the original advocacy map may not have lasted through the entire process. If you adapt it to meet altered situations, however, you should prepare notes to explain why you made those changes; you should also keep the advocacy map updated so that everyone involved can know what the latest plan is.

Working from the latest advocacy map, those evaluating the advocacy effort can determine what was actually done and why. This stage is one of the most important to learning from advocacy efforts—those trying to learn must have a clear understanding of what was done and why. Documenting how these decisions were made is also important.

FIGURE 9.1 Example Advocacy Map

DATE: _____

Problem/Issue: My client is engaging in risky behavior (unprotected sex and recreational use of marijuana) after school and before her mother gets home from work.

Desired Outcome(s) for Client: My client will not engage in risky behavior (unprotected sex and recreational use of marijuana) after school and before her mother gets home from work.

Ultimate Social Justice–Related Outcome(s) for Society: All children will be in safe situations with nearby adult support.

Resources (col. 1)	Tasks (col. 2)	Short-term Outcomes (col. 3)	Medium-term Outcomes (col. 4)	Long-term Outcomes (col. 5)	Ultimate Social Justice–Related Outcomes for Society (col. 6)
Student Client	• Search for acceptable alternative activities to the current risky behaviors. • Research potential consequences of engaging in unprotected sex and recreational use of marijuana. • Learn skills of advocacy for self and others.	• Student will engage in other activities that do not put her at risk. • Student will know negative potential consequences of unprotected sex, negative effects of pregnancy on student and her child in the future, and effects of marijuana on self and unborn child.	• This student will have no more (or at least reduced) engagement in risky behaviors such as unprotected sex and drug use.	• This student will not become pregnant and will discontinue use of all illegal drugs.	• All children will be in safe situations with nearby adult support.

Resources (col. 1)	Tasks (col. 2)	Short-term Outcomes (col. 3)	Medium-term Outcomes (col. 4)	Long-term Outcomes (col. 5)	Ultimate Social Justice–Related Outcomes for Society (col. 6)
Student Client's Parents	• Search for acceptable alternative activities to the current risky behaviors. • Try to arrange situation so that greater supervision of client can be done by a parent or other trusted adult. • If the afterschool program is considered the best spot for the child, advocate for her to be placed in an appropriate situation (either at school or elsewhere).	• Student will engage in other activities that do not put her at risk. • A parent or other trusted adult will be identified to supervise the student each day.	• This student will have no more (or at least reduced) engagement in risky behaviors such as unprotected sex and drug use.	• This student will not become pregnant and will discontinue use of all illegal drugs.	• All children will be in safe situations with nearby adult support.

Social Worker	• Search for acceptable alternative activities to the current risky behaviors. • If the afterschool program is considered the best spot for the client, advocate for client's inclusion in afterschool activities program.	• Student will engage in other activities that do not put her at risk. • Program staff will allow student into program.	• This student will have no more (or at least reduced) engagement in risky behaviors such as unprotected sex and drug use.	• This student will not become pregnant and will discontinue use of all illegal drugs.	• All children will be in safe situations with nearby adult support.
Staff running the afterschool activities program	• Allow this student into the program. • Expand size of program to include all students who would benefit from the program.	• Program staff will allow student into program. • Program staff will have resources to work with all students who would benefit from the program.	• This student will have no more (or at least reduced) engagement in risky behaviors such as unprotected sex and drug use.	• This student will not become pregnant and will discontinue use of all illegal drugs. • Female students in the program will not become pregnant and will not use illegal drugs.	• All children will be in safe situations with nearby adult support.

FIGURE 9.2 Example Advocacy Map

DATE:

Problem/Issue: My client and her family experience hunger regularly at the end of the month when cash runs low, and they have been ruled ineligible for continued assistance because they have received groceries from the emergency food bank three times already this year.

Desired Outcome(s) for Client: My client and her family will have adequate amounts of nutritious food throughout the month.

Ultimate Social Justice–Related Outcome(s) for Society: A society where everyone has adequate amounts of nutritious food.

Resources (col. 1)	Tasks (col. 2)	Short-term Outcomes (col. 3)	Medium-term Outcomes (col. 4)	Long-term Outcomes (col. 5)	Ultimate Social Justice–Related Outcomes for Society (col. 6)
Client and family members	• Conduct research about other sources of resources. • Fill in other program applications.	• Are informed about other resources. • Complete applications.	• Clients are deemed eligible for food assistance.	• Receive adequate amounts of nutritious food. • Self-supporting, in terms of food.	• A society where everyone has adequate amounts of nutritious food.
Social worker	• Provides knowledge of programs to clients. • Assists client in program applications.	• Client learns about possible programs. • Social worker is aware of policies of program and the constraints of the agency.	• Clients make choices about how to overcome lack of food.	• Client has improved knowledge of system and how to access it appropriately.	• A society where everyone has adequate amounts of nutritious food.

Resources (col. 1)	Tasks (col. 2)	Short-term Outcomes (col. 3)	Medium-term Outcomes (col. 4)	Long-term Outcomes (col. 5)	Ultimate Social Justice-Related Outcomes for Society (col. 6)
	• Advocates to emergency relief program to see if family can receive additional food. • Pushes for more adequate funding for food programs.	• Social worker knows of need for more funding of program.	• Social worker tries to influence policies in other organizations and advocates for larger program budgets.	• Advocacy targets learn more about program needs. • Agencies receive additional resources for food aid programs.	
Community programs, such as food banks	• Agencies disclose all rules and procedures for collecting and distributing food.	• Agencies agree to review rules and procedures to determine if they could be improved.	• Within agency constraints, benefits are increased—in any case, benefits are distributed as equitably as possible.	• Agencies self-monitor their policies and procedures, putting social justice at the fore.	• A society where everyone has adequate amounts of nutritious food.
Government programs, such as food stamps	• Advocates legislators and agency to examine laws, rules, and procedures for providing benefits.	• Legislators/program staff agree to review rules and procedures.	• Within agency constraints, benefits are increased—in any case, they are distributed as equitably as possible.	• Agencies self-monitor their policies and procedures, putting social justice at the fore.	• A society where everyone has adequate amounts of nutritious food.

It may be that certain people were the key decision makers in the effort, even if the decision-making process was supposed to be egalitarian. Was this small group of decision makers necessary, or did it detract from the process for others involved?

It may not be immediately obvious how to collect the information needed to describe the implementation of the advocacy map. I discuss the most common approaches to data collection in the next few paragraphs. I recommend that you use more than one approach, particularly for observing the most important aspects of the advocacy effort.

The methods to determine if the planned activities were conducted can be broken into two primary types: direct observation and indirect observation. Direct observation is when the evaluators observe the activity for themselves. If the activity on the advocacy map is that classes will cover a certain curriculum, a direct observation approach is for the evaluator to sit in on the class to determine how often the class met and what it covered. Another advocacy effort might rely on talking to a legislative aide about the importance of changing a particular policy. Again, a direct observation method would be for the evaluator to be a part of that meeting, noting the extent to which the advocate presented the desired material. Direct observation can be a powerful way to collect information, because the evaluator can note much about the situation, how the recipients react to the advocacy activities, and other contextual information. This approach is time consuming and expensive, however, if used to evaluate any but the smallest advocacy effort.

Indirect observation requires the use of proxies to tell the tale. It relies on interviews, surveys, and/or records to provide evidence that the planned activities took place. Advocacy efforts may involve many actors, pursuing a common goal simultaneously in different locations, which makes it impossible for one person to observe directly the activities taking place. In addition, resource constraints may prevent the evaluator from directly observing most aspects of the process.

We now use the same examples of activities as we used to illustrate direct observation methods: An indirect way to determine if classes were held would be to ask the targeted participants face to face which classes they went to and what was covered in them. It may be that the respondents will remember being in a class but have difficulty describing what was covered. In this case, the activity was performed, but the students' inability to recall the content bodes poorly for achieving the planned outcomes, which rely on students mastering the information presented in class. Instead of a face-to-face interview, an evaluator could conduct a written or telephone survey of former students, collecting information on the same topics. Another approach would be to rely on contemporaneous records collected as the advocacy effort was put into effect (roll-call lists, sign-in sheets, lesson plans, etc.) to determine what was offered and to whom. If the advocacy plan was to meet with a legislative aide, indirect observation techniques could include face-to-face interviews, reports written by those involved after the fact, or surveys of advocacy participants' feelings and thoughts about the effort.

How is this information to be used in practice? Examining figure 9.1, we see that the following tasks were to be accomplished by the student client: search for acceptable alternative activities to the current risky behaviors, research potential consequences of engaging in unprotected sex and recreational use of marijuana, and learn skills of advocacy for self and others. There are various options for measurement: The client could keep a process log describing where she looked, when, and with what results. Or the evaluator could interview the client to ask what she had learned. The evaluator can use similar measurement approaches for the client's second task. And for the third task, the evaluator can use direct observation: the worker could put the student in a role-play situation to evaluate if she had learned how to use advocacy skills.

In many cases, examination of the tasks to be completed shows that the tasks were done, after a fashion, but perhaps not to the extent that was envisioned when the advocacy map was developed. For example, perhaps a task to be completed was the creation of an advisory council and frequent consultation with its members. The monitoring process might show results ranging from one extreme to the other: from no council being instituted, to the council holding monthly meetings with high attendance rates and considerable discussion that resulted in useful input for the advocacy effort. More likely are findings that the council was created but met rarely and had only desultory conversations that had little impact on the effort. Or, if using the example of the student in figure 9.1 again, the student might have asked her friends about alternative activities but found nothing of interest, said she already knew about the consequences of unprotected sex and so did not do that task, and thought that the training in advocacy skills was sort of stupid and so did not pay much attention to it.

In either case, the evaluator of the advocacy should assign some identifier to the level of task accomplishment. This can be a grade (such as A to F) or percentage of accomplishment (0% to 100%). It is helpful to have more than one person make these assessments whenever possible, with discussion of each person's results culminating in a final assessment.

Observing the level of task accomplishment and asking how it was accomplished or what could have resulted in a greater level of accomplishment provides considerable opportunity for learning. The idea is not to find ways to assign blame for lack of implementation, but rather to look for ways to do better the next time.

The final product of observing advocacy efforts is to know with considerable clarity what tasks happened, to which targets, who did them, and to what extent. Only after this information is gathered can the evaluators appropriately begin to determine if the desired outcomes occurred.

Context Observation

Although advocacy observation can be completed using indicators from the advocacy map only, other indicators may also be used that relate to the broader context within which advocacy is pursued. Such indicators may be germane to more than the advocacy effort at hand; they may impact future advocacy efforts as well and are thus helpful to track over time. These indicators are shown in figure 9.3. The six suggested categories of context observation are observing your organization, observing your reputation, observing your target, observing your relationships, observing the media, and observing public opinion. Although these categories will not fit every advocacy situation, they apply to many and can be important precursors to future success or failure. It may not be wise to win a particular advocacy battle if the long-term war is lost due to, for example, public opinion turning against your organization.

FIGURE 9.3   Context Observation Indicators

Observing Your Organization

Do the concepts of case and cause advocacy seem to be becoming more acceptable to staff in your organization?

Do the concepts of case and cause advocacy seem to be becoming more acceptable to board members of your organization?

Are staff members using their time, continuing education opportunities, and other resources to become more expert in advocacy?

Is advocacy becoming integrated into the organizational culture?

Observing Your Reputation

Record the sources and numbers of inquiries that you receive as a result of your work.

Are you getting to the people you wanted to get to?

How and where have they heard of your work?

How accurate are their preconceptions about you and your work?

Are you seen by targets and others as being legitimately involved in the situation?

Observing Your Target

Record and observe changes in the rhetoric of your target audience. Keep a file of their statements over time.

What are they saying about you and your campaign?

Are they moving closer to your position, adapting to or adopting any of your language or philosophy?

Observing Your Relationships

Record the frequency and content of conversations with external sources and target audiences.

Are you discussing new ideas?

Are you becoming a confidante or a source of information or advice?

Observing the Media

Count column inches on your issue and the balance of pro and anti sentiment.

Count the number of mentions for your organization.

Count the number of times you are contacted by representatives of the media to give information for their stories.

Analyze whether media are adopting your language.

Observing Public Opinion

Analyze the popular climate through telephone polling or through commissioning surveys.

Count the number of "way-out" negative or positive communications from the public, including hate mail, donations, and so on. Are they increasing or decreasing?

Count the number of volunteers coming to assist the organization. Is it growing or declining?

Source: Adapted and expanded by the author from Laney, M., Scobie, J., & Fraser, A. (2005). *The how and why of advocacy. Guidance Notes 2.1.* London: British Overseas NGOs for Development. Used with permission.

The first category is to observe your organization. One of the primary reasons things are done or not done in most organizations is the organization's culture. Advocacy may be something that is "simply not done around here." This is particularly true for cause advocacy, in which the target for change is located outside the organization. In order to build a clear mandate for future advocacy, it may be necessary to address internal issues of perceived acceptability and desirability of advocacy.

Because individuals and organizations exist in the real world, it is important to observe your reputation. Even if advocates think they have angels on their side, the outside world may have a different opinion. As representatives of an organization that must compete for funds, staff, accommodations, friends, and other benefits that come from outside the organization, it is important to observe your reputation. Even individuals must have concern for their reputation. If you acquire a negative reputation, you may be shut out of decision-making processes regardless of your expertise, interest, and other signs of high ability and dedication.

Reputation can be a two-edged sword. An advocate may want to develop a reputation among members of the elite for being hard to work with, while having a high status among oppressed people for being a tough proponent of their causes. Still, an advocate can overdo this dichotomy, making it likely that another advocate or organization will emerge that can work more easily to achieve the same results.

It is also important to observe your target. Many advocacy efforts are long-term affairs. Targets do not often change their views or positions immediately upon hearing your ideas, especially if the situation you are debating is not new. Still, change happens. Stories emerge. Evidence accumulates. Pressures build. Positions evolve. Over time, observations help remind advocates of what has changed and can be used to maintain commitment to and energy for the efforts toward social justice.

Relationships are one key to successful advocacy, and therefore you must observe them as well. Most advocacy relies on using the bonds of existing relationships (individual and organizational) to achieve change. You should, therefore, invest energy in these relationships and not allow them to wither. In addition, advocacy efforts often require building new relationships. New and different people are called on for their strength, inspiration, knowledge, ideas, skills, and connections. As issues, people, and institutions evolve, targets may also change, which means you will have to create and manage another set of new relationships. You should periodically assess all of these sets of relationships.

You must also observe the media. If the advocacy effort in question is external to the advocate's organization, the media may latch onto the story. In fact, you may be the one who alerted them to the situation. If the media respond to the idea you pitch to them, your advocacy efforts can be greatly facilitated. You can easily count the number of stories and column inches in newspapers and magazines. You can make a rough estimate of the amount of this material that is positive and negative to your position or organization. An important aspect of your relationship with the media is also the number of times they turn to you as a source of information or a viewpoint worth including in a story. Finally, because editorials can be persuasive to readers, if an editorial writer begins to use the same language as you do, it is a sign that the issue is being framed the way you desire. When the media see the situation as you do, the public will be more likely to adopt that viewpoint as well.

Finally, you must observe public opinion. As noted above, public opinion may be shaped by how an issue is presented in the media and on social media. Positive public opinion is very helpful in an advocacy effort, to be sure, but media attention to your viewpoint may also bring out people who are working outside the bounds of rational discourse. Such people may resort to intimidation, threats, and violence. Advocates for causes such as reproductive choice or civil rights for oppressed minorities have found the courage to continue their work in the face of death threats, bombings, and personal attacks. Advocates will not be able to guard against every threat, but you should follow common-sense security measures when intense passion animates opponents. The ways suggested to observe public opinion range from the expensive (polls and surveys) to the free (simply noting the number of letters and donations received, e.g., as well as comments and other forms of engagement on social media).

Once the observation phase of the advocacy effort (checking that the tasks described in the advocacy map were carried out and/or checking on the context of the advocacy effort) is complete, the evaluator can move to the next phase—that of judging how well the outcomes were accomplished. It is worth repeating that evaluating an advocacy effort must include a clear observation of what occurred. Little learning regarding the effectiveness of an effort can be done if it is not clear what was done to achieve the desired outcomes.

JUDGMENT PHASE

In the judgment phase of the advocacy effort we turn to the short-, medium-, and long-term outcomes, as well as the ultimate social justice outcomes, displayed on the advocacy map to determine if they have been achieved. For example, the advocacy map shown in figure 9.1 states that one short-term outcome of the advocacy effort was "Student will engage in other activities (not unprotected sex and recreational use of marijuana) that do not put her at risk." The advocacy map in figure 9.2 lists a long-term outcome of "Client has improved knowledge of system and how to access it appropriately." The judgment phase of an evaluation starts with such outcome statements and uses them to determine what to examine in this phase of the evaluation process.

An important aspect of the judgment process is answering the following question: What is a success? As described in terms of the completion of tasks, the evaluation process may indicate a partial accomplishment of an outcome. The female student in the advocacy map in figure 9.1 may be doing some new things that are not risky (volunteering in a tutoring program for third graders, for example) but also continue smoking marijuana with friends on weekend nights. The food assistance programs in figure 9.2 may have examined their policies and procedures but decided that they are fine the way they are. Are these advocacy outcomes successful? To what extent do the tasks need to be fully accomplished for us to believe that the overall effort was a success? I have stressed above that we cannot expect to achieve everything we set out to do—so this should apply in the judgment of outcomes phase, too. Advocacy is a tool used to move toward social justice; we should not need to achieve all of our desired outcomes before we judge that we have made important progress.

Still, in assessing the worth of any particular advocacy effort, we cannot be too easy, either. A lot of time and other resources go into most advocacy efforts—if we could have used these resources more successfully in different ways, that conclusion should be part of the final judgment. Before the advocacy effort begins, it is useful to try to determine what level of accomplishment will be considered satisfactory, if not ideal. If this level is determined, the final judgment will be easier to make.

Measurement in the Judgment Phase

Measurement approaches in the judgment phase are similar to those I describe in the section on observation. We can use both direct and indirect methods, but outcome measurement does have another tool in the arsenal of indirect measurement: standardized instruments. Standardized instruments are measures that can be administered and scored in uniform ways. Because the instrument is administered and scored identically across subjects, the scores can be usefully compared to the norms that have been developed in the process of standardizing the instrument. In other words, when you have the score of an individual with whom you are working, you can compare that score to the scores of many other people to whom you have administered the instrument in the same way. For example, you may be working with a client who you suspect is using drugs (as in figure 9.1). If you administer a standardized instrument designed to detect drug use or favorable attitudes toward drug use, you can tell if your client is doing better or worse than the others who have provided answers to the instrument. The Substance Abuse Subtle Screening Inventory (SASSI) is, for example, "a brief and easily administered psychological screening measure that helps identify individuals who have a high probability of having a substance use disorder" (SASSI Institute, n.d.). Separate scales exist for adults and adolescents so that we can compare the scores generated to more-comparable subpopulations. Although generally used as a clinical tool, the SASSI might be useful to measure one medium- or long-term outcome on an advocacy map (as in figure 9.1) as well. The importance of the standardization process is the comparison numbers that allow the worker to have a basis for judging how well the client is doing. The worker can give the same measure more than once and then also judge if the client is doing better or worse in comparison with herself.

Standardized instruments have two other attributes that are important to measuring outcomes: they have known levels of validity and reliability. Validity means that "the concept we think we are measuring (e.g., depression) is actually what we are measuring rather than some other concept (e.g. anxiety, anger)" (Jordan & Hoefer, 2001, p. 57). Reliability is "the degree to which the same instrument provides a similar score when used repeatedly" (Jordan & Hoefer, p. 60). High levels of validity and reliability are both important in using measures, because they give us more confidence that what we want to measure is what we are actually measuring, with as little error as possible.

Standardized measures tend to focus on individual or family relationship issues. Many of the issues on which advocacy focuses, however, are measured at a different level—they are community or social problems. Outcome measures that are made up especially for evaluation of a particular advocacy effort (sometimes called ad hoc measures) may be good enough because no standardized measures exist. Another type of measure that can be used to assess advocacy efforts at this larger scale is a social indicator.

The term "social indicator" has no generally accepted single definition, though most definitions are somewhat similar. One definition states, "An indicator is an individual or composite statistic that relates to a basic construct in [a policy field] and is useful in a policy context" (Shavelson, McDonnell, & Oakes, 1991). Not all information is an indicator: "Statistics qualify as indicators only if they serve as yardsticks. That is, they must tell a great deal about the entire system by reporting the condition of a few particularly significant features of it" (Shavelson et al.). Examples of social indicators include life expectancy, educational achievement, poverty level, juvenile drug-related arrest rates, and divorce rates.

Social indicators are most useful when we are looking for progress in long-term or ultimate social justice–related outcomes. In the two advocacy map examples (figures 9.1 and 9.2), the ultimate social justice–related outcomes deal with all children being in safe situations and everyone having adequate amounts of nutritious food. It may be difficult to find social indicators at the correct level of potential impact. Many indicators, for example, cannot be disaggregated to less than a county or even state level. In these situations, indicators are nearly useless to judge the worth of an advocacy effort unless the anticipated outcomes were also county- or statewide in scope. Changes in indicators at such large levels may be caused by many macrovariables, including the unemployment rate, business cycles, and even weather patterns. Thus, it is difficult to link conclusively a smaller-scale advocacy effort to shifts in such indicators.

On the other hand, advocacy efforts at the state level should be examined in light of changes in state-level indicators. When advocates work to gain new funding for state programs dealing with health issues, it may be appropriate to link changes in health indicators (such as low-birth-weight babies, accessibility of prenatal care, rates of teenage pregnancy, etc.) to advocacy efforts.

Coffman and Reed (2009) describe four methodologies that they argue are unique to evaluating advocacy:

Bellwether Methodology. Essentially, this is a series of qualitative interviews with influential people who do not know the purpose of the interview beforehand. These interviews are used "to determine where a policy issue or proposal is positioned on the policy agenda; how decision makers and other influentials are thinking and talking about it; and how likely policymakers are to act on it" (Coffman & Reed, 2009, p. 3). This technique is useful to gauge how successfully an advocacy effort has been in getting its agenda in the consciousness of influential decision makers, and the level of and gaps in decision makers' knowledge base regarding the issue of interest.

Policy-Maker Ratings. In this technique, advocates rate decision makers on their levels of support for the policy desired by advocates, their level of influence, and the raters' level of confidence in their ratings. If a policy maker is confidently considered to be supportive and influential, then he or she can be expected to support a policy position. These ratings can be repeated over time to determine if a particular decision maker is moving toward or away from supporting an organization's key policy positions.

Intense Policy Debriefs. According to Coffman and Reed (2009), a policy debrief is a set of individual interviews or a meeting with persons involved in the advocacy effort "to capture data about advocates' recent experiences" (p. 7). Questions can focus on why the period of intense activity occurred, who made the decisions during this intense period and how, what results happened that were positive, what happened that was negative, and what key lessons could be learned from the experience to improve future advocacy efforts.

System Mapping. System mapping "involves the visual mapping of a system, identifying the parts and relationships in that system that are expected to change and how they will change, and then identifying ways of measuring or capturing whether those changes have occurred" (Coffman & Reed, 2009, p. 8).

The most important element of any advocacy effort evaluation is to match carefully the measures to be used with the outcomes that are expected as a result of the efforts made. The advocacy map is the first and best place to look to answer the question, What should we be seeking information about?

DIFFICULTIES IN EVALUATION

Although conducting a formal evaluation of all advocacy efforts is the right thing to do and this chapter has explained how to conduct such an evaluation, it would be misleading to end without discussing possible difficulties that you may encounter during evaluation. Three main difficulties are finding time and resources to conduct an evaluation, resistance on the part of those being evaluated, and disagreement during the judgment phase.

Finding Time and Resources to Conduct an Evaluation

People who are advocates are usually something else, too: case manager, agency executive, volunteer, student, and so on. Such advocates have many demands on their time, and advocacy may be only a small part of their lives. Few social workers are full-time advocates, and even those who are have many other tasks. Thus, it is easy to think that evaluation will get done later, after a new project is completed. As the advocacy effort to be evaluated recedes in time, the pressure to evaluate it fades.

Because "time is money," a lack of staff or volunteer time could be ameliorated if more money was provided for evaluation and someone was hired to complete an evaluation. Unfortunately, most advocacy efforts directed at improving social justice are as short of funds as they are of time, so it is difficult for them to throw money at the problem to make it go away.

This problem can be reduced by using volunteer evaluators, such as those from a local university class or others who are willing to take on such a specialized role. The problem can also be reduced by explicit support from the advocacy effort's leaders who build evaluation into the effort's staffing and budget. Ongoing measurement of the activities and outcomes also assists in keeping the advocacy going in the planned direction; therefore, a well-implemented effort should already have many of the important data collected by the end of the project. Compiling information already in records, while not time or cost free, is also not very expensive. Using the advocacy map helps to make evaluation an integral part of the entire process.

Resistance on the Part of Those Being Evaluated

Few people like to be graded. Not many people like to grade others, either. No matter how often an evaluator repeats, "This is not an evaluation of the people involved: it is an evaluation of how closely we came to achieving our desired outcomes," the people involved think that they are being scrutinized for mistakes they may have made. Few organizations have such a strong learning culture as to be able to avoid this situation and these feelings. Resistance to the idea of a formal evaluation thus arises from personal feelings, even if the expressed problem is something else, such as a lack of time or funds.

At its heart, this problem is nearly impossible to eliminate. The best that can be done is to have strong leadership support for evaluation and to insist that the evaluation is for learning, and not for punishing. This position is difficult to maintain, however, if clear evidence of bungling or lack of effort emerges. Another element that reduces staff resistance is if the organization's culture embraces improved performance based on feedback, rather than advancement based on mistakes going unnoticed.

Disagreement during the Judgment Phase

One of the most difficult evaluation questions is, What is success? Several people can look at the same information and make different assessments as to whether an advocacy project was successful. When do we judge partial success as good enough? Whose opinion about the level of success will we adopt? People with vested interests and hidden agendas may want to overstate or understate the degree of success. It is almost a given that any one advocacy effort will not achieve everything desired, so this issue also usually comes up when evaluating advocacy.

The best way to reduce this problem is to agree after the advocacy map is developed but before the advocacy begins as to which level of accomplishment will be labeled which level of success. With this agreement recorded and distributed, the final judgment phase becomes easier. Assessment is made simpler by having an agreement in place before people's reactions are colored by what actually happens.

CONCLUSION

The evaluation of advocacy efforts is essential to learning how to perform advocacy better. In the model used in this book, evaluation is closely linked to planning of advocacy. The advocacy map is used to observe whether appropriate and needed resources were present and whether the planned tasks were attempted and completed. Only after a reckoning of the level of resources and extent of task completion is made can the evaluator move to examining whether outcomes were achieved and judging how well the advocacy effort's desired outcomes were accomplished.

Evaluators use both direct and indirect approaches to measure what they want to be able to count. Evaluators can observe for themselves or rely on others to observe and report accurately what they see, feel, or think. Standardized instruments and social indicators can also help to determine if desired outcomes have been achieved.

Advocates, like most others, want to do the best job they can but may be leery of actually finding out how well they did. Although it can be difficult to evaluate advocacy efforts, the possibility to learn from past successes and failures is too important to ignore. Advocates must take a position in which their ethical responsibility for growth and choice for all is large enough to risk hearing some bad news about what they have done. Only by testing what has been done will we ever know what works, when, and why.

Suggested Further Reading

Clark, C. (2001). *Making change happen: Advocacy and citizen participation.* Washington, DC: Just Associates.

This short publication presents a range of issues around advocacy and has a good section on evaluation of advocacy efforts. The author's description of the need for evaluation of organizational learning is especially strong.

Coffman, J. (n. d.). *Monitoring and evaluating advocacy: Companion to the Advocacy Toolkit.* Retrieved from http://www.unicef.org/evaluation/files /Advocacy_Toolkit_Companion.pdf

Intended for an international practitioner audience, this fifty-page pdf has a clear approach and plentiful examples. It is similar to the advocacy-map approach used in this book.

Discussion Questions and Exercises

1. How is evaluating an advocacy effort similar to evaluating treatment of an individual or family? How is it different?
2. How is evaluating an advocacy effort similar to evaluating the impact of a program on client outcomes? How is it different?
3. Develop a comprehensive plan to evaluate your advocacy effort. Discuss your plan with another person. Revise your plan, if needed, after your discussion.
4. What have you learned about constructing an advocacy map now that you have used it all the way through the evaluation process? How would you change it now if you were to begin again? Why?

Chapter 10

ONGOING MONITORING

The client advocacy role, which social workers increasingly carry out through legislative lobbying, should be expanded in concept and practice to include monitoring the implementation of social legislation. Monitoring the bureaucracy, the agency of legislative implementation, is a concomitant responsibility to legislative lobbying; it adds a measure of assurance that change sought by legislation will take place. W. Bell & B. Bell, "Monitoring the Bureaucracy"

Social workers must monitor the advocacy situation on an ongoing basis. Even after an advocacy plan has been implemented and the battle seemingly finished, hard-won gains can be lost. Laws may be passed, but not implemented. Laws may be implemented, but then be hamstrung by counterproductive rules, low resource allocations, bureaucratic indifference, and so on. On the other hand, the legislative battle might not have gone very well. Advocates may be able to achieve some of their goals by working through the postlegislative policy-making phase. The information in this chapter can help in either situation by ensuring that advocates understand the importance of monitoring.

A key lesson from research on advocacy is that, generally, more is accomplished when people work together in coalitions or interest groups than when they work on their own (Brown, Langenegger, Garcia, Lewis, & Biles, 2014). Nowhere is this more true than when monitoring the bureaucracy, for two reasons. First, a great deal of expertise is required to understand the processes and the details involved in bureaucracy. Sometimes, the insertion of just one or two words can make a large difference in the outcome of an advocacy effort. Social workers, for example, were excluded from the list of people who could receive reimbursement from certain federal government programs that provide mental health services, unless the social worker was supervised by a psychologist or psychiatrist. NASW worked diligently to have two words, "social worker," along with an appropriate definition of what a social worker is, included in the regulations that defined who could be directly reimbursed for their work. (See exhibit 10.1 to read the Medicare regulations current as of this writing.)

Exhibit 10.1   Definition of Clinical Social Worker and Clinical Social Work Services by Centers for Medicare and Medicaid Services

TITLE 42—PUBLIC HEALTH
CHAPTER IV—CENTERS FOR MEDICARE & MEDICAID SERVICES,
DEPARTMENT OF HEALTH AND HUMAN SERVICES

PART 410—SUPPLEMENTARY MEDICAL INSURANCE (SMI) BENEFITS—
Table of Contents

Subpart B—Medical and Other Health Services

Sec. 410.73 Clinical social worker services.

(a) Definition: clinical social worker. For purposes of this part, a clinical social worker is defined as an individual who—
   (1) Possesses a master's or doctor's degree in social work;
   (2) After obtaining the degree, has performed at least 2 years of supervised clinical social work; and
   (3) Either is licensed or certified as a clinical social worker by the State in which the services are performed or, in the case of an individual in a State that does not provide for licensure or certification as a clinical social worker—
      (i) Is licensed or certified at the highest level of practice provided by the laws of the State in which the services are performed; and
      (ii) Has completed at least 2 years or 3,000 hours of post master's degree supervised clinical social work practice under the supervision of a master's degree level social worker in an appropriate setting such as a hospital, SNF, or clinic.
(b) Covered clinical social worker services. Medicare Part B covers clinical social worker services.
   (1) Definition. "Clinical social worker services" means, except as specified in paragraph (b)(2) of this section, the services of a clinical social worker furnished for the diagnosis and treatment of mental illness that the clinical social worker is legally authorized to perform under State law (or the State regulatory

mechanism provided by State law) of the State in which the services are performed. The services must be of a type that would be covered if they were furnished by a physician or as an incident to a physician's professional service and must meet the requirements of this section.

    (2) Exception. The following services are not clinical social worker services for purposes of billing Medicare Part B:

        (i) Services furnished by a clinical social worker to an inpatient of a Medicare-participating hospital.

        (ii) Services furnished by a clinical social worker to an inpatient of a Medicare-participating SNF.

        (iii) Services furnished by a clinical social worker to a patient in a Medicare-participating dialysis facility if the services are those required by the conditions for coverage for ESRD facilities under Sec. 405.2163 of this chapter.

  (c) Agreement to consult. A clinical social worker must comply with the consultation requirements set forth at Sec. 410.71(f) (reading "clinical psychologist" as "clinical social worker").

  (d) Prohibited billing.

    (1) A clinical social worker may not bill Medicare for the services specified in paragraph (b)(2) of this section.

    (2) A clinical social worker or an attending or primary care physician may not bill Medicare or the beneficiary for the consultation that is required under paragraph (c) of this section.

[63 FR 20128, Apr. 23, 1998]

Source: U.S. Government Printing Office. (2003). Clinical social worker services. *Code of Federal Regulations, Title 42, Vol. 2* (42CFR410.73). Washington, DC: U.S. Government Printing Office.

Compare the definition of clinical social worker in the Medicare regulations with the definition of clinical social worker in the Civilian Health and Medical Program of the Uniformed Services regulations in exhibit 10.2. What variances do you see? What difference would those variances make to members of NASW? Those who try to influence the regulation-writing process must excel at this type of analysis.

Second, because monitoring work is extremely detailed and relies on a nuanced understanding of what specific words will result in what outcomes, it is both high stakes and often of little interest to individuals and unseasoned advocates (Haynes & Mickelson, 2009). Groups, organizations, and coalitions are thus more likely to be able to conduct

Exhibit 10.2 Definition of a Certified Clinical Social Worker by the Civilian Health and Medical Program of the Uniformed Services

TITLE 32—NATIONAL DEFENSE
  CHAPTER I—OFFICE OF THE SECRETARY OF DEFENSE (CONTINUED)

PART 199_CIVILIAN HEALTH AND MEDICAL PROGRAM OF THE UNI-FORMED SERVICES (CHAMPUS)

Sec. 199.6 Authorized providers.

(F) Certified Clinical Social Worker. A clinical social worker may provide covered services independent of physician referral and supervision, provided the clinical social worker:

  (1) Is licensed or certified as a clinical social worker by the jurisdiction where practicing; or, if the jurisdiction does not provide for licensure or certification of clinical social workers, is certified by a national professional organization offering certification of clinical social workers; and

  (2) Has at least a master's degree in social work from a graduate school of social work accredited by the Council on Social Work Education; and

  (3) Has had a minimum of 2 years or 3,000 hours of post-master's degree supervised clinical social work practice under the supervision of a master's level social worker in an appropriate clinical setting, as determined by the Director, OCHAMPUS, or a designee.

Note: Patients' organic medical problems must receive appropriate concurrent management by a physician.

Source: U.S. Government Printing Office. (2004). Authorized providers. *Code of Federal Regulations, Title 32, Vol. 2* (32CFR199.6). Washington, DC: U.S. Government Printing Office.

monitoring work than are individuals working on their own, because the groups have a continuing presence in the policy arena and can hire expertise, rather than having to learn from experience. No matter how boring the work may seem to some, others find such tasks highly interesting because they involve promoting social justice in this specialized way. Interest groups with staff, such as NASW or the Disability Rights Education and Defense Fund (DREDF), are natural sources for people to monitor the regulation-writing process, because their members have much to gain or lose from the way regulations are written.

All nonprofit organizations, however, are able to monitor the executive side of the policy process and should do so based on their concern for social justice in general or for certain populations. This type of work has become a more important part of what the nonprofit sector does. In fact, "the monitoring and influencing of government may be emerging as one of the single most important and effective functions of the private nonprofit sector" (Commission on Private Philanthropy and Public Needs, 1975, p. 45). Despite the importance of the subject matter, little research has been done to evaluate this prediction.

Two of the earliest social work authors to write about monitoring social policy implementation define the activity of monitoring as "scrutinizing the actions and performances of both public and private social agencies as they implement social legislation" (Bell & Bell, 1982, p. 120). Furthermore, this scrutiny includes such activities as reviewing and attempting to influence the direction and content of bureaucratic rules, administrative or legal decisions, program guidelines, and similar matters related to the implementation of social legislation. The aim of this form of monitoring is to protect the interests of clients targeted by the legislation and to ensure that the benefits intended by the legislation are obtained by the target population (Bell & Bell, p. 120).

Although monitoring the bureaucracy has many different components, three methods stand out as most important for advocates: influencing the regulation-writing process, influencing the budgetary process, and influencing the implementation process. These tools are useful when monitoring government at all levels—local, state, and national—as well as when monitoring how private organizations implement government policies. We will turn to these after exploring the differences in advocacy between the legislative and executive branches of government.

DIFFERENCES IN ADVOCACY BETWEEN LEGISLATIVE AND EXECUTIVE BRANCHES

Advocates who do not understand the need to work with people in the executive branch (at whatever level of organization) are missing a large part of the picture. To be interested only in the legislative arena is like convincing a nonprofit agency board of directors to vote to adopt a new policy and then ignoring what the staff members of the agency do to follow, or not follow, that policy.

Two key differences exist between trying to influence the legislative branch and trying to influence the executive branch (Wolpe & Levine, 1996). The first difference is that it is frequently more difficult to identify and reach the key decision makers in the executive branch. I have stressed how important it is to find the person who can give you what you want—that is, the ultimate target. But because most people in the executive branch are not elected to their positions, they are not as likely to be known to the public. Civil servants in relatively low-ranking positions may be the most influential people on any given issue. It takes time and persistence to find out who they are and to determine the most effective ways to influence them. In addition, their meetings and discussions do not have to be open to the public, and so the formal avenues of input into decision making are limited. This problem is exacerbated by the second difference between the legislative and executive branches—their cultures.

The culture of the legislative branch is politics—24/7. People who visit legislators and their staff are presumed to want something, and it is no surprise when lobbying occurs. Elected officials try to be responsive to their constituents by listening to their concerns, so paying attention to efforts at persuasion and negotiation is considered all in a day's work. Decisions are driven, in large part, by what is good for the people of the district who are most persuasive, not necessarily by what the "truth" is about what the best policy would be. Legislators look out for their district, if only to maintain a majority of voters in the next election. Workers in the executive branch, on the other hand, generally are there because of their expertise in a particular policy arena. Lobbying based on political argument is not expected in this arena. Civil servants are generally hired because of what they know and are promoted by length of service and higher levels of expertise. If you wish to convince them of your case, you need to bring additional expertise and rational arguments to the table, because knowledge is what is supposed to drive decisions in this branch.

While these comments apply to governmental systems, they are also appropriate for nonprofit organizations. People on the board (e.g., the organization's policy-making body) of a nonprofit are often selected based on who they know and the fund-raising sources to which they are connected. Some are selected because of their personal history with the organization. Board members' names are often listed on an organization's Web site or letterhead. Staff members' names (other than the executive director), however, are frequently not mentioned. If you wanted to know, for example, how to get the local affiliate of a national child mentoring program to change its policy regarding what it does with the children on its waiting list, you might have a hard time finding out what is currently being done and who is able to provide data on what is happening to the unmatched children. If you called the agency phone number and started asking questions about this topic, you might be met with suspicion and questions about why you want the information. If, as an outsider to the organization, you tried to get them to provide more services to the unmatched children, your right to be involved might be questioned or you might be told that the topic is being discussed internally. If you were able to have a conversation with the organization, they would probably mention resource constraints as a reason for not doing more.

This example illustrates the nature of working on an advocacy effort that is focused on the executive side of the policy equation. Let's now turn to the three most important types of executive branch advocacy: influencing the regulation-writing process, influencing the budgetary process, and influencing the implementation process.

INFLUENCING THE REGULATION-WRITING PROCESS

Although there is considerable research on group influence on the legislative branch available, much less research concerning group influence on the executive branch is available, especially in relationship to the rulemaking process. This omission is curious because the importance of understanding how regulations are created is well known. Indeed, "regulatory politics—the struggle for control over the administrative levers of power and policy shaped within government agencies—is central to government activity in the United States" (Harris & Milkis, 1989, p. viii).

Although nonlegislative policy making is a very important aspect of influence over policy, it is still a neglected area of research, especially in social welfare where changes in program rules can have dramatic impacts on individual recipients of aid and services. Changing social welfare regulations without going through the legislative process first became an important way to alter policy during President Reagan's administrations, beginning in the early 1980s.

The following four suggested guidelines for improving the effectiveness of monitoring activities are based on years of experience in monitoring bureaucracy:

1. Know the process by which policy is implemented in state government.
2. Develop credibility with legislators and legislative staff.
3. Neutralize the potential resistance and hostility of bureaucrats.
4. Organize and develop linkages with citizen groups. (Bell & Bell, 1982, pp. 131–132)

What Is the Regulation-Writing Process?

Regulations, also known as rules, are written as described in the Administrative Procedures Act of 1946. The process has been described as consisting of eleven steps (Kerwin & Furlong, 2010). For this chapter, I condense these steps into three stages (see figure 10.1).

The first stage, prepublication, sets the process in motion. This stage ends only when the draft rule is published in the *Federal Register*. The agency drafting the rule makes decisions regarding the legislative authority of the rule, discusses ideas for what might be in the rule, and grants authorization to proceed. Staff members are assigned, and the goal of the regulation is established. The draft rule is developed and reviewed by both internal and external actors. Although much of this stage is seemingly invisible, as with any project, the quality of the preparation has a strong impact on the quality of the results.

The second stage, postpublication, consists of public participation and taking action on the draft rule. At this stage, the agency decides how to manage public input, such as choosing between requesting written comments and holding public hearings. After input is received, the agency must read, analyze, and fold it into the proposed rule or refute it. There are many alternative courses of action, ranging from preparing the final rule with no changes from the draft rule, making

FIGURE 10.1   Steps and Stages of the Regulation-Writing Process

Kerwin's Steps	Condensed Stages
1. Origin of rule-making activity	1. Prepublication
2. Origin of individual rule making	
3. Authorization to proceed with rule making	
4. Planning the rule making	
5. Developing the draft rule	
6. Internal review of the draft rule	
7. External review of the draft rule	
8. Revision and publication of a draft rule	
9. Public participation	2. Postpublication
10. Action on the draft rule	
11. Post-rule-making activities	3. Postadoption

Source: Kerwin, C., & Furlong, S. (2010). *Rulemaking: How government agencies write law and make policy*, 4th ed. Washington, DC: Congressional Quarterly Press.

minor or major changes, abandoning the rule-making effort, and beginning over, to the most extreme case—deciding that no rule making will take place at all (Kerwin & Furlong, 2010).

The final stage of the regulation-writing process, postadoption, takes place after the final rule is adopted. Actions that take place in this stage include interpreting vague or unclear portions of the rule, making corrections, responding to petitions for reconsideration of the rule, and preparing for litigation.

What Are the Best Ways to Influence the Regulation-Writing Process?

Hoefer (2000) conducted research regarding the most effective way to influence the regulation-writing process by surveying organizations in Washington, D.C., that were actively trying to influence social welfare program regulations during the Clinton administration. His results show that the following are significant predictors of a higher level of group influence:

- Having greater access to information from the executive branch,
- Having policy positions that are in line with the administration,
- Using a prepublication strategy (i.e., bringing current regulations to the attention of Congress and the executive branch and offering drafts of desired regulations prior to publication of draft regulations in the *Federal Register*), and
- Devoting more resources to influence efforts.

These findings indicate that there is considerable hope for organizations, groups, and coalitions wishing to affect federal social programs' regulations, if they understand the pathways and barriers to effective action.

One of the most important findings for advocates is that using a prepublication strategy is very important to being effective. Many groups do not become active until the later stages of the process, once the rules are essentially completed. At this time, it is usually too late for considerable change to occur. Groups that build a coalition and share information before publication of a rule will be the most effective, because they have the greatest opportunities to shape the terms of the discussion by acting in concert and early in the process.

Another implication of this study for social workers is to be prepared with ideas about how to change current or proposed regulations. Proactivity leads to success. This action requires developing networks within the executive branch and reaching out to the persons writing the regulations to discover the issues that they see as likely to be controversial or problematic.

In the American system, there are multiple pathways in policy making; in some cases, different agencies within the federal bureaucracy may be assigned the job of writing the regulations that govern the implementation of a law. Human service interest groups who want certain regulations written should thus work to influence members of Congress who have the authority to assign the job of writing the regulations to a federal agency sympathetic to the group's cause. Interest groups that influence which staff member of an agency drafts the regulations may have an easy time persuading the staffer to adopt the group's ideas. This decision is frequently heavily influenced by the congressional committee that developed the legislation, and even by the most influential author of the bill, which implies that a long-term view of the governmental process must be in place even before potential legislation is discussed with possible sponsors of a bill.

We must also understand the connection between what makes an agency friendly and social work lobbying groups' policy positions. The reason that a liberal policy position may have been helpful to effectively influence the executive branch during Hoefer's (2000) study is that the Clinton administration's policy positions were liberal. The opposite was true during the more conservative administrations of Presidents Ronald Reagan, George H. W. Bush, and George W. Bush. One interest group representative for gay, lesbian, and transgendered individuals indicated that his group had had no access to the regulation-writing civil servants during the elder Bush's years in the White House. In other words, you are more likely to be successful if your policy positions are similar to those of the president in office. Social workers should therefore realize the importance of national electoral politics' influence on what sometimes is seen as an obscure and unimportant element of the policy process—the writing of regulations.

A final implication of Hoefer's (2000) research is that success in influencing social program regulations requires resources, and the more the better. Money is translated into staff and other key resources for making a difference. Social workers, if they are to create a more effective voice for themselves and their clients, must be willing to devote their funds to supporting the organizations that represent them in the halls of power.

INFLUENCING THE BUDGETARY PROCESS

The budgetary process allocates the primary resource of all programs—money—to the different agencies responsible for implementing programs and to the individual programs within an agency. If an individual program has gone through the legislative process, has had regulations written for it, and is ready to move forward to provide services, but does not have sufficient resources to serve those who are eligible, something negative has happened. People will wonder why they are not getting the benefits they thought would be available to them.

Decision makers who are against the program will make an issue of its limited success, ignoring the reality of the skimpy funding. These reactions may eventually lead to significant cuts in the program's remaining budget or a dismantling of the program altogether. In order to prevent this cycle from occurring, it is important to try to influence the budgetary process.

An example of the power of the budget process at the highest levels is when the U.S. Congress took the government over the fiscal cliff in January 2013 by not passing a budget by a self-imposed deadline. After a brief delay, an automatic series of cuts, called sequestration, took effect. In its first year (fiscal year 2013), federal government expenditures were cut $85 billion, taken equally from defense and nondefense spending (Mahnken, 2013). The sequester is set to continue until 2021, taking away $109 billion in spending every year until then, unless modified by Congress and the president. The upshot of this process is much less spending for discretionary human services (as well as defense efforts), which means greater competition for fewer dollars for social work–related programs.

While it might appear that the damage done to human services is limited to only federal government programs, the reality is worse. Many states receive funding from Washington to conduct programs at the local level. The money passes through the states to localities. When federal funding is decreased, the cuts show up at the local level. Advocates who understand the budget allocation process will be able to protect their clients better than others.

As you can understand, the budgetary process is both a legislative and an administrative process. Legislative advocacy as I have discussed it elsewhere in the book is applicable in the legislative arena, but advocacy in the making of administrative budgeting decisions is quite different. One of the most important differences between the executive branch and the legislative branch is that it is more difficult to obtain and influence information in the executive branch than in the legislative branch. This circumstance again shows the importance of having specialized information about the budgetary process and an extensive network of contacts within the agency.

The budgetary process varies from agency to agency. Most governmental agencies are asked to develop a budget that the top persons in the executive branch then adjust and approve, aggregated with the budgets for other agencies, and further adjusted before approval by the legislative branch. The level of discretion may be small once the budget bill is passed for any given agency. In these cases, the best way to influence the budget process is to be involved in setting the agency priorities in the early budgetary discussions. If you want more funding for homeless veterans, for example, you will have to make your case early so that executive branch decision makers can reorder priorities in the initial budgetary request.

For many nonprofit agencies, budget processes are highly dependent on what funding sources will pay for. If a grant is obtained for a particular service, that service will be provided. If donors can be motivated to support a program, it will probably continue. Thus, the advocate in this situation may need to work with the agency to find income sources.

In either of these scenarios, the most important element of being persuasive is to have up-to-date and reliable information about any unmet need. Evidence of need, such as the number and percent of children without health insurance, can be found in social indicators. It can also be found in the size of client waiting lists for services, in systematic surveys, or in community needs assessments. Often government and agency officials do not take the time to look for additional problems to address. They sense that their hands are full already. It is the job of advocates to bring forward such information and to advocate for monetary resources to be allocated to fix the identified problems.

INFLUENCING THE IMPLEMENTATION PROCESS

Implementation is the actual running of a program. Monitoring is vital at this point, because it is when real clients meet real agency workers that the program comes alive. If patterns of discrimination or omission can be observed, it is up to advocates to try to bring attention to these problems and have them rectified.

Up until now, the focus of this book has been on changing policy in a legislative or policy-setting context. Although I have used many examples to show that the same process applies in advocating for individuals, groups, or communities, more of the examples have focused on influencing decision makers who can change policy (laws and rules) than decision makers who work in a policy implementation capacity where following rules laid down by others is the norm.

The public administration literature has a long history of discussing the supposed legislative/executive dichotomy. At its core, the dichotomy states that the legislative branch makes policy and the executive branch merely puts the policies into effect (Wilson, 1887). Subsequent research and theory casts doubt on the degree to which this division is true. Because many laws or other policies that are enacted are ambiguous or vague, those who administer them have considerable latitude in how to proceed. Street-level bureaucrats are low-level workers whose jobs give them direct contact with people who are affected by their decisions (Lipsky, 1980). They also have considerable latitude in interpreting laws and rules and a large amount of freedom because they are not directly observable by supervisors who might want to enforce a certain interpretation of the law or rules. A basic tension exists for managers of street-level bureaucrats. On the one hand, managers want to encourage a single way of acting, in order to be fair to all. On the other hand, the situations that street-level bureaucrats encounter often require being able to take into account the individual circumstances of the case, and so flexibility is a requirement for effective implementation. A simple example is the case of the highway speed limit. The speed limit posted is the law. The use of radar makes measuring a car's speed easy and accurate. Why, then, do so many drivers speed? Police officers decide independently who to pull over for speeding and, once they have stopped someone, whether to issue a ticket. Sometimes a police officer will only give a warning if the driver's powers of persuasion are effective.

Human service workers have similar discretion at times. Different child welfare workers, for example, will make different decisions regarding the removal of children from a home. Different intake workers encourage or discourage individual clients from applying for benefits available from an agency. Social work education stresses learning principles and models of behavior, rather than a cookbook approach to helping clients, because of the need to respond to individuals. "Start with the client" is a mantra of social work. This flexible approach means that similar clients will inevitably be treated differently. It is impossible to mandate that clients be treated the same because no two cases are identical. Clients deserve someone taking into account their special circumstances in order to provide them with the best service possible. Effective supervision can assist in ensuring that similar clients are treated similarly. Social workers should always try to use their discretion in a way that benefits clients rather than making their lives more difficult.

The existence of the street-level bureaucrat phenomenon has an important implication for advocacy. The decisions made by individual workers may have an overt impact on certain categories of people. Monitoring of worker behavior is imperative to ensure that the flexibility inherent in many social service jobs is used to further social justice, not hinder it. The use of formal or informal racial profiling by police departments may, for example, mean that they stop African Americans or Hispanics who are driving in a predominantly white area. Advocates can fight this practice, but only if they have appropriate information. In many cases, the first goal of an advocate is to compel an agency to start gathering certain information. If police departments never collect or report information on the race of the people officers stop, it is impossible to ascertain whether any biased behavior is occurring.

Human service agencies are not immune to such problems, either. For many years, in some Southern states, when African Americans tried to apply for the Aid to Families with Dependent Children program, their applications were denied. The agency staff would report that an inquiry, but not an application, had been made. Because states had to report by race the number of applications that were turned down—but not the race of people who only inquired about applying—it did not appear that African Americans were being targeted by discriminatory behavior. Only after advocates had made considerable effort to uncover the subterfuge was this shameful practice curtailed.

Another type of required monitoring is to spot action that *should* be taken, but is not. Sometimes making a formal complaint is sufficient to resolve an issue, but sometimes it requires a great deal more effort. A prime example occurred in California, beginning in 2004. The DREDF sent a letter to the California Department of Education, alleging that the state was not doing its job in overseeing the implementation of the Individuals with Disabilities Education Act and the Americans with Disabilities Act. Specifically, local school districts did not allow school personnel to assist in the administration of insulin to diabetic children. DREDF noted the need for insulin injections for the children with diabetes and the safety of allowing trained, though not licensed, personnel to give injections, when authorized by the child's physician. Without this action, children with diabetes were forced to take their own blood sugar readings and give themselves shots, no matter their age (Egelko, 2007).

The California Department of Education eventually did allow for nonlicensed personnel to administer insulin injections. The permission was challenged, however, by several associations of nurses who stated that this was an unlawful practice of nursing by nonlicensed people. In the end, the California State Supreme Court ruled against the nurses and in favor of allowing school personnel to inject insulin (California Supreme Court, 2013).

There are several reasons that implementation may be different from what the underlying law states (Haynes & Mickelson, 2009). Of these, we should be especially mindful that agencies usually try to protect their own interests, and these do not always coincide with clients' needs. Thus, advocates from inside and outside the organization may be needed to work for social justice. Outside advocates often have more freedom of action than do agency employees, but insiders often have access to information that is required to make a good case. In addition, we should remember that different people can have legitimate differences in opinion as to what a law or regulation means.

CONCLUSION

Advocates for social justice must realize that legislation, or policy enactment, is only part of the fight. Follow-up through influencing the writing of regulations, the size and composition of budgets, and the actual implementation of programs is also required. Such monitoring work may not seem as glamorous as working in the legislative arena, but it is just as vital. In most cases, an organization, group, or coalition that can devote considerable attention to the task should coordinate such efforts. Monitoring requires time to develop both expertise and relationships, without which effective advocacy cannot take place.

This chapter has provided specific recommendations for how to be an effective advocate in each of these three areas of follow-up. Recommendations for influencing regulation writing include being proactive and working to influence the content of regulations before they are printed in the *Federal Register*. In addition, it is important to influence the following steps: developing a network of contacts within the executive branch, finding common ground with administration officials, and devoting more resources to the effort.

Influencing the budget and implementation of policies requires gathering information relating to the unmet need and current outcomes of the program. In both cases, advocates can profit from having friends inside the agency who will provide appropriate and helpful information about internal processes. Without such help, outside advocates will find it very difficult to make an impact.

Suggested Further Reading

Kerwin, C., & Furlong, S. (2010). *Rulemaking: How government agencies write law and make policy* (4th ed.). Washington, DC: Congressional Quarterly Press.

This book provides a thorough description of the process and theory of the regulation-writing process. It contains essential information for anyone wanting to advocate in this important arena of policy making.

Wolpe, B., & Levine, B. (1996). *Lobbying Congress: How the system works.* Washington, DC: Congressional Quarterly Press.

This book provides an in-depth view of how to lobby Congress, as suggested by its title, but it also provides important information on lobbying the executive branch of government. This book is very hands-on, and readers will be able to easily apply what it says to their advocacy efforts.

Discussion Questions and Exercises

1. For advocates, why is the concept of termination less relevant than it is for direct practice social workers?
2. For your advocacy effort, what are the likely areas where ongoing monitoring will be needed? How would you plan to do this?
3. Research the identity of a person in the executive branch of government (federal, state, or local) who plays an important

part in determining the rules, budget, or implementation of a policy you are interested in. Report to your class how you discovered this person's importance. If you want to explore this topic more, contact this person and talk about the ways that he or she decides on issues relevant to your interest.

Chapter 11

INTEGRATING ADVOCACY PRACTICE INTO YOUR SOCIAL WORK PRACTICE

Today's social workers are the heirs of a powerful tradition of social action. K. Haynes & J. Mickelson, *Affecting Change*

Advocacy in social work has a long, if not continuous, history. In some ways, it is the beginning point of the profession, and by any measure it is one of the most influential and enduring ideas within social work. By understanding the ideas and practicing the skills presented in this book, anyone can join in the rich history of advocacy for social justice. It is not a tradition that is limited by age, gender, race, or sexual preference—indeed, some of the major victories in advancing social justice have been achieved by people who were considered "too old," "too female," "too minority," or "too gay" to be full-fledged members of society.

This chapter looks at some of the high points in the history of social workers advocating for social justice and closes with suggestions for integrating this type of practice into whatever you do as a social worker.

THE PROGRESSIVE ERA

The history of the social work profession in the United States is usually traced to the Progressive Era of American politics, roughly 1895 to 1920. During those years Americans experienced several important trends: Industrialization continued to bring people from rural areas to urban areas. Immigration continued to bring people from other countries to the United States. Life for average citizens improved with new roads, better communication systems, and the advent of electricity in homes and businesses. Even necessities such as food and housing were improving for vast numbers of people.

During this time, government—often derided as little more than a jobs program filled with friends, family members, and cronies of elected officials—was being reformed to eliminate many of the worst abuses of the spoils system. Direct democracy was creating and institutionalizing the way laws were passed, as initiatives and referenda voted on in general elections were just being introduced as ways to enact a law. Direct democracy was also changing who served in the government, with direct elections of U.S. senators beginning with the Seventeenth Amendment in 1914 and recall elections being allowed in many places.

Amidst these conditions and changes, poverty and need continued. Two approaches were developed to alleviate these problems. The Charity Organization Societies were designed to assess through careful diagnosis the needs of potential clients (Jansson, 2011, p. 157). This charity work became, in time, institutionalized as casework, a method central to the social work profession even today. Mary Richmond, who wrote the classic book *Social Diagnosis* in 1917 on this technique (Richmond, 1917/1955), was one of the primary leaders of this approach to the new profession of social work.

The other approach, the settlement house movement, brought a different perspective to social workers' efforts. They tried to understand issues and problems by living side by side with potential clients. They often thought that change needed to take place at a social level, rather than at the level of the individuals affected (Jansson, 2011).

Jane Addams, the cofounder of Hull House in Chicago, is considered one of the most famous proponents of this view of fighting social problems. Progressives fought hard to establish the principle that government could be used to combat social problems and be a force for uplifting its citizens. Issues involving women and children came to the forefront of public attention, and Congress and President Taft adopted government-based solutions. The U.S. Children's Bureau was established in 1912, initially headed by Julia Lathrop from Hull House. States began programs called widows' pensions that provided financial assistance to widowed mothers; Missouri started the first such program, in

1911. Other topics of advocacy during this period were promoting women's right to vote and civil rights for African Americans. School social work started with visiting teachers who went to children's houses to work with their parents on various problems.

Additional advocates during this period included Jeannette Rankin, a social worker and the first woman elected to Congress. She introduced a bill in 1918 that—when later passed in 1921, after Rankin was no longer in Congress—provided funds for local health authorities to provide maternal and infant health services. Florence Kelly and other settlement house workers advocated diligently to reform child labor laws, and Congress passed a law in 1916 that eliminated many forms of child labor.

From the beginning of the profession's existence, then, social workers have been involved in advocacy for increased social justice. Shortly after the Progressive Era, however, concerns over professionalization and wanting to shed the stigma of working with the poor took hold of social workers. The next era of significant advocacy by social workers began with the Great Depression of the 1930s.

THE GREAT DEPRESSION AND THE NEW DEAL

The nascent profession of social work turned away from large-scale advocacy during World War I and throughout the 1920s, pursuing legitimacy through the adoption of psychoanalytic techniques pioneered by psychiatrists such as Sigmund Freud. Also new during the 1920s were opportunities for college-based education in social work at places such as Smith College and Columbia University. Gaining legitimacy and a place in the world of higher education took away most of the impetus for advocacy from social workers, although prior reforms such as the Children's Bureau and mothers' (formerly widows') pensions continued.

The widespread devastation caused by economic collapse in 1929 shook some social work leaders out of their desire to focus on casework and professionalization issues. Bertha Reynolds, director of the Smith College of Psychiatric Social Work, stated that focusing on emotional problems was absurd when so many people were going hungry (Huff, 2002). Lobbying Congress by social work groups, such as the

American Association of Social Workers, attempted to make clear the extent of hunger and the need for government action. Unfortunately, little was done during Herbert Hoover's presidency.

With his election in 1932, however, Franklin Delano Roosevelt (FDR) brought a new attitude about government to the White House. While governor of New York, FDR had established many social programs aimed to provide relief to the unemployed. Social workers such as Harry Hopkins and Frances Perkins were a part of his team in Albany when he was governor. When he became president, these social workers went with him to Washington. Even FDR's wife, Eleanor Roosevelt, had been a settlement house worker. At perhaps no other time were so many social workers involved at the top levels of government, advocating for and running programs that assisted a large portion of the American population. Indeed, Director Hopkins of the Federal Emergency Relief Administration, and Secretary of Labor Perkins were instrumental in crafting the Social Security Act of 1935, the foundation for the social welfare system in the United States.

Although FDR's programs, collectively known as the New Deal, assisted millions of Americans, only the massive spending and recruitment of men into the armed forces during World War II really ended the Depression. After the war, government programs providing veterans with opportunities for education and housing helped set the stage for a time of prosperity. International concerns, such as the Cold War and the conflict in Korea, took over much of the political spotlight. It was not until the 1960s that social work became an activist profession again.

THE 1960S: WAR ON POVERTY AND THE GREAT SOCIETY

Although the 1950s are a time blurred by memories of poodle skirts, the birth of rock and roll, and postwar prosperity, facts often contradict our idealized images of that era. Social conditions for minorities and rural people of all races did not keep pace with improvements in newly developed suburbs. Educational inequality was exposed by the 1954 *Brown v. Topeka Board of Education* case: the Supreme Court decided that case by determining that separate schools for blacks and whites were inherently unequal. Civil rights groups were organizing across the land. Women, many of whom had worked successfully in the military, in industry, and in other jobs during World War II, now were encouraged to stay home and raise families. By the start of the 1960s, poverty was back in the media spotlight. Robert Kennedy, John F. Kennedy's brother, had traveled through Appalachia while campaigning for his brother. In addition, Michael Harrington (1963) wrote *The Other America,* a detailed exploration of poverty in America, that became a best-seller after its publication in 1963.

As the 1960s progressed, racial tensions and other problems increased. School desegregation had not proven easy at any level, from elementary to university. Voting and other civil rights still were not guaranteed for people of color. Peaceful protests were held in all parts of the country, particularly in the South, in order to achieve true racial equality. Violence sometimes erupted, and because change was slow, frustrations mounted. Riots sometimes broke out, with buildings being burned and stores looted.

At least in part to calm these problems, President Lyndon B. Johnson sought to build on the legacy of President Kennedy's vision for civil rights and more support for disadvantaged Americans. Many laws were passed and programs created that promised improvement. The Civil Rights Act of 1964 was an important guarantee of voting rights, desegregated facilities, and fair employment procedures. The Voting Rights Act of 1965, which allowed federal authorities to administer elections directly, strengthened the earlier law and made enforcement easier.

After his election in 1964 by a landslide majority, President Johnson sought legislation to promote his vision of a Great Society. Medicare, a program to ensure health care for the elderly, and Medicaid, a program to ensure health care for the poor, were two programs that broke new ground in establishing the federal government's responsibility to assist Americans in receiving these vital services. Other programs were created to assist local education efforts, provide services to senior citizens, employ youth, make legal advice available to the poor, open medical clinics in low-income areas, and organize neighborhoods and communities. This last goal was implemented by setting up the Office of Economic Opportunity, which oversaw the development of Community Action Agencies.

All of this activity to promote social justice was influenced by social workers and had an influence on the profession. Two social work professors from Columbia University, Richard Cloward and Lloyd Ohlia, laid the groundwork for the Economic Opportunity Act through their earlier work with the Mobilization for Youth program (Schneider & Lester, 2001). This program was developed, with support from the Ford Foundation, to reduce delinquency and crime. Other social workers were active in the civil rights movement and provided leadership in community organizing projects sponsored by various Community Action Agencies. Community organization courses, including material on advocacy, were offered in many social work schools, and graduates of these programs were the staff implementing many of the Great Society's efforts. The Ad Hoc Committee on Advocacy, organized by NASW, declared that social workers should engage in advocacy practice (Schneider & Lester, 2001).

BETWEEN THE 1960S AND THE END OF THE TWENTIETH CENTURY: KEEPING HOPE ALIVE

Activism and the use of advocacy in social work did not die in the decades between the 1960s and the start of the new century, but they became less prominent. Since the election of President Ronald Reagan in 1980, social programs have been under more or less constant attack, and social work advocacy has had to focus more on stemming losses than on breaking new ground (with the notable exception of the Affordable Care Act). Welfare reform, culminating in the largest change in domestic policy since the 1930s occurred while President Bill Clinton, a Democrat, was in office. He had campaigned to "end welfare as we have come to know it" and worked with a Republican-controlled Congress to achieve that goal. A neoliberal consensus to rely on market mechanisms and jobs to reduce poverty emerged in the last two decades of the twentieth century.

Nonetheless, social workers were important participants in the movements for equal rights for women; people with disabilities; and gay, lesbian, bisexual, and transgendered people, among other causes. Without social work advocates and the skillful use of their knowledge to maintain client services, social programs, and legal rights, the prospects for social justice would be far grimmer than they were as the twenty-first century began.

ADVOCACY PRACTICE IN THE TWENTY-FIRST CENTURY

The first decade of this century saw the continuation of trends begun in the 1990s. But American society has also been buffeted by many storms, both literal and figurative. The attacks by extremists on September 11, 2001, set off long-term changes in laws and beliefs about national security and are ultimately related to wars in both Afghanistan and Iraq and a war against terror that seems likely to never end. The economy suffered several lasting downturns in the first years of the twenty-first century, leading to considerable wealth being lost in the stock market, large numbers of people being unemployed for long periods of time, increased need among the populace, lower levels of support for nonprofits, debt being piled up at the national government level, and difficult decisions at the state and local levels as tax revenues failed to keep pace with spending needs.

Natural disasters such as Hurricanes Katrina in 2005 and Ike in 2008 battered the Gulf Coast, as did an oil spill by British Petroleum that lasted for weeks, fouling beaches and wildlife across the region. Hurricane Sandy devastated parts of the Caribbean, the Northeastern United States, and the Canadian Eastern Seaboard in 2012. Climate change may mean such storms will be more frequent and cause even more damage in the years to come.

In 2008 a community organizer was elected president of the United States and was reelected in 2012. Although Barack Obama does not have social work training, nor has he ever identified himself as a social worker, many social workers supported the elections of the first African American to the top office in the country. Obama's election fulfilled many of the aspirations of the social work profession for greater involvement of minorities in American politics.

Yet advocacy within the field of social work continues to face challenges, despite its acknowledged status in the CSWE's *Educational policies and accreditation standards* (2012). Chief among these is just fitting information into programs of study so that graduates are confident enough in their skills to become part of this wonderful social work heritage. Now that you are nearing the end of this book, you have a great deal of knowledge and should feel empowered to be an advocate for social justice on your own terms.

INTEGRATING ADVOCACY PRACTICE INTO YOUR SOCIAL WORK PRACTICE

At this point, you may wonder where social work advocates find work. Hopefully, the most accurate answer to this question is that social work advocates find work in all areas of the profession. The major thrust of this book is that advocacy, as a problem-solving practice technique with steps similar to other practice techniques, can and should be used in many situations and places. Advocacy is needed in dealing with client problems at micro-, mezzo-, and macrolevels. Advocacy should be part of every social worker's job tasks, and not restricted to the job title of an advocate.

Still, some jobs may allow you more time to work on macrolevel advocacy than others. Examples of this type of job include working for a professional organization, such as NASW, or a state mental health association, as a government relations specialist or lobbyist. (See exhibit 11.1 for a position description of a government relations coordinator for an NASW chapter.)

Another job that allows you to spend considerable time working on policy and advocating is legislative aide. Legislative aides work for elected officials and frequently become the real experts on certain types of policy for their legislator. Some of their job duties include preparing drafts of bills, monitoring legislation, recommending actions that their legislator should take, and frequently representing their legislator in contacts with lobbyists, constituents, and other legislators and their staff. These jobs require very long hours during legislative sessions and can be quite stressful. You may see an unpleasant side to others in a highly partisan atmosphere where other people's egos are large. Most legislative aides are young and are in this position for only a few years. Still, the rewards can be great, particularly if you work for a powerful legislator. By working for social justice in this way, you can have a large impact. You can actually help set policy for thousands, if not millions, of people. It can also be a stepping-stone to becoming an

EXHIBIT 11.1   Job Description for a Government Relations Coordinator

---

NASW/Texas Chapter

Job Opening Announcement

POSITION TITLE: Government Relations Coordinator

Exempt Position: Salary commensurate with experience.

Function: To initiate, organize, and coordinate legislative and political action by Chapter members. The goal of this position is to mobilize and communicate to membership in order to build political power on behalf of NASW membership and their clients.

Basic Duties and Responsibilities

1. Coordinate, activate and involve Chapter membership on legislative and political activity as approved by the Board of Directors and Texas Political Action for Candidate Election Committee (TPACE).
2. Organize members on legislative issues and TPACE endorsed electoral campaigns, targeting key constituents.
3. Organize and coordinate events throughout the state to facilitate interaction and information sharing between members and legislators and/or candidates. Facilitate interaction between legislators and membership on legislative priorities.
4. Produce and distribute timely legislative alerts on an as-needed basis to members and related organizations. Ensure Chapter testimony on key legislative issues.
5. Provide education and training to social workers and social work students on legislative and political action through newsletters, website, house parties, Lobby Days, and other presentations as requested. Assist with production of newsletter/website.
6. Work closely with policy faculty at schools of social work to coordinate student involvement in NASW/Texas legislative initiatives, including speaking at classes and coordinating Student Day at the Legislature.
7. Providing staffing functions to TPACE and NASW/TX selected committees.
8. Work with national PACE staff and national legislative staff on critical federal legislation and federal candidate races.
9. Work toward identification and recruitment of chapter members to run for elective office.
10. Represent NASW/Texas on coalitions as assigned by Executive Director.
11. Keep members informed on all activities.
12. Coordinate sessions and events for state conference and chapter annual leadership meeting.

13. Supervise student interns as directed.
14. Other related duties as assigned by Executive Director.

These statements are intended to describe the general nature and level of work being performed. They are not intended as exhaustive of all responsibilities.

Qualifications: MSW preferred. Demonstrated ability in community organization and political action required. Knowledge of legislative, electoral and political process at the local/state/federal level. Experience in health and human services policy analysis and/or program administration. Basic computer skills, good organizational skills, able to work with high level of independence. Demonstrated ability in public relations, excellent oral and written communication. Experience working with volunteers. Ability to work collaboratively with professionals, administrative staff, committee leaders and chapter members. Strong commitment to membership involvement and membership services. Texas license and NASW membership required.

Physical and Sensory Requirements: Must be willing to travel, be able to work under florescent lighting, able to lift 25 pounds, able to withstand prolonged sitting, standing, ability to manage stress.

Benefits

• Health insurance, including dental, PPO paid for by employer
• Life insurance premium (3%) paid for by employer
• Pension plan (401-K) (6%) paid for by employer
• Flexible work schedule
• Convenient downtown Austin location with free parking and private office
• 2 weeks vacation for first 2 years, plus 11 paid holidays

Used with permission. Hansen, V. (2005). *Job opening announcement.* Austin, TX: National Association of Social Workers, Texas Chapter.

---

elected official yourself, as it was for Hillary Rodham Clinton, who was elected U.S. senator, ran for nomination as the Democratic Party nominee for president, and served as secretary of state for President Obama. (See exhibit 11.2 for a job posting for a legislative aide for a state representative in Texas.)

Sometimes large organizations hire social workers as advocates. One example is a large nonprofit hospital, Children's Health (formerly Children's Medical Center) in Dallas, Texas, that employs an advocacy

EXHIBIT 11.2   Job Announcement for a Legislative Aide

POSITION AVAILABLE

Legislative Aide for State Representative Helen Giddings

General Description:

Position available for full-time legislative aide for the 79th Legislative Session. It will require daily contact with constituents, elected officials, lobbyists, and other Capitol staff. This person will be responsible for legislative research, correspondence, and analyzing legislation.

Requirements:

Legislative Aide must be familiar with legislative issues. Position requires strong demonstrated writing and effective oral communication skills; strong organizational skills and the ability to meet critical deadlines; the ability to interact with all levels of people and maintain confidentiality; the ability to work effectively with others and maximize available resources. The position requires great flexibility in scheduling as it will be necessary to represent the Representative in various functions; sometimes on short notice; must be familiar with community, organizations and institutions.

LEGISLATIVE SESSION EXPERIENCE REQUIRED.

Salary:

Salary will be commensurate with experience.

Source: Texas House of Representatives. (2005, March). House Personnel Department, Texas House of Representatives, Austin.

---

manager. Their Web site lists the following information under the heading "Public Relations": "Children don't vote so they rely on adults and organizations like Children's Medical Center to be their advocates. Children's takes this charge seriously through a combined effort of legislative, grassroots and media strategies. Efforts include sponsoring twice-a-year advocacy trips to the state Capitol. The goal is to make sure that children's needs are kept at the forefront of public policy debates" (Children's Health, 2014).

A final example of a job that allows a social worker to spend considerable time conducting advocacy for social justice is any elected position. NASW lists nearly 200 social workers who serve as elected officials at some level (NASW, 2014). NASW encourages social workers to be on public boards and to run for office because social workers have the background to understand social problems and the skills to help fix them. Many state chapters of NASW have a political action committee that may endorse and/or donate funding to people who support NASW's positions, including, of course, social workers.

Most people begin their electoral careers at a local level, such as on a school board or city council. This step is often preceded by time spent on appointed committees, such as those at a municipal level, those working to distribute Community Development Block Grant funds, or oversight boards, such as a citizen's police department panel. Other political careers have been started from being a community or neighborhood activist or working within the Parent-Teacher Association. These experiences definitely move people from being spectators in politics to being gladiators.

Recent research can give hope to current social work students that running for election is not a "crazy idea." Lane and Humphreys (2011) surveyed 270 social workers involved in political social work. Their findings suggest that the same variables that lead others to become active in advocacy (see chapter 3) are strongly present among this group of politically active social workers that we discussed earlier. They have resources of income and time in greater doses than the average American. They have more self-perceived skills (63% agreed or strongly agreed that their social work degree prepared them for their elected office).

They have more experience with political activities than typical citizens even before they run for election. Due to their involvement in the political system, the most important source of recruitment to becoming an elected official was a person who had already been elected to office. These social workers ran for many different levels of offices but had the most success when running for the state legislature, city councils, county boards, and boards of education. The areas where they considered they had the most knowledge were education, mental health, and health care. This study should help you see yourself in this role—as with much in life, once you start down the path of advocacy and engagement in the political realm, you may find yourself enjoying yourself and continuing on to what at first may seem unimaginable heights of success.

This book provides you with the tools required to become a part of the social work advocacy tradition. You have learned these key points:

- Advocacy practice is compatible with the generalist practice model of social work taught in many social work programs and follows a parallel set of steps, as do other types of social work practice.
- Social justice is the most important aim of the social work profession and thus of advocacy practice.
- NASW's Code of Ethics declares that social workers should do advocacy.
- The factors that influence whether a person is an advocate can be altered to increase the probability that a person will engage in advocacy practice.
- Understanding an issue results from answering five questions: What is the issue? Who is affected and how? What are the causes of the issue? What are possible solutions to the issue? and How do proposed solutions lead to social justice?
- Advocacy planning is facilitated by using an advocacy map, which explicitly connects proposed actions with the outcomes desired for the advocacy effort.
- Advocates must sometimes educate their targets on issues of concern, using techniques such as consciousness-raising and social liberation, in order to get action taken.
- Advocacy practice often involves the use of negotiation skills, such as setting forth an initial position and various fallback positions and knowing your limit.
- Advocacy practitioners use skills in persuasion to achieve their desired outcomes. They try to understand the variables of context, message, sender, and receiver to achieve the highest level of persuasive power possible.
- Presenting useful information in an effective way to your advocacy targets is vital to success. Information can be presented in various ways, and advocates should choose their method carefully for maximum effect.
- Evaluators should evaluate advocacy efforts to document suc-

cess and to learn what was more and less successful. The advocacy map developed in the planning stage is useful in evaluation efforts because it guides the evaluator's monitoring and judgment processes.

- Advocates must monitor what happens to the changes they accomplish through policy change—if not, clients may not receive the benefit of what was won through advocacy. Areas of monitoring include the creation of regulations, program budgeting, and program implementation.

This list is a great deal to have covered and to remember. As with all new skills, it takes a willingness to go beyond what you are comfortable doing in order to become adept at using your new knowledge. Several suggestions can help in moving from being an advocacy novice to being an advocacy master:

1. Allow yourself to be nervous as you engage in the process.
2. Try to find a teacher or mentor who can lead you through the process. Your mentor, to be most useful, should already be a master in the art. If there is no one person who has all the skills you wish to learn, find different people who have some of the skills you are looking for.
3. Be open to learning from anyone, but be sure to check his or her suggestions against reality by monitoring your progress on a regular basis.
4. Do not be afraid to make mistakes—it means you are trying something new to improve your skills.
5. Learn from your errors, but try not to make the same ones again.
6. Advocate, advocate, and advocate some more.
7. After you have some experience, teach others what you know. Nothing forces you to deepen your own knowledge and analyze your own practice like teaching someone else.

As you move through your social work career, whether you work primarily with individuals in a direct practice setting or with groups or communities, and whether you work with children, women, the elderly, teens, or other populations, be sure to be an advocacy practitioner. It is on that basis and that basis alone that social work values will become a stronger part of our world.

Suggested Further Reading

National Association of Social Workers (NASW). (2013). *NASW News: Social workers in public office.* Retrieved from http://youtu.be/yeVxtGTKcnE

This is a video that NASW has developed that compiles interviews with social workers who are elected officials.

Day, P., & Schiele, J. (2012). *A new history of social welfare* (7th ed.). Boston: Allyn & Bacon.

Jansson, B. (2011). *The reluctant welfare state: American social welfare policies—past, present, and future* (7th ed.). Belmont, CA: Wadsworth.

Several good books on the history of social policy in the United States and the forces that shaped it are available. All will provide insight into the historical roots of current social policy and the effect of individual and group efforts to make governmental policy more just. Two of the more thorough ones are listed here.

Discussion Questions and Exercises

1. Some people have suggested that this chapter should be the first one in the book, rather than the last. Which placement do you think makes the most sense? Why?

2. To what extent do you identify with this aspect of social work history in the United States? What aspects of advocacy practice do you see yourself conducting in the next few years?

References

Abbott, A. (1988). *Professional choices: Values at work.* Silver Spring, MD: NASW Press.

Administrative Procedure Act, PL 79-404, 60 Stat. 237 (1946).

Ailes, R. (with Kraushar, J.) (1988). *You are the message.* Homewood, IL: Dow Jones-Irwin.

Albert, R. (1983). Social work advocacy in the regulatory process. *Social Casework, 64*(8), 473-481.

Alinsky, S. (1972). Of means and ends. In *Rules for radicals.* New York: Vintage Books.

Allingham, M. (2014). *Distributive justice.* New York: Routledge.

Almog-Bar, M., & Schmid, H. (2014). Advocacy activities of nonprofit human service organizations: A critical review. *Nonprofit and Voluntary Sector Quarterly, 43*(1), 1-43.

Americans with Disabilities Act, PL 101-336 (1990).

Amidei, N. (1987). The new activism picks up steam. *Public Welfare, 45*(3), 21-26.

Aune, R., & Basil, M. (1994). A relational obligations approach to the foot-in-the-mouth effect. *Journal of Applied Social Psychology, 24*(6), 546-556.

Baines, D. (Ed.). (2007). *Doing anti-oppressive practice. Building transformative politicized social work.* Halifax, NS: Fernwood.

Barker, R. (1995). *The social work dictionary* (3rd ed.). Washington, DC: NASW Press.

Barker, R. (2003). *The social work dictionary* (5th ed.). Washington, DC: NASW Press.

Barnoff, L. (2001). Moving beyond words: Integrating anti-oppression practice into feminist social service organizations. *Canadian Social Work Review, 18*(1), 67-86.

Barrett, S. (2001). *The dark side of Linus Pauling's legacy.* Retrieved from http://www.quackwatch.org/01QuackeryRelatedTopics/pauling.html

Baumgartner, F., & Jones, B. (1993). *Agendas and instability in American politics.* Chicago: University of Chicago Press.

Bedell, G. (2002). *Three steps to yes: The gentle art of getting your way.* New York: Crown Business.

Bell, W., & Bell, B. (1982). Monitoring the bureaucracy: An extension of legislative lobbying. In M. Mahaffey & J. Hanks (Eds.), *Practical politics: Social work and political responsibility* (pp. 118-135). Silver Spring, MD: NASW Press.

Benson, M. (2004, April 11). Tax time renews cries of class warfare. *Austin American Statesman,* pp. E1, E4.

Best, J. (2012). *Damned lies and statistics: Untangling numbers from the media, politicians and activists* (2nd ed.). Berkeley: University of California Press.

Bipartisan Policy Center (2012, November 8). *2012 voter turnout.* Retrieved from http://bipartisanpolicy.org/library/report/2012-voter-turnout

Bonchek, M. S. (1995, April). Grassroots in cyberspace: Using computer networks to facilitate political participation. Paper presented at the 53rd Annual meeting of the Midwest Political Science Association, Chicago.

Brady, H., Verba, S., & Schlozman, K. (1995). Beyond SES: A resource model of political participation. *American Political Science Review, 89*(2), 271-294.

Briggs, H. E., & Rzepnicki, T. L. (Eds.). (2004). *Using evidence in social work practice: Behavioral perspectives.* Chicago: Lyceum Books.

Brown v. Topeka Board of Education, 347 U.S. 483 (1954).

Brown, L., Langenegger, J., Garcia, S., Lewis, T., & Biles, R. (2014). *Practicing Texas politics: 2013-2014 edition.* Boston: Wadsworth.

Browning, G. (1996). *Electronic democracy: Using the Internet to influence American politics.* Wilton, CT: Pemberton Press.

Burg, B. (2011). *The art of persuasion: Winning without intimidation.* Shippensburg, PA: Sound Wisdom.

BusinessDictionary.com. (2014). *Negotiation.* Retrieved from http://www.businessdictionary.com/definition/negotiation.html

California Supreme Court. (2013). American Nursing Association et al. v. Torlakson. S184583, Ct.App. 3 C061150, Sacramento County, Super. Ct. No. 07AS04631

Chaiken, S., Liberman, A., & Eagly, A. (1989). Heuristic and systematic information processing within and beyond the persuasion context. In J. Uleman & J. Bargh (Eds.), *Unintended thought* (pp. 212-252). New York: Guilford.

Children's Health. (2014). *Public relations.* Retrieved from https://www.childrens.com/keeping-families-healthy/child-advocacy/public-relations

Christakis, N., & Fowler, J. (2011). *Connected: The surprising power of our social networks and how they shape our lives—how your friends' friends' friends affect everything you feel, think, and do.* New York: Back Bay Books.

Cialdini, R. (2001, February). The science of persuasion. *Scientific American,* 76-81.

Cialdini, R. (2008). *Influence: Science and practice* (5th ed.). Boston: Allyn & Bacon.

Citizens United v. Federal Elections Commission, 558 U.S. 310 (2010).

Civil Rights Act, PL 88-352 (1964).

Clark, C. (2001). *Making change happen:Advocacy and citizen participation.* Washington, DC: Just Associates.

Coffman, J., & Reed, E. (2009). *Unique methods in advocacy evaluation.* Retrieved from http://www.alnap.org/resource/8709

Cohen, W. (1966). What every social worker should know about political action. *Social Work, 11*(4), 7-11.

Comart, J. (2011, November 17). *Can Occupy Wall Street match the Tea Party's offline effectiveness?* Retrieved from http://mashable.com/2011/11/17/ows-tea-party/

Commission on Private Philanthropy and Public Needs. (1975). *Giving in America: Toward a stronger voluntary sector.* Washington, DC: Commission on Private Philanthropy and Public Needs.

Cooper, J., Bennett, E., & Sukel, H. (1996). Complex scientific testimony: How do jurors make decisions? *Law and Human Behavior, 20,* 379-394.

Cornfield, M., & Rainie, L. (2006, November 6). *The Internet and politics: No revolution, yet.* Retrieved from http://www.pewresearch.org/2006/11/06/the-internet-and-politics-no-revolution-yet/

Council on Social Work Education (CSWE). (2012). *Educational policies and accreditation standards.* Retrieved from http://www.cswe.org/File.aspx?id=41861

Crabtree, S. (2014, October 25). *Tea Party allies launch social media turnout effort.* Retrieved from http://www.washingtonexaminer.com/tea-party-allies-launch-social-media-turnout-effort/article/2555283

Csikai, E., & Rozensky, C. (1997). "Social work idealism" and students' perceived reasons for entering social work. *Journal of Social Work Education, 33*(3), 529-538.

Dahl, R. (1961). *Who governs?* New Haven, CT: Yale University Press.

Daly, J. (2012). *Advocacy: Championing ideas and influencing others.* New Haven, CT: Yale University Press.

Day, B. (2000). Media campaigns. In B. Day & M. Monroe (Eds.), *Environmental education and communication for a sustainable world* (pp. 79-84). Princeton, NJ: Academy for Educational Development.

De Bono, E. (1999). *Six thinking hats.* Boston: Little, Brown.

Dear, R., & Patti, R. (1981). Legislative advocacy: Seven effective tactics. *Social Work, 26*(4), 289-296.

Dickinson, J. (2004). The views of NASW members in one state toward social action. *Professional Development: The International Journal of Continuing Social Work Education, 7*(2), 12-26.

Dillard, J., & Shen, L. (2013). *Sage handbook of persuasion* (2nd ed.). Thousand Oaks, CA: Sage.

Doe Network. (2008). *Officials haunted by cold cases.* Retrieved from http://www.doenetwork.org/media/news219.html

Dunn, W. (1981). *Public policy analysis:An introduction.* Englewood Cliffs, NJ: Prentice Hall.

Economic Opportunity Act, PL 88-452 (1964).

Egelko, B. (2007). *Settlement entitles California's diabetic kids to care at school.* Retrieved from http://dredf.org/settlement-entitles-californias-diabetic-kids-to-care-at-school/

Eiseley, L. (1979). *The star thrower.* New York: Harvest.

Eisenhower, D. (1954, January 28). *Address recorded for the Republican Lincoln Day dinners.* Retrieved from http://www.presidency.ucsb.edu/ws/?pid=10008

Ezell, M. (1991). Administrators as advocates. *Administration in Social Work, 15*(4), 1-18.

Ezell, M. (1993). The political activity of social workers: A post-Reagan update. *Journal of Sociology and Social Welfare, 20*(4), 81-97.

Ezell, M. (1994). Advocacy practice of social workers. *Families in Society: The Journal of Contemporary Human Services, 75*(1), 36-46.

Ezell, M. (2001). *Advocacy in the human services.* Belmont, CA: Brooks/Cole.

Facebook (n.d.) *Statistics.* Retrieved May 5, 2015, from https://newsroom.fb.com/company-info/

Felderhoff, B., Hoefer, R., & Watson L. (2014, July). Political activity and engagement of Texas social workers. Paper presented at 2014 NASW conference, Social work: Courage, hope & leadership, Washington, DC.

Finn, J., & Jacobson, M. (2008). Social justice. In T. Mizrahi & L. Davis (Eds.), *The encyclopedia of social work* (20th ed., pp. 44-52). New York: Oxford University Press.

Fitzgerald, E., & McNutt, J. (1997, March). Electronic advocacy in policy practice: A framework for teaching technologically based practice. Paper presented at the 1997 CSWE annual program meeting, Chicago.

Friedman, T. (2007a). *The world is flat.* (Release 3.0). New York: Picador.

Friedman, T. (2007b, March 16). Marching with a mouse. *New York Times.* Retrieved from http://www.nytimes.com/2007/03/16/opinion/16friedman.html?_r=0

Gass, R., & Seiter, J. (2013). *Persuasion, social influence and compliance gaining* (5th ed.). New York: Pearson.

Ghonim invigorates crowd with speech after release. (2011, Feb. 2). *Dallas Morning News Briefing,* p. 8.

Gibelman, M., & Kraft, S. (1996). Advocacy as a core agency program: Planning considerations for voluntary human service agencies. *Administration in Social Work, 20*(4), 43-59.

Ginsberg, L. (1988). Social workers and politics: Lessons from practice. *Social Work, 33*(3), 245-247.

Goldkind, L. (2014). E-advocacy in human services: The impact of organizational conditions and characteristics on electronic advocacy activities among nonprofits. *Journal of Policy Practice, 13*(4), 300-315. DOI: 10.1080/15588742.2014.929073

Guo, C., & Saxton, G. (2014). Tweeting social change: How social media are changing nonprofit advocacy. *Nonprofit and Voluntary Sector Quarterly,* 43(1), 57-79.

Hansen, V. (2005). *Job opening announcement.* Austin: National Association of Social Workers, Texas Chapter.

Harrington, M. (1963). *The other America.* New York: Penguin.

Harris, R., & Milkis, S. (1989). *The politics of regulatory change.* New York: Oxford University Press.

Haynes, K., & Mickelson, J. (2009). *Affecting change* (7th ed.). Boston: Allyn & Bacon.

Health Care and Education Reconciliation Act, PL 111-152 (2010).

Hoefer, R. (2000). Making a difference: Human service interest group influence on social welfare program regulations. *Journal of Sociology and Social Welfare, 27*(3), 21-38.

Hoefer, R. (2001). Highly effective human services interest groups: Seven key practices. *Journal of Community Practice, 9*(2), 1-14.

Hoefer, R. (2010). *Decision-making flow chart.* [video] Retrieved from https://www.youtube.com/watch?v=8ptq1SR0wok

Hoefer, R., & Felderhoff, B. (2014, October). Do social workers support political advocacy? Paper presented at the Texas NASW chapter annual conference, San Marcos, TX.

Huff, D. (2002). *The social work history station.* Retrieved from http://www.socialworkhistorystation.org/

Iatridis, D. (1993). *Social policy: Institutional context of social development and human services.* Belmont, CA: Brooks/Cole.

Individuals with Disabilities Education Act, PL 101-476 (2004).

Jansson, B. (1994). *Social policy: From theory to policy practice* (2nd ed.). Pacific Grove, CA: Brooks/Cole.

Jansson, B. (2003). *Becoming an effective policy advocate: From policy practice to social justice* (4th ed.). Pacific Grove, CA: Brooks/Cole.

Jansson, B. (2011). *The reluctant welfare state* (7th ed.). Belmont, CA: Wadsworth/Thomson Learning.

Jordan, C., & Hoefer, R. (2001). Reliability and validity in quantitative measurement. In B. Thyer (Ed.), *The handbook of social work research* (pp. 53-67). Thousand Oaks, CA: Sage.

Kahneman, D., & Tversky, A. (1990). Prospect theory: An analysis of decision under risk. In P. Moser (Ed.), *Rationality in action: Contemporary approaches* (pp. 140-170). New York: Cambridge University Press.

Kanter, B., & Fine, A. (2010). *The networked nonprofit: Connecting with social media to drive change.* San Francisco: Jossey-Bass.

Kerwin, C., & Furlong, S. (2010). *Rulemaking: How government agencies write law and make policy* (4th ed.). Washington, DC: Congressional Quarterly Press.

Kingdon, J. (1995). *Agendas, alternatives and public policies* (2nd ed.). New York: Harper Collins.

Kirst-Ashman, K., & Hull, G. Jr. (2011). *Understanding generalist practice* (6th ed.). Belmont, CA: Brooks/Cole.

KWCH12 News (2014, February 12). *Hutchison high school athletes suspended for drinking party.* Retrieved from http://www.kwch.com /news/local-news/hutchinson-high-school-athletes-suspended-for-drinking-party/24446860

Lane, S., & Humphreys, N. (2011). Social workers in politics: A national survey of social work candidates and elected officials. *Journal of Policy Practice, 10*(3), 225–244.

Laney, M., Scobie, J., & Fraser, A. (2005). *The how and why of advocacy. Guidance Notes 2.1.* London: British Overseas NGOs for Development.

Lasswell, H. (1936). *Politics: Who gets what, when, and how.* New York: Free Press.

Lens, V. (2005). Advocacy and argumentation in the public arena: A guide for social workers. *Social Work, 50*(3), 231–238.

Levine, J., & Valle, R. (1975). The convert as a credible communicator. *Social Behavior and Personality, 3,* 81–90.

Liasson, M. (1996, August 26). Politics in America. Presentation to NASW Political Action Institute, Washington, DC.

Lindsey, R. (2013, July 29). *What the Arab Spring tells us about the future of social media in revolutionary movements.* Retrieved from http:// smallwarsjournal.com/jrnl/art/what-the-arab-spring-tells-us-about-the-future-of-social-media-in-revolutionary-movements

Lipsky, M. (1980). *Street-level bureaucracy: Dilemmas of the individual and public service.* New York: Russell Sage Foundation.

Mahaffey, M., & Hanks, J. W. (1982). *Practical politics: Social work and political responsibility.* Silver Spring, MD: NASW Press.

Mahnken, K. (2013, September 29). To understand the budget debate, you need to understand the sequester: Here's a quick primer. *The New Republic.* Retrieved from http://www.newrepublic.com/article/114892/what-sequester-2013-sequestration-guide

Mary, N., Ellano, C., & Newell, J. (1993). Political activism in social work: A study of social work educators. In T. Mizrahi & J. Morrison (Eds.), *Community organization and social administration* (pp. 203–223). New York: Haworth.

Mathews, G. (1982). Social workers and political influence. *Social Service Review, 56*(4), 616–628.

May, P. (1981). Hints for crafting alternative policies. *Policy Analysis, 7*(2), 227–244.

McCutcheon v. Federal Elections Commission, 572 U.S. (2014).

McDavid, J., Huse, I., & Hawthorne, L. (2013). *Program evaluation and performance measurement: An introduction to practice* (2nd ed.). Thousand Oaks, CA: Sage.

McNutt, J., & Menon, G. (2008). The rise of cyberactivism: Implications for the future of advocacy in human services organizations. *Families in Society,* *89*(1), 33–38.

Mertens, D., & Wilson, A. (2012). *Program evaluation theory and practice: A comprehensive guide.* New York: Guilford.

Messing, N. (2013). *The art of advocacy: Briefs, motions and writing strategies of America's best lawyers.* New York: Aspen.

Mickelson, J. S. (1995). Advocacy. In R. Edwards (Ed.), *The encyclopedia of social work* (19th ed., pp. 95–100). Washington, DC: NASW Press.

Milbrath, L. (1965). *Political participation.* Chicago: Rand McNally.

Mills, H. (2000). *Artful persuasion: The new psychology of influence.* New York: AMACOM.

Mosteller, F. (1977). Assessing unknown numbers: Order of magnitude estimation. In W. Fairley & F. Mosteller (Eds.), *Statistics and public policy* (pp. 163–164). Reading, MA: Addison-Wesley.

Nagel, S. (2002). *Handbook of public policy evaluation.* Thousand Oaks, CA: Sage.

National Association of Social Workers (NASW). (1995). Political involvement high. *NASW News, 40*(9), 1.

National Association of Social Workers (NASW). (2008). *Code of ethics.* Washington, DC: NASW Press.

National Association of Social Workers (NASW). (2014). *Social workers in state and local office.* Retrieved from https://www.socialworkers.org/pace /state.asp

Nozick, R. (1974). *Anarchy, state and utopia.* New York: Basic Books.

O'Donnell, C. (2011, September 12). *New study quantifies use of social media in Arab Spring.* Retrieved from http://www.washington.edu/news/2011 /09/12/new-study-quantifies-use-of-social-media-in-arab-spring/

Osborn, A. (1963). *Applied imagination* (3rd ed.). New York: Scribner.

Patient Protection and Affordable Care Act, PL 111-148 (2010) (Affordable Care Act).

Patton, C., & Sawicki, D. (2012). *Basic methods of policy analysis and planning* (3rd ed.). Englewood Cliffs, NJ: Prentice Hall.

Pawlak, E., & Flynn, J. (1990). Executive directors' political activities. *Social Work, 35*(4), 307–312.

PBS NewsHour (2014, November 10). *2014 midterm election turnout lowest in 70 years.* Retrieved from http://www.pbs.org/newshour/updates /2014-midterm-election-turnout-lowest-in-70-years/

Perlman, H. (1957). *Casework: A problem-solving process.* Chicago: University of Chicago Press.

Perloff, R. (1993). *The dynamics of persuasion.* Hillsdale, NJ: Lawrence Erlbaum.

Pew Research Center. (2012a, Feb. 2). *Cable leads the pack as campaign news source.* Retrieved from http://www.people-press.org/2012/02/07 /cable-leads-the-pack-as-campaign-news-source/

Pew Research Center. (2012b, September 4). *Politics on social networking sites.* Retrieved from http://www.pewinternet.org/2012/09/04/politics-on-social-networking-sites/

Pew Research Center. (2014, June 12). *Political polarization in the American public.* Retrieved from http://www.people-press.org/2014/06/12/section-1-growing-ideological-consistency/

Prochaska, J., Norcross, J., & DiClemente, C. (1994). *Changing for good: The revolutionary program that explains the six stages of change and teaches you how to free yourself from bad habits.* New York: William Morrow.

Puzo, M. (1969). *The Godfather.* New York: G. P. Putnam.

Rainie, L., Cornfield, M., & Horrigan, J. (2005). *The Internet and campaign 2004.* Washington, DC: The Pew Research Center for the People and the Press.

Rawls, J. (1971). *A theory of justice.* Cambridge, MA: Harvard University Press.

Reamer, F. (1993). *The philosophical foundations of social work.* New York: Columbia University Press.

Reeser, L., & Epstein, I. (1987). Social workers' attitudes toward poverty and social action: 1968-1984. *Social Service Review, 61*(4), 610-622.

Reingen, P., & Kernan, J. (1993). Social perception and interpersonal influence: Some consequences of the physical attractiveness stereotype in a personal selling setting. *Journal of Consumer Psychology, 2*(1), 25-38.

Reisch, M. (1995). If you think you're not political, guess again. *NASW Network, 21*(13), 1, 10.

Reisch, M., & Jani, J. (2012). The new politics of social work practice: Understanding context to promote social change. *British Journal of Social Work, 42*, 1132-1150.

Rhoads, K. (1997). *What's in a frame? Working Psychology.* Retrieved from www.workingpsychology.com/whatfram.html

Rhoads, K., & Cialdini, R. (2002). The business of influence: Principles that lead to success in commercial settings. In J. Dillard & M. Pfau (Eds.), *The persuasion handbook* (pp. 513-542). Thousand Oaks, CA: Sage.

Richan, W. (1996). *Lobbying for social change* (2nd ed.). New York: Haworth Press.

Richmond, M. (1955). *Social diagnosis* New York: Russell Sage Foundation. Original work published 1917.

Ritter, J. (2007). Evaluating the political participation of licensed social workers in the new millennium. *Policy Practice Journal, 6*(4), 61-78.

Ritter, J. (2008). A national study predicting licensed social workers' levels of political participation: The role of resources, psychological engagement, and recruitment networks. *Social Work, 53*(4), 347-357.

Robert, H. III, Evans, H., Honeman, D., & Balch, T. (2000). *Robert's rules of order* (10th ed.). New York: HarperCollins.

Roberts, A., & Yeager, K. (Eds.). (2004). *Evidence-based practice manual:*

Research and outcome measures in health and human services. New York: Oxford University Press.

Rogers, E. M. (2003). *The diffusion of innovation* (5th ed.). New York: Free Press.

Rosenthal, A. (1993). *The third house: Lobbyists and lobbying in the states*. Washington, DC: CQ Press.

Rubin, B. (2000). *A citizen's guide to politics in America*. Armonk, NY: M. E. Sharpe.

Rybacki, K., & Rybacki, D. (2011). *Advocacy and opposition: An introduction to argumentation* (7th ed.). New York: Pearson Higher Education.

Salcido, R. M. (1984). Social work practice in political campaigns. *Social Work, 29*(2), 189–191.

SASSI [Substance Abuse Subtle Screening Inventory] Institute. (n.d.). *Welcome to the SASSI Web site*. Retrieved from https://www.sassionline.com/

Schein, E. H. (1997). *Organizational culture and leadership* (2nd ed.). San Francisco: Jossey-Bass.

Schiller, B. (2007). *The economics of poverty and discrimination* (10th ed.). Upper Saddle River, NJ: Prentice Hall.

Schneider, R., & Lester, L. (2001). *Social work advocacy: A new framework for action*. Belmont, CA: Brooks/Cole.

Schwartz, E. (1996). *NetActivism: How citizens use the Internet*. Sebastopol, CA: O'Reilly.

Shavelson, R., McDonnell, L., & Oakes, J. (1991). What are educational indicators and indicator systems? *Practical Assessment, Research & Evaluation, 2*(11). Retrieved from http://PAREonline.net/getvn.asp?v=2&n=11

Silverman, R. (2014, October 2). Some ice bucket challenge funds will go to research. *Wall Street Journal*. Retrieved from http://online.wsj.com/articles/some-ice-bucket-challenge-funds-will-go-to-research-1412280063

Smith, A. (2011, January 27). *22% of online Americans used social networking or Twitter for politics in 2010 campaign*. Retrieved from http://www.pewinternet.org/2011/01/27/22-of-online-americans-used-social-networking-or-twitter-for-politics-in-2010-campaign/

Smith, A. (2014, November 3). *Cell phones, social media and campaign 2014*. Retrieved from http://www.pewinternet.org/2014/11/03/cell-phones-social-media-and-campaign-2014/

Social Security Act, PL 74-271 (1935).

Stanley, H., & Niemi, R. (1995). *Vital statistics on American politics* (5th ed.). Washington, DC: Congressional Quarterly Press.

Tester, F. (2003). Anti-oppressive theory and practice as the organizing theme for social work education. *Canadian Social Work Review, 20*(1), 127–132.

Texas House of Representatives. (2005, March). House Personnel Department, Texas House of Representatives, Austin.

U.S. Government Printing Office. (2003). Clinical social worker services. *Code of Federal Regulations, Title 42, Vol. 2* (42CFR410. 73). Washington, DC: U.S. Government Printing Office.

U.S. Government Printing Office. (2004). Authorized providers. *Code of Federal Regulations, Title 32, Vol. 2* (32CFR199.6). Washington, DC: U.S. Government Printing Office.

Van Soest, D. (1995). Peace and social justice. In R. Edwards (Ed.), *The encyclopedia of social work* (19th ed., pp. 1810-1817). Washington, DC: NASW Press.

Verba, S., Schlozman, K., & Brady, H. (1995). *Voice and equality: Civic voluntarism in American politics.* Cambridge, MA: Harvard University Press.

W. K. Kellogg Foundation. (2004). *Logic model development guide.* Battle Creek, MI: W. K. Kellogg Foundation.

Webster, M. Jr., & Driskell, J. Jr. (1983). Beauty as status. *American Journal of Sociology, 89,* 140-165.

Wheeler, M. (2013). *The art of negotiation: How to improvise agreement in a chaotic world.* New York: Simon & Schuster.

Wilson, R. (2002). *Seeking and resisting compliance: Why people say what they do when trying to influence others.* Thousand Oaks, CA: Sage.

Wilson, W. (1887). The study of administration. *Political Science Quarterly, 2*(2), 197-222.

Wolk, J. L. (1981). Are social workers politically active? *Social Work, 26*(4), 283-288.

Wolpe, B., & Levine, B. (1996). *Lobbying Congress: How the system works.* Washington, DC: Congressional Quarterly Press.

Young, I., & Allen, D. (1990). *Justice and the politics of difference.* Princeton, NJ: Princeton University Press.

INDEX

Note: Page numbers followed by "e" refer to exhibits. Page numbers followed by "f" refer to figures. Page numbers followed by "t" refer to tables.

accuracy, presentations and, 136
action
    calls to, in advocacy campaigns, 173
    taking, planning and, 101-102
Ad Hoc Committee on Advocacy, 225
Addams, Jane, 221
advocacy. *See also* electronic advocacy;
        evaluation, of advocacy;
        presentations
    in Code of Ethics (NASW), 25-27
    defining, 2-3
    differences in, between legislative and
        executive branches, 206-208
    generalist approach and, 2
    goals of social workers with, 35-36
    local, 105-106
    social workers and, 2
    types of, 4
    unified model of, 3-4
advocacy campaigns. *See also* media
        campaigns
    e-mail for, 172-173
    Facebook for, 173-174
    key concepts in, 167-170
    possible frames in, 156-157
    Twitter for, 174-175
    Web sites for, 170-172
    YouTube for, 175-178
advocacy maps
    columns in, 89f, 90-95
    examples, 91-93, 96-98
    line items of, 88-90, 89f
    for observation phase, of advocacy
        evaluation, 182-190, 183-187f

prioritizing outcomes for, 99-100
    tips on developing, 98-99
advocacy practice. *See also* social work
        practice
    advocating stage of, 16
    case of Ms. Jones, 8-11
    defining, 3
    education as factor for greater, 50-52
    ethical issues in, 36-40
    evaluating stage of, 16
    factors leading to greater use of, 49-60,
        49f, 51t
        education, 49f, 50-52, 51t
        interest, 49f, 51t, 55-56
        participation in other organizations,
            49f, 51t, 57-58
        sense of professional responsibility,
            49f, 54
        skills, 49f, 51t, 57
        time, 49f, 51t, 58-60
        values, 49f, 51t, 52-54
        wealth, 60
    generalist social work practice and,
        5-8, 5t
    getting involved stage, 12-13
    integrating, into social work practice,
        227-234
    interest as factor for greater, 55-56
    ongoing monitoring stage of, 16-17
    participation in organization as factor
        for greater, 57-58
    planning stage of, 14-16
    skills as factor for greater, 57
    social justice and, 2
    social responsibility as factor for
        greater, 54
    social workers and, 24
    targets of, 3
    time as factor for greater, 58-59

trends affecting, 17-21
in twenty-first century, 226-227
understanding the issue stage of, 13-14
values as factor for greater, 52-54
wealth as factor for greater, 60
advocates. *See also* social workers
Internet-based tools and, 166
social work, possible jobs for, 227-231
advocating stage, of advocacy practice, 5t, 6, 16
case of Ms. Jones, 9-10
Alinsky, Saul, 37
Allen, D., 33
American Association of Social Workers, 223
American public, levels of political participation of, 44-45
antioppression framework, 32-35
arguments versus cues message styles, 137
assessment stage, of generalist social work practice, 5t, 6
case of Ms. Jones, 8-9

bat listening tactic, in negotiation, 128
bellwether methodology, 197
biases, of senders, 119-120
black hat thinking style, 80
blogging, 171
blue hat thinking style, 80-81
body language, senders and, 120
brainstorming, for developing solutions, 75-76
brevity, presentations and, 136
Brown v. Topeka Board of Education, 223-224
budgetary process, influence, 212-214

calls to action, in advocacy campaigns, 173
campaigns. *See* advocacy campaigns; media campaigns
case advocacy, 4
casework, 221
cause advocacy, 4
Charity Organization Societies, 221
Children's Health (Dallas, Texas), 229-230
Citizens United v. Federal Elections Commission, 20
civic human (*homo civicus*), 44

Civil Rights Act of 1964, 224
clinical social workers, definition of. *See also* social workers
by Centers for Medicare and Medicaid Services, 203-204e
by Civilian Health and Medical Program of the Uniform Services, 205e
Clinton, Bill, 225
Clinton, Hillary Rodham, 229
Cloward, Richard, 225
coalitions, monitoring and, 202-205
Code of Ethics (NASW)
advocacy in, 25-27
core values of social work, 27
ethical issues and, 37-38
social justice in, 27-29
collaborative versus confrontational message styles, 138
community action agencies, 25
commutative justice, 28
confrontational versus collaborative message styles, 138
consciousness-raising process, 106
context observation, 190-194
indicators, 190-194, 191f
contextual information, 135
credibility, senders and, 117-122
cues versus arguments message styles, 137
cultural imperialism, oppression and, 34

Dahl, Robert, 44
decision makers, 24
Democratic Party, 18-19
direct observation, 188-189
Disability Rights Education and Defense Fund (DREDF), 205
distributive justice, 28. *See also* social justice
defining, 28
Nozick's views on, 30-32
Rawls's views on, 29-30
Rawls's versus Nozick's views of, 32
theories of, 28-29
Doc Network, 164-165

e-mail
for electronic advocacy, 172-173
for presentations, 148

echolocation tactic, in negotiation, 128
Economic Opportunity Act, 225
editorials, for presentations, 149–150
education, advocating through. *See also*
    social work education
  consciousness raising and, 106
  as factor for greater advocacy practice,
    49f, 50–52, 51t
  local advocacy and, 104–106
  social liberation and, 107
  "what's in it for me?" (WII-FM) and,
    107–108
Educational policies and accreditation
    standards (CSWE), 226
elected officials, social workers as,
    230–231
electronic advocacy. *See also* advocacy
  blogging for, 171
  defined, 160–162
  e-mail for, 172–173
  Facebook for, 172–173
  growing influence of, 163–167
  organizational attributes of use of,
    162–163
  social media campaigns, 167–170
  Twitter for, 174–175
  Web sites for, 170–172
  YouTube for, 175–178
engagement stage, of generalist social
    work practice, 5–6, 5t
  case of Ms. Jones, 8
evaluating stage, of advocacy practice, 5t,
    7, 16
  case of Ms. Jones, 10
evaluation, of advocacy, 180–181
  difficulties in, 198–200
  judgment phase, 194–198
  observation phase, 182–194
evaluation stage, of generalist social work
    practice, 5t, 7
  case of Ms. Jones, 10
evidence-based advocacy practice, trend
    of increased support for, 17–18
executive branch, differences in advocacy
    between legislative branch and,
    206–208
expertise, senders and, 117–118. *See also*
    knowledge biases

experts
  talking like, 118
  use of, 73
exploitation, oppression and, 33–34

Facebook, for electronic advocacy,
    172–173
fallback positions, in negotiation, 130–131
faxes, for presentations, 147–148
fear appeals principle, of messages,
    116–117
Federal Register, 209
follow-up stage, of generalist social work
    practice, 5t, 7
  case of Ms. Jones, 11
frames/framing, 109–110. *See also*
    persuasion
  possible, in advocacy campaigns,
    156–157
  types of, 110–113

generalist social work practice, 2, 4–5
  case of Ms. Jones, 8–11
  stages of, 5–8, 5t
  unified model of advocacy and, 5–8, 5t
"George Constanza" approach, for
    developing solutions, 76
getting involved stage, of advocacy
    practice, 5–6, 5t, 12–13
  case of Ms. Jones, 8
goal setting, 65
  articulating problem and, 65
good-looking people, persuasion and,
    121–122
government relations coordinator, job
    description for, 228–229
Great Depression, social work practice
    during, 222–223
Great Society programs, 224
green hat thinking style, 80
group visits, 141
guesses, 73

Harrington, Michael, 224
heuristic thinking, 124
homo civicus (civic human), 44
homo politicus (political human), 44
Hopkins, Harry, 223
Hull House (Chicago), 221

imperialism, cultural, defining, 34
implementation process, influencing,
214-217
implementation stage, of generalist social
work practice, 5t, 6
case of Ms. Jones, 9-10
in-person advocacy, 140-142
in-person visits, 141
indirect observation, 188
information, 133-134. *See also* message
styles; presentations
contextual, 135
presenting, 135-140
sharing, 173
substantive, 134-135
useful, 133-134
initial positions, in negotiation, 127-129
intent principle, of messages, 114
interest, as factor for greater advocacy
practice, 49f, 51t, 55-56
interest groups, monitoring and, 206
Internet, advocacy and use of, 164-166.
See also electronic advocacy
issues, 62-63
steps to understanding, 63f
deciding main causes of issue, 74-75
defining issue, 63-65
determining who and how people
are affected by, 71-74
generating possible solutions, 75-79
problem setting, 65-71
reviewing proposed solutions to
determine impact on social
justice, 79-83

jobs, for social work advocates, 227-231
Johnson, Lyndon B., 224
judgment phase, of advocacy evaluation,
194-198
disagreement in, 200
measurement approaches in, 195-197
methodologies for, 197-198
justice, views of, 28. *See also* distributive
justice; social justice

Kelly, Florence, 222
Kennedy, Robert F., 224
knowledge biases, 119. *See also* expertise

Lasswell, Harold, 23
Lathrop, Julia, 221
legal justice, 28
legislative aides, 227-229
job announcement example for, 230e
legislative branch, differences in advocacy
between executive branch and,
206-208
letters
to editors, for presentations, 149
for presentations, 146, 147f, 148-149
Liasson, Mara, 23
likeability, 120
dimensions of, 120-122
limits, negotiation and, 126-127
local advocacy, 105-106
looking back technique, in negotiation,
129
looking forward approach, in negotiation,
128-129

Maheffey, Maryanne, 25, 37
maps. *See* advocacy maps
marginalization, oppression and, 34
*McCutcheon v. Federal Elections
Commission*, 20
Mead, Margaret, 12
media
campaigns, setting up, 157-158
obtaining interest from, 154-156
role of, 151-154
working with, 150-151
media campaigns, setting up, 157-158.
See also advocacy campaigns
Medicare program
definition of clinical social worker by,
203-204
establishment of, 224
message styles, for presenting
information, 136-138
collaborative versus confrontational, 138
cues versus arguments, 137
one-shot versus repetitive exposure, 137
positive versus negative, 121
private versus public, 137-138
messages, 113-114
comparison of, 139-140
fear appeals principle of, 116-117
intent principle of, 114

organization principle of, 114
redundancy principle of, 115
repetition principle of, 115
rhetorical questions principle of, 116
sidedness principle of, 115
template for content of, 138-139
Mikulski, Barbara, 24
Milbraith, L., 44-45, 170
Mobilization for Youth program, 225
Moncrief, Mike, 24
monitoring
    budgetary process, 212-2144
    coalitions/interest groups for, 202-205
    differences in, between legislative and
        executive branches, 206-208
    implementation process, 214-217
    nonprofit organizations and, 206
    regulation-writing process, 208-212

Nagel, Stuart, 76-77
National Association of Social Workers
    (NASW), 205
Natural Resources Defense Council
    (NRDC), 165-166
need, people in, 1-2
needs, personal, 123
negative versus positive message styles,
    121
negotiations
    defined, 126
    fallback positions in, 130-131
    with friends, 129
    initial positions in, 127-129
    limits and, 126-127
New Deal, social work practice during, 223
nonprofit organizations, monitoring and,
    206, 207-208
Nozick, Robert, 28, 29
    versus Rawls, 32
    views on distributive justice of, 30-32

Obama, Barack, 226
observation, of advocacy evaluation,
    182-194
    advocacy maps for, 182-190, 183-187f
    context, 190-194, 191f
    direct, 188-189
    indirect, 188
Ohlia, Lloyd, 225

one-shot versus repetitive message styles,
    137
ongoing monitoring stage, of advocacy
    practice, 5t, 7, 16-17
    case of Ms. Jones, 11
oppression
    defining, 33
    five faces of, 33-35
organization principle, of messages, 114
Other America, The (Harrington), 224
outcomes, prioritizing, in advocacy maps,
    99-100

participation in organizations, as factor
    for greater advocacy practice,
    49f, 51t, 57-58
people in need, 1-2
Perkins, Frances, 223
personal needs, 123
persuasion, 108-109. See also frames/
    framing
    context and, 109-110
    message and, 113-117
    receivers and, 122-126
    senders and, 117-122
petitions, for presentations, 150
planning process, 86-87
    advocacy maps for, 88-100, 89f, 91-93f,
        96-97
    defining, 87
    identifying target in, 100-101
    logic model for, 88
    taking action and, 101-102
planning stage, of advocacy practice, 5t,
    6, 14-16
    case of Ms. Jones, 9
planning stage, of generalist social work
    practice, 5t, 6
    case of Ms. Jones, 9
policy debriefs, 197-198
policy-maker ratings, 197
political behavior, factors leading to levels
    of, 45
political beliefs, trend of rise in ideologi-
    cally consistent, 18-19
political human (homo politicus), 44
politics
    defining, 23-24
    reasons people become active in, 43-46
    social workers and, 46-49

positive versus negative message styles, 121
powerlessness, oppression and, 34
PowerPoint presentations, 143-144
practice. *See* advocacy practice; social work practice
pragmatic approach, to problem definition, 68-69
presentations. *See also* information
  accuracy and, 136
  brevity and, 136
  formats of, 140-142
  of information, 135-140
  message style and, 136-138
  PowerPoint, 143-144
  telephone calls for, 144-146
  tips for giving effective, 143
  written documents and, 146-150
private versus public message styles, 137-138
problems
  accepting client's definition of, 66-68
  approaches to defining, 66-71
  articulating, and goal setting, 65
  defining, 65-66
  pragmatic approach to, 68-69
  social-criterion approach to, 69-71
Progressive Era, social work practice during, 220-222
public versus private message styles, 137-138

Rankin, Jeannette, 222
Rawls, John, 28, 29
  versus Nozick, 32
  views on distributive justice of, 29-30
Reagan, Ronald, 225
receivers
  categories of, 124-125
  persuasion, 122-124
red hat thinking style, 80
redundancy principle, of messages, 115
reference sources, 73-74
reframing, 66
regulation-writing process
  best ways to influence, 210-212
  defined, 209-210

influencing, 208-209
  steps and stages of, 210f
repetition principle, of messages, 115
repetitive versus one-short message styles, 137
reporting biases, 119-120. *See also* expertise
Republic Party, 18-19
Reynolds, Bertha, 222
rhetorical questions principle, of messages, 116
Richmond, Mary, 221
Roosevelt, Eleanor, 223
Roosevelt, Franklin Delano, 223

Scorecards, Social Justice, for evaluating solutions, 81-83, 82t
senders
  biases and, 119-120
  body language and, 120
  clothing and, 120
  credibility and, 117-122
  expertise of, 117-118
  likeability of, 120-122
  trustworthiness of, 118-120
settlement house movement, 221
sidedness principle, of messages, 115
six thinking hats approach, for evaluating solutions, 79-81
skills, as factor for greater advocacy practice, 49f, 51t, 57
social-criterion approach, to problem definition, 69-71
social indicators, 196-197
social justice, 20-21. *See also* distributive justice
  advocacy practice and, 2
  antioppression framework for understanding, 32-35
  in Code of Ethics (NASW), 27-29
  defining, 27-28
Social Justice Scorecards, for evaluating solutions, 81-83, 82t
social liberation, education and, 107
social media campaigns, 167-170
social responsibility, as factor for greater advocacy practice, 49f, 51t, 54

social work advocates, possible jobs for, 227-231
social work education, 1. *See also* education
social work practice. *See also* advocacy practice
  defining element of, 1
  during Great Depression, 222-223
  integrating, into advocacy practice, 227-234
  during New Deal, 223
  during 1950s, 223-224
  during 1960s, 224
  during 1980s to end of twentieth century, 225-226
  during Progressive Era, 220-222
social work values, 35
social workers. *See also* advocates; clinical social workers
  advocacy and, 2
  advocacy practice and, 24
  beliefs of, in social work values, 35
  as elected officials, 230-231
  factors leader to greater use of advocacy practice by, 49-60, 49f
  goals of, with advocacy, 35-36
  people in need and, 1-2
  political activism of, 46-49
solutions
  evaluating
    six thinking hats approach, 79-81
    Social Justice Scorecard for, 81-83, 82t
  generating possible, 75-79
    brainstorming, 75-76
    "George Constanza" approach, 76
    "what can be done?" approach, 77-79
    "win-win" approach, 76-77
spin, 109
standardized measurement instruments, for advocacy evaluation, 195-196
street-level bureaucrat phenomenon, 216
Substance Abuse Subtle Screening Inventory (SASSI), 195

substantive information, 134-135
"super-optimizing" approach, for developing solutions, 76-77
Super PACs, 20
system mapping, 198
systematic surveys, 73, 74
systemic thinking, 124

telephone calls, for presentations, 144-146
termination stage, of generalist social work practice, 5t, 7
  case of Ms. Jones, 10-11
thinking styles, six hats, 79-81
time, as factor for greater advocacy practice, 49f, 51t, 58-60
trustworthiness
  body language and, 120
  clothing and, 120
  likeability and, 120-121
trustworthiness'
  senders and, 118-120
Twitter, for electronic advocacy, 174-175
TXU, 165-166

understanding the issue stage, of advocacy practice, 5t, 6, 13-14
  case of Ms. Jones, 8-9
unified model of advocacy, 3-4. *See also* advocacy practice
  generalist social work practice and, 5-8, 5t
U.S. Children's Bureau, 221
useful information, 133-134

values
  as factor for greater advocacy practice, 49f, 51t, 52-54
  social work, 35
violence, oppression and, 34-35
Voting Rights Act of 1965, 224

wealth
  as factor for greater advocacy practice, 60
  trend of increasing role of, in American politics, 19-21

Web. *See* electronic advocacy; Internet, advocacy and use of
Web sites, for electronic advocacy, 170–172
welfare reform, 225
"what can be done?" approach, for developing solutions, 77–79, 78t
"what do you think of that" approach, in negotiation, 129
"what's in it for me?" (WII-FM), education and, 107–108
white hat thinking style, 80

WII-FM ("what's in it for me?"), education and, 107–108
"win-win" approach, for developing solutions, 76–77, 77t
WordPress.com, 171
written documents, presentations and, 146–150

yellow hat thinking style, 80
Young, I., 33
YouTube, for electronic advocacy, 175–178

About the Author

Richard Hoefer is Roy E. Dulak Professor for Community Practice Research at the University of Texas at Arlington (UTA) School of Social Work. He has been at UTA since 1992, publishing frequently and teaching how to conduct advocacy, evaluate programs, and administer and manage nonprofit organizations. His goal is to provide information to assist nonprofit leaders and social workers in becoming better at their jobs. Professor Hoefer is an award-winning professor and a member of the National Association of Social Workers, the Council on Social Work Education, and the Association for Research on Nonprofit Organizations and Voluntary Action.